THE POOR ALWAYS
PAY BACK

THE POOR ALWAYS PAY BACK

THE GRAMEEN II STORY

Asif Dowla and Dipal Barua

Kumarian
Press, Inc.

The Poor Always Pay Back : The Grameen II Story

Published 2006 in the United States of America by Kumarian Press, Inc., 1294 Blue Hills Avenue, Bloomfield, CT 06002 USA

Design, production, and editorial services were provided by Publication Services, Inc., Champaign, Illinois. The text of this book is set in Baskerville BE 11/14

Printed in Canada on acid-free paper by Transcontinental Gagne.
Text printed with vegetable oil-based ink.

∞" The paper used in this publication meets the minimum requirements of the American National Standard for Information Sciences—Permanence of Paper for printed Library Materials, ANSI Z39.48-1984

Library of Congress Cataloging-in-Publication Data

Dowla, Asif Ud, 1954–
    The poor always pay back : the Grameen II story / by Asif Ud Dowla and Dipal Barua.
        p. cm.
    Includes bibliographical references and index.
    ISBN-13: 978-1-56549-231-8 (pbk. : alk. paper)
    ISBN-10: 1-56549-231-5 (pbk. : alk. paper)
        1. Microfinance—Developing countries.   2. Poor—Services for—Developing countries.   3. Grameen Bank.   I. Barua, Dipal, 1954–II. Title.
    HG178.33.D44D69 2006
    332.109172'4—dc22   2006026415

Contents

To my wife Rubab and my children
Nizar, Nazat, and Abish with love.

To my parents Pulin Behari Barua
and Protiva Barua with respect.

List of Figures, Tables, and Boxes

FIGURES

TABLES

BOXES

Foreword

I am very happy that Asif Dowla and Dipal Barua, two of my former students, joined hands to write this book on Grameen Bank. They were both students at the Economics Department of the institution where I taught during the 1970s and took part in the Grameen initiative in the neighboring village of Jobra. Dipal became an active participant in my work in the village and has continued with me ever since. He is one of the core builders of Grameen Bank and now occupies the number 2 position in the bank. Asif chose the academic path but has retained contact with Grameen Bank. He spent his sabbatical working in Grameen several years back and has widely published articles about various aspects of the bank in professional journals.

The Grameen initiative was a big success in putting a question mark in the minds of people who believed that the poor are not creditworthy. Grameen demonstrated how wrong they were. It also changed the mind-set of the poor women who thought they were no good at earning money and had no capacity to utilize money.

To make it easy for our poor illiterate borrowers, we made our rules very simple. We eliminated all flexibility in the rules. Later we added many extra features into the program to compensate for the lack of flexibility, but we did not touch the basic simple structure because we thought it would be very difficult to undo the rules that were already imbedded in the borrowers' minds. We also had to consider the implications for the Grameen-like programs that had emerged all over the world. All of the programs had adopted the same methodology, and a new version could put them in difficult situation.

A quarter of a century later we decided to revisit our rules, to be bold and take the next step. We felt that all borrowers of Grameen Bank, and those of the Grameen replicators, had matured enough to accept a new, improved version of the methodology if they recognized how it would benefit them. After thorough preparation for the conversion we went full speed ahead with it. I have described this conversion process as moving from Grameen I to Grameen II, Grameen I being the one-size-fits-all version of credit delivery, or classical Grameen, and Grameen II being the "tailor-made" credit operation, or the Grameen generalized system.

This book documents the process of transition, examining the changes to the system and their implications for Grameen Bank, its borrowers, and its staff. I am very happy that we decided to go through with it. The new system has made life much easier for the borrowers, and staff report that their work is far better organized now and their performance can be assessed in a more transparent fashion. This book details Grameen II for policymakers, practitioners, and the larger development community. One can see the strengths of Grameen II in features such as open-access savings, flexible loan products, a range of deposit products attractive to savers, self-reliance at the branch level, freedom from donor dependence for funds, maintenance of the interest rate at close to the commercial rate while keeping each branch profitable from the second year of operation, insurance products, a pension fund, education loans, loans geared to the needs of beggars, total computerization of branch-level accounting and MIS, elimination of the staff's reliance on paperwork, and the uncoupling of microcredit from the myth of group guarantee, joint liability, and legal instruments.

This book captures very well the central message of Grameen— that the poor always pay back, not because they are afraid, but simply because they are smart. They see how their interest is better served by repayment. The poor also demonstrate skill in fund management, balancing short-term and long-term needs. I hope this book will help readers understand the poor better and inspire them to play an active role in creating a world free of poverty.

Muhammad Yunus
Pohela Boishak
April 14, 2006
Grameen Bank

Preface

Grameen Bank, a pioneering microcredit institution that began in the village of Jobra, Bangladesh, has been in existence for more than two decades. The bank and its successes have revolutionized how credit is delivered to the poor. Over the two decades of its existence, the bank has standardized its products and its credit delivery mechanism, and the Grameen Bank model is currently replicated in more than 100 countries around the world.

This book began with an invitation around November 2001, a few months after September 11, 2001, from the founder of the bank, Professor Yunus, to write about Grameen II, an improved and flexible version of the now well-known Grameen model. It was a tumultuous time for the world as well as for the bank. After the devastating flood of 1998, when two-thirds of the country was under water for eleven weeks, the bank was facing repayment problems in certain areas. Although 80% percent of the borrowers were repaying on time, 20% became irregular in their repayment. Grameen Bank took this opportunity to rethink their model. At the time of the invitation, the bank was finally recovering from the repayments problems of 1999–2000. The bank had completely redesigned its model—switching from group lending and savings to individual lending and savings, merging various loan products into one product called the basic loan, providing a temporary reprieve in the form of a flexible loan for borrowers having repayment problems, introducing a contractual savings account later named the Grameen pension scheme (GPS) for its members, and beginning the practice of collecting regular and contractual savings from the general public on a large scale. These changes were collectively dubbed Grameen II.

At the end of 2001, the bank was noticing success with these changes. Even though this was a momentous event for the global microfinance industry, very few outside of Grameen knew what was going on. Even the people involved with the microfinance industry in Bangladesh did not know much about the new model. The first public pronouncement about Grameen II came with the publication of a monograph by Professor Yunus appropriately titled *Grameen Bank II: Designed to Open New Possibilities* in April 2002, which described the various elements of Grameen II. Clearly, the transition to Grameen II and the details of the new loan and savings products could not be delineated within the confines of a booklet. We decided that a book describing the process of arriving at Grameen II along with a detailed description of the various loan and savings products is warranted. More important, we felt that we needed to incorporate stories of real people whose lives were affected and the context that led to the changes, in addition to analytically evaluating the new model. We wanted to tell the story of how the staff were implementing changes to the well-established Grameen model, and how these changes were affecting the lives of the borrowers. Teaching assignments, running a bank with 16,000 staff members, geographical separation of the authors, and family needs precluded the earlier completion of the book. Moreover, in the process of writing and revising the early draft of the book, we found that the circumstances and the model were changing rapidly. We could not resist the temptation to include all of these changes as well as the exciting new initiatives that were added to the initial Grameen II model.

An important thing that readers will learn from reading this book is that Grameen Bank is a dynamic organization. At any moment in time, the bank is involved in two or three major initiatives to improve its model. It is constantly fine-tuning and changing its model of financial service delivery in response to changes in the field. This is because Grameen Bank works with the poor, and its mission is to alleviate poverty. Poverty, however, is a dynamic phenomenon. The process through which people become poor changes, as do the means to alleviate poverty. Providing financial services to the poor so that they can use their ingenuity to get out poverty on their own is an important and effective means of poverty alleviation. The means used to reduce poverty had to be changed and refined constantly to keep up with changes in the poverty dynamics. Flexibility is the hallmark of the new Grameen model.

We know that by the time the book is published, some of the information we have included in the book will have become outdated because of changes in the field. However, we had to stop writing and send the manuscript to the publisher at some point, and we thought this would be the appropriate time. Despite the changing vista, the overall message of the book remains intact: the financial needs of the poor are varied and changing, and an effective financial institution has to devise products that will meet these changing needs.

We feel that we are in a unique and enviable position to write the book. Our association with the bank goes back a long way. Both of us were undergraduate students when the Grameen experiment was taking place in the village of Jobra, adjacent to the university campus. Asif worked in the Rural Economics Program of Chittagong University. One of his tasks was to pay the salaries of the first two employees of the Grameen Bank. At that time Professor Yunus and Dipal were in Tangail putting the finishing touches on the embryonic Grameen model. After the initial association with the bank, we parted ways. Asif left Bangladesh to pursue an academic career, and Dipal continued with the Grameen Bank, rising rapidly through the hierarchy. Asif has maintained contact with the bank through frequent visits to Bangladesh and a year on sabbatical at the bank in the late 1990s. Dipal has been involved with the bank from day 1 and brings the perspective of an insider who was involved with all major changes in the bank. In writing the book, we bring our unique perspective to the story of this tectonic shift in the field of microfinance. We are able to provide fascinating insights into the functions of a flagship microfinance institution by blending theoretical and analytical insights with the day-to-day aspects of managing a bank with 5.5 million borrowers.

The book is about the poor and how they cope with poverty. They are resourceful managers of their limited income and assets. Even though they are not trained in the intricacies of modern finance, they use their limited income efficiently, and are diligent in paying back their loans, and even managing to save. The main message of the book is that, despite the harsh economic and social conditions in which they live, the poor always pay back. They also save a great deal. The poor do not need our sympathy; they only need a helping hand. And a helping hand in the form of financial services is the most important one. They value this window of opportunity provided by thousands of formal and informal institutions all over the world, and it is their self-interest that prompts them to repay mostly on time.

As readers can guess, the book would have been impossible without the support and encouragement of Professor Yunus. We are grateful to him for spending his valuable time reading the manuscript and providing suggestions. We are grateful to our spouses and children for their support and understanding. Ultimately, they are the ones who paid the price for our absences from their lives. Vidar Jorgensen provided financial support so that the book could be finished on time. Vidar was also a source of inspiration for us. He read the chapters and suggested that we include tables and illustrations to make the book more readable. He also paid for a graphic artist to create illustrations that have greatly improved the book, and suggested changes that would make the book more meaningful to readers unfamiliar with the story of Grameen Bank. We are grateful to him for his financial support, suggestions, and encouragement. We are also grateful to Green Children (thegreenchildren.org) for their generous sponsorship of the book. They are two young musicians who are using music to make the youth of the world aware of microfinance.

We are fortunate to have had the support of numerous people. Lindsay Pack read the first version of the manuscript, corrected grammatical mistakes, and provided suggestions to improve the drafts. Adrienne Forrester prepared the bibliography and end notes.

We are grateful to them for there excellent service. Tanweer Akram, Jon Armajani, Lindy McBride, Jonathan Mordoch, and Mark Schriener knew about the plan of the book and made valuable suggestions on how to make the book more attractive. Stuart Rutherford read the earlier version of the manuscript. His incisive comments and questions greatly improved the manuscript. We are grateful to him. Jeffrey Hammond, George B. and Willma Reeves Distinguished Professor in the Liberal Arts at St. Mary's College of Maryland, read the complete manuscript and provided suggestion on how to improve the narratives. Professor Hammond's help is especially noteworthy as the subject matter was completely outside his field of expertise. Still, he cheerfully agreed to read the manuscript, spent time learning about the bank, and developed a new appreciation for financial institutions. The staff of Grameen Bank provided an invaluable service, and this book would have been impossible without their help. Mohammad Abul Hossain went through the manuscript repeatedly, gave his inputs, corrected factual errors, and collected the necessary data from the Monitoring and Evaluation Department of the bank for inclusion in the book. He was helped in this endeavor by Mohammad Danesh Hawlader and Mohammad Mustafizur Rahman. Sabrina Shaab also read the manuscript and provided valuable suggestions. Mohammad Moslem Ali, Mohammad Sarwar Alam, and Mohammad Wasim Reza helped in preparing illustrations for the book. The photographers of Grameen Bank—Salauddin Azizee, Ekramul Haque, and Nurjahan Chaklader—supplied us with the pictures that are included in the book and were used in preparing the illustrations. Dipal Barua's personal assistant, Ranokul Khan, provided overall assistance in collecting the necessary information in support of the book. We are lucky to have these wonderful people on our side and are grateful for their assistance. Jim Lance, the editor of Kumarian Press, was a source of inspiration for us. He skillfully and diplomatically handled difficult negotiations with humor and candor. We are thankful for his support. We are grateful to Susan Yates of Publication Services for her help in preparing the manuscript for publication.

Asif wants to take this opportunity to thank the above-named staff of Grameen Bank for their assistance in reconstructing the story of Grameen II during his frequent visits to the head office of the bank. He is grateful to St. Mary's College of Maryland for awarding several faculty development grants enabling him to spend time at Grameen Bank in Bangladesh and conduct field work there to collect materials for the manuscript. He acknowledges the help of the library staff at St. Mary's College, especially Terry Leonard, Brenda Rodgers, and Jayna Dempsey, in finding valuable research materials that greatly improved the book.

This book is mainly about the millions of borrowers of Grameen Bank. Even though they may be not be able to read this book on their own, we hope that their children will read it and find that we portrayed their parents fairly and with respect. We hope that they will take the stewardship of the bank in the future, and the book will help them in developing their own model of financial services for the poor.

Introduction

Gazi Abdul Malek was a member of Grameen Bank in Fatehabad—the mother branch of the bank since 1983. Gazi joined the bank in his mid-40s. He was a model member and always paid his installments on time. At the end of the year 2001, he had an outstanding balance in his account of 2400 taka.[1] In accordance with the new rule of the bank, he was required to buy insurance by depositing 60 taka (2.5% of the outstanding balance) in a special savings account. In the meantime, Gazi took out more loans from the bank, and because of his stellar performance he was awarded large special investment project loans. Even though he did not know his actual health status, he was worried about taking out such large loans from the bank. He was concerned that he might die leaving a huge debt for his family.

Gazi died on June 26, 2002. At that time, he owed the bank 118,278 taka. Since his death, the bank has repaid the entire amount from the loan insurance fund. In addition, the bank returned the original 60 taka deposit in his insurance savings account.

We begin with this anecdote because it highlights several aspects of the radical rebuilding of Grameen Bank: basic loan, personal savings account, special investment project loan, loan insurance, and most important, the paying off of the outstanding loan amount from the bankwide accumulated insurance fund. In addition to these economic aspects, the story reveals an important social achievement of

Grameen II: providing people with an even greater possibility of dying debt free by virtue of being a member of the bank. In a Muslim-majority country such as Bangladesh, all residents, and especially the poor, aspire to achieve this goal. For Muslims, an important ritual during the funeral prayer is the eldest son asking for forgiveness on behalf of his parents and promising to assume their debts. This allows creditors to forgive the debt of the parents so that the son can bury the parents debt free, which is considered a great honor. Under Grameen I, a long-standing policy was to send a representative to the funeral of a deceased member. At the funeral, the representative would hand the deceased's family a nominal amount from the built-in life insurance benefit program to defray the cost of the funeral and burial. Now, under Grameen II, the branch manager attends the funeral and, prior to the burial, publicly announces freedom from Grameen Bank's debt as well as the decision to even return the money deposited in the loan savings account to the family. Needless to say, the possibility of dying without leaving behind a debt burden is very popular with the members. Even nonmembers are amazed that a bank will forgive loans by the poor. Many female borrowers, including all elected members of the Grameen Bank board, demanded coverage for their husbands under the insurance program; this is necessary to protect the female borrower from destitution after the death of her husband. Recently, the bank has extended the insurance to cover the husbands also.

The successes of Grameen II have built upon the revolutionary concept of the first Grameen. In 1983 in a village near his university campus in Bangladesh, an American-trained economist embarked on an idea that was counter to the established conventional wisdom. The idea was that the poor are creditworthy, their precarious economic condition notwithstanding. He was convinced that if a system could be developed to supply credit to the poor, they would use the money to improve their economic condition by investing the funds in income-generating projects. He also had faith that even without an explicit threat of confiscation of collateral, they would repay their loans on time. In addition, he believed that the poor would know, without training, how to maximize the benefits of their micro-loan; the financial institution would merely have to give them the money on time and get out of the way. The economist, Muhammad Yunus, developed this system, which is now known as the Grameen model.

Imagine for a moment the typical day of a manager of a national-ized or a private bank in Bangladesh. A manager generally sits in an air-conditioned office in an urban area. Most likely he will spend the better part of his day on the phone with borrowers who have defaulted on their loans.[2] He will beg each client to make good on the installment payments on an already rescheduled loan of large size. Instead of being angry, however, the manager has to be polite because he knows that if the borrower does not pay, the bank has lit-tle recourse. The borrowers know that a bank's threats of court bat-tles or reports to the Credit Information Bureau are not credible. They can merely hire an expensive attorney and get a court injunc-tion against the bank as well as against the central bank, preempting the bank's attempt to collect the loan in arrears.[3] Borrowers have also found a way to get around the stigma of having their names placed on the Credit Information Bureau's list of borrowers who have defaulted on loans from the commercial banks. Inclusion in that list should preclude the defaulter's receiving additional loans from any commercial bank; however, a borrower can simply use his relative's name as a proxy to get a loan from another bank. More than likely, this powerful defaulter is already the director of a pri-vate bank, even though he owes money to the government-owned banks. These delinquent borrowers can also reschedule their loans on favorable terms and use their connections on the board to approve new loans.[4,5] The predicament of the private bank man-ager is reminiscent of the famous statement by John Getty, the American oil baron: "When you owe the bank $100, that is your problem. When you owe the bank $100 million, that's the bank's problem."

These defaulters, with large arrears with commercial banks, live in the most prosperous part of town. They own beautiful houses, paid for mostly with the bank's money, and own the latest-model imported sport utility vehicles—all achieved by siphoning off money from the inflated project loans. Their children attend private schools in the country and in the United States, Canada, the United Kingdom, Australia, or India. They can repay the bank if they want, but they do not want to because they know they do not have to.[6]

Now imagine a Grameen bank worker in a remote village in Bangladesh. The bank worker lives on the upstairs floor of the branch building. Every day the worker visits a group of members in the village. The trip takes quite a bit of time, and the bank worker usually rides a bicycle to the villages. The group meets in a pre-designated space called the "center house," built by the members using their own resources. The members sit in groups with the bank worker at the front, and after the initial greetings, the members hand over their weekly installment payments. Occasionally, one or two may miss a payment, but the large majority of them pay their dues on time. Unlike their rich counterparts, these people live with their extended families in modest homes. They usually walk to visit relatives in other villages or to the local market, only occasionally riding in a rickshaw or baby taxi if they can afford it. Their children attend the public primary schools in crowded classrooms. They face all types of crises: flooding, river bank erosion, health problems, and harassment by police and local goons. They may have to walk a few miles to a government health clinic, and when they arrive there is no guarantee that a doctor will be there.[7] Even if the doctor is there, the prescribed medicine may not be on the shelves. The people may have to use bribes to see the doctor or get medicine, forcing many to use up their savings for treatment of chronic illnesses of their family members. They also face natural disasters such as floods, which can destroy their crops, damage their homes, and kill their livestock and even their children. The rise in the river level during a flood might also wash away their land and leave them destitute.

Despite these calamities and the insecure nature of their lives, the poor pay back their loans on time and in large numbers. They are known to repay their loans even after the loans have been written off the bank's books: the bank is now collecting 3.8 million taka a day of "bad debts." There are even instances where a borrower went overseas and, after living there for several years, came home and repaid the loans that had been written off. Others working with the poor in Bangladesh and in many other parts of the world have also found that the poor always pay back their loans.[8]

Grameen Bank, which attained its formal status in 1983, faced a repayment problem in 1998 in the aftermath of an unprecedented flood that inundated two-thirds of Bangladesh for thirteen weeks during June to September. Even though 80% of the borrowers repaid on time, the other 20% lost all contact with the bank. This loss affected the whole system. The rigidity of the rules and the precarious nature of the poor's existence increased the debt burden of the borrowers so much so that they stopped coming to the center meetings to make payments. Unlike the challenge at its inception— to prove that the poor are creditworthy—the bank now faced a different type of challenge: how to get the borrowers to rejoin the bank and motivate them to repay the loans. This time the bank had to prove to the country and the world that the poor will always pay back. The challenge is captured masterfully in the words of the founder of the bank, Professor Yunus:

> On some occasions they may take [a] longer time to pay back than was originally stipulated, but repay they will. There is no reason for a credit institution dedicated to provide financial services to the poor to get uptight because a borrower could not pay back the entire amount of a loan on a date fixed at the beginning of the disbursement of the loan. Many things can go wrong for a poor person during the loan period. After all, the circumstances are beyond the control of the poor people. We see no reason why the sky should fall on anybody's head because a borrower took [a] longer time to pay back her loan. Since she is paying additional interest for the extra time, where is the problem? We always advocated that microcredit program[s] should not fall into the logical trap of the conventional [bank] and start looking at their borrowers as some kind of "time-bombs" who are ticking away and waiting to create big trouble on pre-fixed dates. Please

rest assured that poor people are not going to create any trouble. It is us, the designers of institutions and rules, who keep creating trouble for them. One can benefit enormously by having trust in them, admiring their struggle for and commitment to have decent lives for themselves.[9]

Professor Yunus and the staff of Grameen Bank had to convince everyone that the poor will always pay back. They may be "late" or "at risk" according to conventional banking standards, but this tardiness is due to circumstances beyond their control. The attempt to validate this belief is the genesis of Grameen II. It is a belief reinforced by the rebuilding process itself, because it has been Grameen policy never to take its borrowers to court even though it is allowed to do so by the legal charter of the bank. During the reconstruction, borrowers who lost contact with the bank for years and even left their villages came back, signed a contract, and paid the defaulted amount. Even loans that had been written off and were off the books are now being repaid in large amounts each month. That the poor want to pay back is now a firmly established fact.

The journey to arriving at this new truth was a difficult one. In developing Grameen II, the bank had to explicitly consider the precariousness of the poor. As a result, the poor were allowed an option called a "flexible loan." Needless to say, rebuilding the bank was a more monumental challenge than developing the original model. Grameen had become the flagship for the microfinance revolution and was synonymous with success. Any misstep would have been perceived as another well-intentioned development initiative that failed. Perceived as unsustainable, Grameen would have become another headstone in the cemetery of failed development interventions. The bank never blamed the borrowers during the redesign process. Rather, it saw the fault as resting within the bank and its system: the fact that the poor did not pay on time was because the rigidity of the system discouraged them from doing so. When the system was redesigned to incorporate flexibility, the borrowers who left the bank came back in droves and paid off loans that were long overdue.

The widely popular loan insurance program is only one element of Grameen II. This book will examine Grameen II in all its aspects, including loan consolidation, new loan products, collection of overdue loans, the Grameen Pension Fund, savings products for members and nonmembers, scholarship funds and higher education loans for the children, and a special program for the struggling members (beggars).

Even though the new model is fully implemented and has been in operation for more than three years, very few in the global microfinance community, and even in Bangladesh itself, have a clear idea of how the new system works. The objective of this book is to demystify Grameen II for policymakers, practitioners, and the larger development community. It chronicles the new Grameen and explains how a flagship institution such as Grameen Bank has been able to accomplish a complete overhaul of its system. In addition, the book is the most up-to-date description of the restructured Grameen Bank; its publication will bolster the case for the superiority of Grameen II and represent a valuable addition to the burgeoning literature on microfinance.

Although several books have already explored various aspects of Grameen Bank, including its management structure, its institutional history, and micro- and macro-level impact assessments, most of these books were written before the mid-1990s.[10] Grameen Bank has been making improvements and introducing new policies since it was established, an evolution that these books do not present clearly. And because they depended excessively on field-level experiences from the oldest operational areas of the bank, these books have been unable to document the various modifications that have been made to the classic Grameen model, which began in 1977.[11]

Numerous articles about Grameen Bank have also been published in academic journals. Since many of the academic articles were based on secondary sources, their content was ahistorical in nature and suffered from the same deficiencies as the books. Grameen I, or the classical Grameen, generated a lot of excitement in the development community as an effective means of poverty alleviation. However, no one has yet published a complete account of Grameen II. This book will be the first to accomplish this goal.

In the classical Grameen model, to obtain a loan the borrowers formed a group of five, consisting mostly of poor females. The loans were to be repaid in weekly installments, and the borrowers could receive new loans only if they repaid their previous loans on time. The borrowers also made compulsory deposits in a group fund that was managed by the group. The bank workers met several of these groups on their own premises to collect repayments and savings.

The new structure of Grameen is marked by departures from many of its well-known tenets. Long-term observers and supporters of the bank will be surprised by the new Grameen. For example, the bank has moved away from the idea of group loans; loans are now given to individuals. We will show that, through Grameen II, the bank is addressing microfinance frontier issues: open-access savings, flexible loan products, self-reliance, absence of donor dependency for funds, and product development to cater to the needs of retirees (Grameen pension scheme) and their adult children (higher education loans).

As mentioned earlier, the bank faced repayment problems in some zones of the bank's operation after the flood of 1998. In some areas, a combination of difficult geography, post-flood decline in economic activity, staff neglect, and a breakdown of repayment culture created serious problems for the bank: the members discontinued their installment payments and attendance at the regular weekly meetings, and staff lost contact with members completely. The senior management, however, realized that the flood and the consequential disruption of economic activity were not the root causes of the problem; the flood had also affected areas containing branches that continued to have perfect repayment rates. Together the staff and management came to the conclusion that the rigid rules of Grameen I were the main contributing factor to the problem. The rank and file of the bank rolled up their sleeves, put their heads together, and got to work to change the rules. The result is Grameen II.

This book will provide a detailed description of the structure of the rebuilt bank and the process through which Grameen II was created "brick by brick."[12] We hope that the book will appeal to a wide range of audiences. Students of development will be interested in finding out how Grameen II was established and learning about the fascinating process through which a huge development organization goes about restructuring and redesigning itself. The book is also of potential benefit to development practitioners, who presumably would be interested in knowing how a large flagship institution like Grameen Bank reinvents itself. Management theorists will be intrigued as well with how the bank created an internal market for winning ideas by creating task forces to develop solutions for rehabilitating the worst-performing branches. Another important aspect of the book is its account of how the bank persuaded its 13,000 staff at the time to abandon the principles of credit delivery inculcated through training and practice over long periods in favor of a completely new form of banking for the poor. This will prove helpful to the managers of microfinance institutions and policymakers assigned the task of developing new institutions for credit delivery to the poor. The book will also appeal to microfinance specialists, who will be curious as to how an institution with very little interest in voluntary savings has changed course to such a degree that it rewards branches with stars for acquiring more deposits than loans. Overall, the book provides a balanced narrative on how the bank recognized the problem it faced and chose to move forward toward an exciting new day.

The authors are in an enviable position to tell the story of Grameen Bank. Both of us were students at Chittagong University when the Grameen experiment was taking place in the adjacent village of Jobra. After graduation, we went our separate ways. One of us went to the United States to purse higher education in economics, and the other started a long and distinguished career with Grameen Bank. We kept in constant contact, however. In addition, one author is originally from the village of Jobra, where the bank was born. This book gave us an opportunity to collaborate and relate the unique and fascinating story of Grameen II using our respective areas of expertise.

Chapter 2 examines the key features of classical Grameen. It provides a brief review of the emergence of Grameen I. It also provides an up-to-date survey of the various impacts of Grameen Bank. This chapter will be useful to readers unfamiliar with the bank. We have cited and described all published and unpublished research on the impact of Grameen I using language that even people who are unfamiliar with Grameen can understand. The objective of this chapter is to give a clear background of Grameen I as a basis for understanding what Grameen II entailed. Readers familiar with the original Grameen model will also benefit from this chapter, as it includes a full description of the changes that were made to the original model and that are not reported elsewhere.

Chapter 3 explains the salient features of Grameen II. It presents examples to illustrate the workings of various loan products. We also provide context and justification for the changes that were made to the loan products.

A unique feature of the new credit delivery mechanism is the collection of savings from members and nonmembers. Chapter 4 deals exclusively with the various savings-related products and the strategy used to mobilize savings, especially from nonmembers. In particular, this chapter explains the differences between various compulsory and voluntary savings products. Finally, this chapter explains how Grameen II differs from the classical Grameen system (Grameen I).

Chapter 5 explores how the various building blocks of Grameen II came about—an archeology of Grameen II. Here we suggest that some of the ingredients of Grameen II were already in existence on a piecemeal basis. During the last two decades, many ideas and innovations were tried and discarded. The hallmark of Grameen II is that all of the innovations and changes to the classical Grameen system were integrated to create a new financial service delivery mechanism. Instead of merely tinkering with Grameen I, Grameen II built a new and more generalized framework. This chapter tells how Grameen managed its redesign process despite the built-in inertia of the system and how the intellectual struggle for ideas within this institution was settled. In addition, the chapter suggests some broader guidelines for institutions contemplating radical changes of their own.

Chapter 6 explores how staff members were trained to implement the changes entailed in Grameen II, along with the incentives system provided for the staff to carry out the rebuilding. The chapter also describes how an important element of Grameen II—the rewriting of the rules—was done in a participatory manner. Moreover, to facilitate quick transition, the bank published implementation guidelines. In this chapter, we provide a detailed description of how this process worked.

Chapter 7 describes some of the innovative programs of the bank that were launched along with Grameen II. We describe how the bank is trying to serve the poorest of the poor—the beggars—by creating a special program for them. The chapter also describes the highly innovative program of higher education loan for the borrowers' children. Further, it describes how the bank is encouraging education of the borrowers' children by giving them scholarships for excellence in studies and extracurricular activities in secondary and higher secondary levels.

The final chapter examines the lessons that Grameen's rebuilding holds for the industry as a whole, as well as and the challenges that it will face in the future.

NOTES

1. The taka is the Bangladeshi currency; approximately 67 takas are equal to 1 US dollar.
2. We are using a male pronoun to refer to the manager and the borrower of a commercial bank as these individuals are more likely to be male.
3. The government has recently made amendments to the Bank Company Act of 1991 that preclude bank directors from issuing an injunction against the central bank in lower courts. "Bank Turns to 'Unfair Means' to Dodge Rules," *Daily Star Web Edition* 5(103), September 5, 2004; available at http://www.the dailystar.net/2004/09/05/d40905050252.htm.
4. The *Daily Star* reports that the major nationalized bank rescheduled the loan of a top defaulter by waiving off 46 crore taka, including 11 crore of applied interest. (A crore is equal to 10 million.) The loan of this business group alone represented about 15% of the paid-up capital of the bank. The commercial banks use dubious techniques to extend fresh loans to powerful defaulters. "We sanctioned a fresh loan to a party who, as we know, is a defaulter," admitted a credit officer of a private commercial bank, requesting anonymity. "What we do is make sure that the party's overdue loans have been rescheduled, taking money from the fresh loan." "SB Gets Kind to Tk 170cr Loan Defaulter," *Daily Star Web Edition* 3(928), April 19, 2002 (available at http://www.thedailystar.net/dailystarnews/200204/19/n2041901.htm#BODY4).
5. The bank helped the client reschedule the previous loan by paying 10% of the loan as a down payment, revised the Bangladesh Bank's Credit Information Bureau (CIB) report to indicate that he was no longer a defaulter, and then activated the fresh loan at a deferred date. "Banks Turn to 'Unfair Means' to Dodge Rules," *Daily Star Web Edition* 5(103), September 5, 2004 (available at http://www.thedailystar. net/2004/09/05/d40905050252.htm).
6. This is not a fictional account. The description is based on actual events and was told to the authors by friends who are top-level bankers in Bangladesh.
7. A recent World Bank study reports that the absentee rate for doctors at the larger clinics is 40%. The rate is even higher, at 74%, in smaller subcenters with only one doctor. See Nazmul Chaudhury and Jeffrey S. Hammer, *Ghost Doctors: Doctor Absenteeism in Bangladeshi Heath Centers,* Policy Research Working Paper no. 3065 (World Bank, 2003).

8. The repayment rates for Grameen Bank and other credit-granting NGOs in Bangladesh are significantly higher than the repayment rates for government-owned banks and other financial institutions. Even though the nonperforming loan (NPL) rate for nationalized commercial banks has gone down, these banks were still burdened with 29.7% NPL as of September 2004. Shahidur Khandker, *Fighting Poverty with Microcredit: Experience in Bangladesh,* Tables 6.2 and 6.3. (New York: Oxford University Press for the World Bank, 1998); M. A. Khalily and Richard L. Meyer, "The Political Economy of Rural Loan Recovery: Evidence from Bangladesh," *Savings and Development* 17(1), 1993, pp. 23–38.

9. Muhammad Yunus, *Grameen Bank II: Designed to Open New Possibilities* (Dhaka: Grameen Bank, 1998).

10. David Bornstein, *The Price of a Dream* (New York: Simon & Schuster, 1996); Alex Counts, *Give Us Credit* (New York: Times Books, 1996); Susan Holcombe, *Managing to Empower: The Grameen Bank's Experience of Poverty Alleviation* (London: Zed Books, 1995); Helen Todd, *Women at the Center: Grameen Bank Borrowers after One Decade* (Boulder, CO: Westview Press, 1996); Abu Wahid, *The Grameen Bank: Poverty Relief in Bangladesh* (Boulder, CO: Westview Press, 1993).

11. For a firsthand description of the evolution of the classical Grameen model, see Muhammad Yunus, *Banker to the Poor: Micro-Lending and the Battle against World Poverty* (New York: Public Affairs, 1999).

12. The best way to assess these changes is to draw a parallel—for example, with IBM and how it turned itself around. In the 1990s IBM, the flagship organization of the computer industry, was in the midst of a devastating slump. Many critics predicted the imminent demise of the company. Then a new manger, Louis Gerstner, took bold steps resulting in the company's turnaround. His firsthand chronicle of this extraordinary achievement is found in the book *Who Says Elephants Can't Dance? Inside IBM's Historic Turnaround* (New York: HarperCollins, 2002).

Classical Grameen and Its Impacts

The story of how Grameen Bank began is now well known (Yunus, 1999). The bank's origin goes back to a chance meeting of the founder, Mohammad Yunus, with a bamboo stool maker, Sufia Khatoon, in the village of Jobra in the southern part of rural Bangladesh. Sufia was making bamboo stools with raw materials supplied on credit by a money lender, who then bought the finished product.[1] The money lender set both the price of the raw materials and the price of the finished product, and after paying for the raw materials, Sufia had hardly enough left to feed her family of five. To be exact, Sufia made two cents from each stool, which was the difference between the payment for the raw materials and the low price paid by the money lender for the finished product. This meant that she had to return to the same lender to produce her next batch of stools. Sufia seemed destined to repeat and unable to escape this vicious cycle. Yunus asked her if she could borrow the money from the money lender to buy the raw materials and sell the product on her own. Sufia explained that the usurious interest rate charged by the money lender would make that exchange even worse than the current deal. Yunus, who had a freshly minted Ph.D. in economics from the United States, was dismayed that a hard-working human being should be condemned in such inhumane conditions simply because she was unable to borrow a mere twenty-two cents. He tried to find out how many other people were in the same situation as Sufia in the village. A quick survey taken with the help of his students from the local university identified forty-two such people, who altogether borrowed twenty-seven dollars from the traders. It made Yunus even angrier to think that all of these hard-working people were in misery because they could not scrounge up twenty-seven dollars. He gave money out of his pocket so that the people could pay off the traders. Yunus reasoned that these people were poor not because they were lazy or stupid, but because they did not have credit and could not get any from a formal financial institution because they had no collateral. For Yunus, this was a "Eureka" moment.

The initial loan that Yunus made was repaid in full. This strengthened his belief in the poor's ability and willingness to repay. He realized, however, that his out-of-pocket solution would not work on a larger scale. He believed that to make credit truly effective as a catalyst for poverty alleviation, large numbers of people should have access to it—and for that, an institutional setup would be necessary. Every attempt Yunus made to get the commercial bank to loan the money to the poor, however, was met with resistance. Undeterred, Yunus kept pounding, and gradually doors began to open. Initially he received help from the Agricultural Bank. This bank created a special window for borrowers for whom Yunus acted as guarantor.

Although this first experiment was successful, the bankers were still not convinced. They argued that success in one village close to the university where Yunus was a professor of economics did not prove that it could work in another part of the country. Consequently, Yunus had to take a leave of absence from his teaching to replicate and fine-tune the method of credit delivery in Tangail, a district north of the capital city of Dhaka. The pilot project in Tangail, the crucible for Grameen Bank, was funded by the Central Bank of Bangladesh. Major elements of Grameen I emerged from the experimentation in that area.

Despite this success in the quite diverse setting of Tangail, bankers were still skeptical. It was then that Yunus realized that banking for the poor cannot be conducted using the formal banking apparatus.

They needed a bank of their own. Through the help of supportive civil servants in the government and some central bank officials, the pilot project became an independent financial institution with the passage of the Special Grameen Bank Ordinance of 1983. This ordinance was later ratified by the Bangladesh Parliament. The new institution was named Grameen (meaning "village" in Bengali, the local language) Bank. The ordinance specified that "the Bank shall provide credit with or without collateral security, in cash or in kind, for such term and subject to such conditions as may be prescribed, to landless persons for all types of economic activity, including housing."[2] The ordinance also permitted the bank to accept deposits, issue and sell bonds, and borrow money against security of its assets or otherwise for the purpose of the bank's business.[3]

The classical Grameen model was based on loan without collateral; membership in the bank was limited to poor people from households owning less than half an acre of medium-quality cultivatable land, or assets not exceeding the value of one acre of medium-quality land. An academic, Yunus did not know how to run a bank. However, he wanted to make sure to avoid the mistakes of conventional banks and credit cooperatives. He reasoned that the requirement of one-time repayment of loans used by conventional banks and credit cooperatives was psychologically trying for the borrowers as they grew attached to the money. Over time, they would start to believe that the money belonged to them. Also, in many cases, it was hard for borrowers to gather the full amount owed. Moreover, Yunus felt that lump-sum payments allowed both borrowers and lenders to ignore difficulties that might arise early on.[4]

Consequently, he divided the loan repayments into weekly installments and gave all of the loans a one-year duration. Initially, the borrowers were required to pay installments daily to a local shopkeeper, whose place of business was a natural meeting place for the villagers. Soon, however, this loan collection scheme ran into trouble. There were claims and counterclaims of payment and nonpayment, respectively, between the borrowers and the grocery shop owner. The condition did not improve much even with the use of a ledger by the grocer, because the borrower would complain that he or she had paid but the shop owner had failed to enter it into the ledger.[5] Yunus realized that there had to be another means of collecting repayment; the method should be public so that there would be witnesses to the repayment, and this would demand honesty from the loan collector. So he suggested that the borrowers meet in groups after the weekly Friday prayer and make repayment at the group meeting.

This was the genesis of the now famous group lending scheme that is used all over the world. Initially, the groups were based on loan activity. For example, all borrowers using credit for rearing goats were organized into a group. This innovation soon became unworkable, because the bank worker could not find enough people using credit for the same purpose to form a group.[6] Then the bank developed the idea of allowing groups with members who used credit for different purposes. After a period of trial and error, a group size of five was settled on. A major reason for the prior failure of credit cooperatives in Bangladesh was that the groups were too big and consisted of people with varied economic backgrounds. These large groups did not work because the more affluent members captured the organizations. Yunus wanted to avoid this fate by keeping the groups small and preventing the rich from joining them by using a maximum amount of land ownership as the condition for membership.

To avoid the mistakes of the cooperatives, the bank insisted that the group members have similar economic backgrounds, as well as trust and confidence in each other's ability to repay loans. The bank also stipulated that only one member per household be allowed in the group to prevent a particular family from having undue influence in any one group. The selection and training of members and the function of the group remained the same in the new model. Each group is required to elect a group chairperson and a secretary. The chairperson's main task is to collect the payments from other members and hand them over to the bank worker. The groups had to go through a period of rigorous training while they learned the rules and regulations of the bank, including learning how to sign their names and memorizing the bank's "Sixteen Decisions" regarding social conduct. The "Sixteen Decisions," a social charter for the borrowers, was adopted in a national workshop of center chiefs in 1984. This social development program is the bank's attempt to deal with the social aspects of being poor. It includes pledges from the borrowers to limit the size of their families, educate their children, not accept or give dowry, plant vegetable gardens, and other resolutions (see Appendix 2A).[7]

After training, each member of the group is required to pass an oral test, and then the group is recognized formally. Six to eight such groups are federated into a center, which holds weekly meetings. These centers elect center chiefs and deputy center chiefs, whose task is to maintain the discipline of the center. In the center meetings, the center manager (bank worker) collects savings deposits and loan installments, and approves loan proposals (see Figure 2.1). The approved loan is disbursed at the branch office. Part of the meeting time is also used to discuss problems that borrowers might be facing in the utilization of the loan and how to resolve them. In the meeting, the bank workers might distribute seeds and treesaplings at cost, give advice to the borrowers about hygiene and other social issues such as family planning, and urge them to immunize their children

Initially, loans were given to the two neediest borrowers in the group; depending on their performance, two more received loans. Generally, the chairperson was the last one to get a loan. Successful repayment of one loan led to the sanctioning of new and larger loans. A loan was given for the stated purpose of income generation and housing rather than consumption. Each member's loan contract was cosigned by the group chairperson, and other members were expected to behave responsibly by urging the borrower to repay the loan on time.[8]

To receive a loan, borrowers were required to save. One component of this saving was the deposit of a fixed amount weekly; the other was a 5% deduction from a loan to go toward what was known as the group tax. The compulsory weekly savings and loan deductions were used to create a group fund, and the borrowers were paid 8.5% interest on their deposits. The fund was managed by the group; borrowers could withdraw money from the group fund

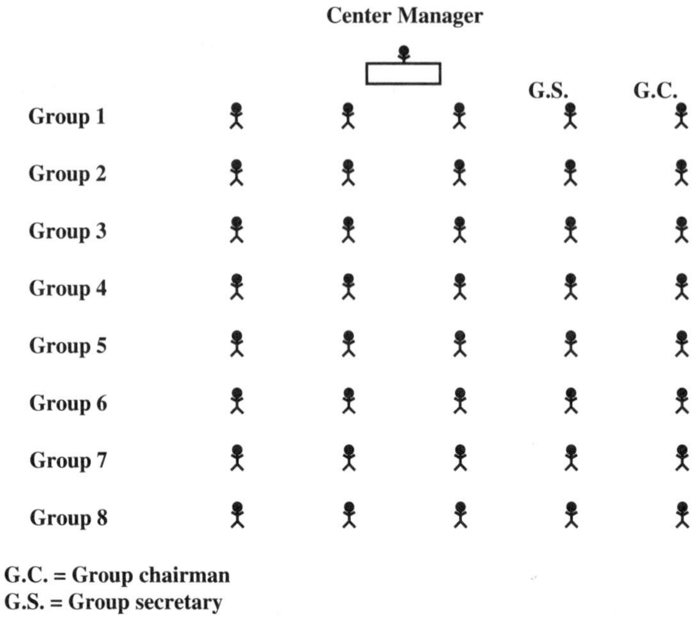

Center Manager

				G.S.	G.C.
Group 1	🧍	🧍	🧍	🧍	🧍
Group 2	🧍	🧍	🧍	🧍	🧍
Group 3	🧍	🧍	🧍	🧍	🧍
Group 4	🧍	🧍	🧍	🧍	🧍
Group 5	🧍	🧍	🧍	🧍	🧍
Group 6	🧍	🧍	🧍	🧍	🧍
Group 7	🧍	🧍	🧍	🧍	🧍
Group 8	🧍	🧍	🧍	🧍	🧍

G.C. = Group chairman
G.S. = Group secretary

Figure 2.1   Center meeting under the classical Grameen model

temporarily, provided that the loan amount did not exceed more than half of the group fund and that the group approved the purpose of the loan. In case of a disaster such as prolonged flooding, the full amount accumulated in the group fund could be withdrawn. The group fund was used for numerous purposes, such as paying school tuition and buying food during the lean season. The accumulated group fund of the bank exceeded the net worth of many companies in Bangladesh.

In February 2001 Grameen Bank was planning to take these accumulated funds and use them to float a mutual fund. A private asset management company was slated to issue a mutual fund in which the group funds would be used to buy blue-chip stocks. The asset management company was willing to guarantee a 10% minimum rate of return on the mutual fund, which is higher than what the borrowers could get (8.5%) by keeping their money with the bank. Initially, about 120 to 150 million taka would have been floated out of the 10 billion taka accumulated in the group fund at that time. However, after a scandal and the collapse of stock market bubble in 1996, activity in the market became rather thin and the private asset company did not feel that it would be prudent to issue the fund until an upturn occurred in the market.

Recently, the bank has revived this plan, as activity in the share market has picked up. The bank has given seed money of 16.5 million taka to the same asset management company to float a mutual fund. The company raised another 103.5 million taka through selling the fund privately to the leading financial institutions of the country, plus another 50 million by selling it to the public through the stock market. The fund is called Grameen Mutual Fund One (or Grameen One), with a size of 170 million taka. The initial public offering of the fund in the local market was oversubscribed by about nine and a half times in the primary market, and ownership had to be determined through a lottery.[9] On the first day of trading, the closing price of a share of Grameen One was 18 taka against the face value of 10 taka.

A recent paper by the former chairman of Grameen Bank, Professor Rehman Sobhan, notes

> Whatever may be the fate of the Grameen Fund, the concept of mutual funds for the poor provides significant institutional mechanisms to move the poor out of the village economy and into the more dynamic corporate sector, to a stage where a significant share of corporate wealth could be owned by the poor. The savings of the poor can not only augment the savings base but also broaden the investment capacity of the economy, whilst transforming the poorest rural household into stakeholders in the process of national economic growth.[10]

Before 1995 Grameen borrowers could not access group funds other than for short-term withdrawal subject to approval by the group that had to be repaid. Even though borrowing from the group fund was interest free, borrowers had to pay a 5% group tax, known as Group Tax 2, on these loans. More important, borrowers who dropped out could not claim their share of the group fund. When the group was small, the policy of restricted access was acceptable to the borrowers. As the group fund became larger, however, borrowers colluded to access these funds on a regular basis. For example, if 2000 taka accumulated in the group fund, the group would approve withdrawal of the total amount from the fund and split it equally among them. However, when the group fund started to become substantial, this ad hoc arrangement became unacceptable to borrowers, who demanded open access to these funds. Moreover, the policy of not allowing borrowers to claim their accumulated contributions to the group fund when they dropped out was seen as unfair. Thus, in response to the borrowers' demand, Grameen changed its policy in 1995. Under the new policy, the borrowers' contributions to the group fund were transferred to their individual savings accounts if they had been members of the bank for ten years. If a borrower left the institution before ten years, she or he could take out the contribution after it was adjusted for any outstanding loan amount. The bank has also abandoned collecting a group tax (Group Tax 2) on loans from the group fund.

In addition to the compulsory saving related to the group fund, the borrower can save voluntarily as well. Until recently, the bank did not pursue voluntary deposit collection vigorously, even though this would have enabled it to collect savings from members and nonmembers alike.

As a part of initial Grameen model, borrowers were required to contribute 25% of interest due on the principal to an emergency fund. The accumulated funds were used to provide life insurance to all members and to support activities to improve members' welfare. In 1991 the contribution to the emergency fund was reduced to 5 taka for every 1000 taka borrowed for loan amounts exceeding 1000 taka; in 1995 the bank stopped collecting contributions to the emergency fund altogether. The income from the accumulated funds is now used to pay death benefits of 2000 taka to those who have been members since 1995 and 1000 taka to newer members. As of January 2005, all members will receive a 1500 taka death benefit from the proceeds of the fund irrespective of membership duration. In addition, the return from the fund is used to pay for the disaster fund for each center, which provides relief during and after floods or other natural disasters.

Each borrower is required to buy a share of the bank, which has a face value of 100 taka; the first 100 taka accumulated in the group fund is used to buy the share. The borrowers receive 8.5% interest on funds accumulated in the group fund except for the 100 taka used to buy the share. The bank has not yet paid any dividends on the shares; its long-term plan is to allow the borrowers to swap these shares for shares of other, sister organizations of the bank. In a recent directive, Bangladesh Bank, the central bank of the country, has urged the bank to pay dividends for share ownership.[11] The government granted tax-exempt status to Grameen Bank with the stipulation that the payable dividends be transferred to a rehabilitation fund. Grameen Bank's tax-exempt status expired in December 2005. On the other hand, Grameen Bank's competitors, such as the credit-granting NGOs, enjoy unconditional tax-exempt status and they also charge higher interest rates than the bank. The bank pointed out to the government that forcing it to pay tax and dividends will make it difficult to compete with its rivals. The bank suggested that if the government is ready to grant it unconditional tax-exempt status, it will distribute dividends to its shareholders.

In addition to owning shares of the bank, the borrowers collectively elect the majority of the members of the board of directors: nine out of the thirteen board members are directly elected by the borrowers, and currently they own 94% of shares of the bank (see Figure 2.2).

One exciting possible use of the shares currently owned by the borrowers would be to exchange them for shares of for-profit sister organizations of Grameen Bank, such as Grameen Telecom. Grameen Telecom owns 38% of the shares of Grameen Phone, with Telenor, the largest mobile phone company in Norway, owning the remaining 62%. Grameen Phone, an extremely profitable company with 6 million subscribers, is the largest multinational corporation in the country. When the company goes public, the share swap could make Grameen Bank members direct stakeholders of this large multinational corporation.

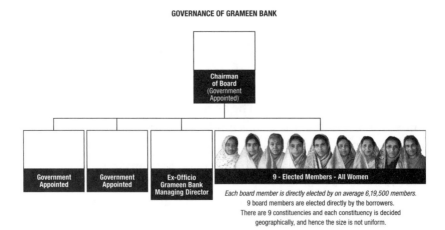

GOVERNANCE OF GRAMEEN BANK

Chairman
of Board
(Government
Appointed)

Government
Appointed

Government
Appointed

Ex-Officio
Grameen Bank
Managing Director

9 - Elected Members - All Women

Each board member is directly elected by on average 6,19,500 members.
9 board members are elected directly by the borrowers.
There are 9 constituencies and each constituency is decided
geographically, and hence the size is not uniform.

Figure 2.2   Board of directors of Grameen Bank.

So far, we have examined the savings side of classical Grameen, where a portion of the compulsory savings was used to buy ownership in the bank. The most important business of the bank, however, is disbursement of credit. Under classical Grameen, there were several types of loans a borrower could obtain, and the borrower could also have several loans outstanding. The typical loan of Grameen Bank, known as the "general loan," had duration of one year and was to be repaid in fifty-two equal installments. The repayment started a week after the disbursement of the loan. This loan product, which was fine-tuned based on earlier experiences in Chittagong and Tangail, is widely used in replications of the Grameen Bank model throughout the world. In the earlier years of Grameen, the last two installments were set aside to count as interest payments. Later the arrangement was changed to include principal and interest payments in each installment. Each of these installments consists of 2% of the principal amount and 2 taka interest per week for every 1000 taka of the loan amount, with an interest rate of 20% on a declining-balance basis. These loans were—and still are—supposed to be used for non-farm activities.

Initially, the majority of the loans were used for activities that were safe and would yield quick returns, such as milch cow raising, paddy husking, cattle fattening, seasonal crop trading, and handloom weaving. Now that the average size of the loan is larger, loan funds are increasingly used for high value-added (in the sense that these activities are more profitable but require large investments) activities such as buying agricultural equipment, cellular phones, and small irrigation equipment.

As Grameen progressed, new loan products were introduced, many of which were variations of the general loan. These new loan products were prompted by the realization that the credit needs of borrowers change and the bank has to let borrowers take advantage of new opportunities. For example, seasonal loans were introduced to allow borrowers to buy a product for a low price during the harvesting seasons and sell it during the lean season at a higher price. Many of these new loan products were suggested by the borrowers themselves. In Arihazar, an area near Dhaka, the capital city, the borrowers of the bank noticed that many of their competitors were using power looms; they, on the other hand, were producing fabrics for local markets with handlooms. They suggested that the bank help them acquire power looms. Initially, the bank bought the power looms and rented them out to the borrowers. The bank manager soon realized that the borrowers would be better served if the machines were leased to them, as borrowers could then pay the cost plus the leasing fee with income from these machines. After a year of piloting leasing loans in another part of the country, leasing was introduced in 1994 in all zones of the bank.

Clearly, the repayment conditions for newer products such as leasing loans had to be different from those for the general loan. For example, livestock leasing loans were introduced so that the borrower could buy an animal and fatten it to sell during the Muslim holiday of *Qurbani*. Generally, the duration of these loans was six months, and borrowers repaid with a one-time payment. This leasing loan was more flexible than the general loan, as the repayment commenced a month after the loan disbursement. Moreover, the installment payments for pure leasing loans were flexible enough to be synchronized with the demand cycle for the equipment, allowing for low repayment during the lean season and high repayment during the peak period.[12]

In the early 1980s Grameen Bank also experimented with the collective loan, a bigger loan given to a group instead of to the individual. The motivation for these larger loans was that they would enable members to fund more profitable activities that required greater capital, such as installation of rice, oil, and weaving mills and leasing of markets, orchards, and bodies of water. However, some members felt that they were doing most of the work while others enjoyed the benefits. Conflict among the group members resulted in the limited success of these loans, and the bank eventually abandoned them.

Another important loan of classical Grameen was the housing loan. This loan was introduced on a small scale in 1984, but was expanded rapidly after the devastating flood of 1987. Grameen felt that better housing for the poor should be categorized as an investment rather than as consumption, as the borrower can use a good house both as factory space and as protection from natural calamities detrimental to health. The housing loan, which exists to this day, is a long-term loan to be repaid by weekly installments over several years, with an annual interest rate of 8% per year. Initially, a sum of up to 15,000 taka was introduced as the "Moderate Housing" loan. The amount was raised to 25,000 taka to account for the rising cost of building materials. The houses built with the loans must meet certain minimum standards to protect this investment: the loan must be used to purchase four reinforced concrete pillars, a sanitary latrine, and corrugated iron roofing sheets. Each house must have a reinforced concrete pillar on a brick foundation at each corner, and six intermediary bamboo posts, with bamboo tie beams, wooden rafters and purlins supporting the corrugated iron roofing sheets. The approved structure of the house provides protection against floods, cyclones, strong monsoon winds, and rain. The pillars and the corrugated sheets are more likely to survive natural disasters such as floods and can be used to rebuild the house fairly quickly afterward.

The housing loan is given exclusively to women. The land on which the house is built has to be in the woman's name. Grameen included this condition to make sure that the woman would not be evicted from her home in case of dissolution of the marriage. There is a common misperception among the uneducated poor that a Muslim male can divorce his wife just by uttering "I divorce thee" three times. Even though such divorces are illegal and do not conform to the religious texts, most people in the rural areas accept this edict. Registering the land in the names of the women protects them from such circumstances. Even though women are entitled to land through inheritance from their paternal families, they rarely exercise such rights. They voluntarily waive these rights and, in some cases, involuntarily waive them in favor of their brothers. They need the goodwill and the protection of their brothers in case of a breakdown of the marriage, and waiving the rights to family land is a means of guaranteeing that protection. Owning a piece of land through a housing loan from Grameen Bank may be the only way for a woman to have "a house of her own."

After the flood of 1987, the bank realized that the borrowers needed money to rebuild homes that were damaged. As a result, a new type of housing loan, the "Basic Housing Loan," was introduced. The loan amount was raised from 7000 taka to 12,000 taka to account for the rise in prices of building materials. Initially, the repayment period for a housing loan was a multiple of one-thousandth of the amount; for example, a 10,000 taka loan would have to be repaid in ten years. Later on, the maximum period for repayment of a housing loan was fixed at ten years irrespective of the amount borrowed, because the bank felt that the previous method of computing loan duration was extending the period of repayment too far into the future. Now the maximum period for repayment of a housing loan is five years and the maximum loan size is 15,000 taka.

The key objectives of Grameen I, or classical Grameen, were to prove that the poor are creditworthy and that a lack of capital is the primary obstacle to productive self-employment among the poor.

The persistent high repayment rates and the documented positive impacts examined in later chapters will show that Grameen I has satisfied these objectives. We can summarize the salient features of Grameen I as follows:[13]

- It is targeted at the poor, particularly poor women, as identified by land ownership.
- It is offered to create self-employment for income-generating activities and housing for the poor, as opposed to consumption.
- It is based on "trust" rather than collateral or legally enforceable contracts.
- All loans are to be paid back in installments (weekly or bi-weekly).
- To receive loans, a borrower must join a group of borrowers.
- A borrower can receive a new loan, often of larger size, if the previous loan is repaid. A borrower can also have more than one loan outstanding.
- Grameen I comes with both obligatory and voluntary savings programs for the borrowers.
- The model is based on a democratic governance structure. The borrowers elect group and center leaders and board members through regular elections. The behavior of the borrowers is regulated by "Sixteen Decisions," the social development charter drawn up mainly by the borrowers.

These key features of Grameen I, including loans structured for the poor and the other features mentioned above, have changed since the bank's institution. There are, however, aspects of classic Grameen that have remained unchanged.

The management structure of the bank is one characteristic that has retained its original form. The lowest administrative unit of the bank is the branch, which typically consists of a branch manager, a senior assistant, several bank workers, and a peon cum guard. A branch usually manages eighty centers, each of which consists of six to eight groups. The bank worker known as the center manager is in charge of ten centers (see Figure 2.3).

GRAMEEN BANK ORGANIZATIONAL DESIGN
January 2006

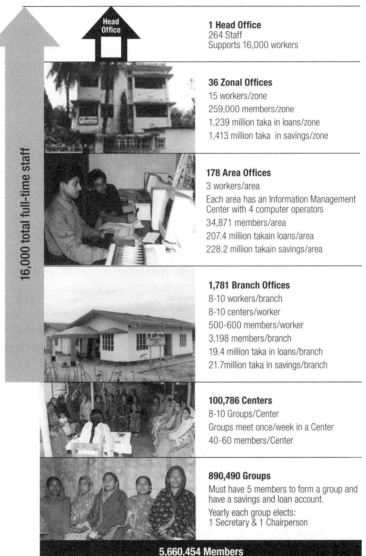

1 Head Office
264 Staff
Supports 16,000 workers

36 Zonal Offices
15 workers/zone
259,000 members/zone
1,239 million taka in loans/zone
1,413 million taka in savings/zone

178 Area Offices
3 workers/area
Each area has an Information Management
Center with 4 computer operators
34,871 members/area
207.4 million takain loans/area
228.2 million takain savings/area

1,781 Branch Offices
8-10 workers/branch
8-10 centers/worker
500-600 members/worker
3,198 members/branch
19.4 million taka in loans/branch
21.7million taka in savings/branch

100,786 Centers
8-10 Groups/Center
Groups meet once/week in a Center
40-60 members/Center

890,490 Groups
Must have 5 members to form a group and
have a savings and loan account.
Yearly each group elects:
1 Secretary & 1 Chairperson

5,660,454 Members

16,000 total full-time staff

Head Office

Figure 2.3   Organizational structure of Grameen Bank.

The next administrative level of the bank's operation is an area office, which supervises ten branches. Ten area offices constitute a zonal office. The zonal offices are managed by the head office, which is situated in the capital city of Dhaka. Each branch of the bank borrows money from the head office at 12% and on-lends it to borrowers at 20%. The branch office is supposed to cover all its costs from the 8% margin; after three to fours years of operation, the branch usually starts making profit. One or two zonal manager conferences are held in the head office every year. A conference lasts for three days and all zonal managers participate—one area manager from each zone and all department and section heads from the head office, including the managing director, deputy managing director and general managers. Usually, zonal audit officers are also invited to attend these all-important meetings. Under the supervision of the managing director, participants discuss the crucial issues facing the bank. Many of the major decisions, such as those involving the introduction of new products, the development of important policy, and rule changes, are made in these meetings. The meetings are also used to hammer out differences on major policy and implementation issues across zones.

Grameen now has a staff of over 16,000 employees. Branch managers and bank workers are directly recruited. These managers are required to hold a master's degree, whereas non-officers must have passed the higher secondary school certification exams. Since most of the borrowers are female, special preference is given to female candidates. The recruitment process is highly competitive and involves passing a rigorous written test and attending a face-to-face interview. Once selected, the staff must undergo an intensive twelve-month training program divided into two six-month periods. During the first period, staff spend time at the Training Institute at the head office and also undergo classroom training and field visits. At the end of this period, the trainee must pass an examination, after which he or she is posted for on-the-job training in the branch. At the end of this training period, trainees must pass another exam so that they can be accorded permanent status. About 35% of the original recruits do not make it to the end of the training period. Such a high dropout rate during the training stage may be construed as expensive, but once one realizes the difficult and complex nature of the job, the expense appears justified. This rigorous training also instills in the staff a sense of pride and genuine concern for the poor. Once staff survive the provisionary period, only a very negligible fraction leave the institution, and there have been only minor cases of embezzlement of funds by the staff. In fact, staff have been known to protect the funds despite the threat of physical injury and even death. They are fervently loyal to the institution and its mission, despite the demanding nature of the job.

World Bank social scientist Michael Woolcock aptly describes the challenges faced by a branch manager at Grameen. He notes that in the course of a single day the manager is "likely to find himself assuming the roles of marriage counselor, conflict negotiator, training officer, civic leader, and bank manager. From 6 am until 10 pm, a day in the life of this young rural banker at times seems more demanding and intense than that of an emergency room doctor."[14] Successful branch managers who have accumulated diverse experience are eventually promoted to area and zonal mangers.[15]

The interests of the staff are represented by the Staff Association, which was established June 19, 1991. The Staff Association is registered under the Societies Act, which regulates the conduct of nonpolitical, nongovernmental, and nonprofit associations. All non-officers are members of the association, and they elect their representative by direct voting at each level of the bank's hierarchy: branch, area, and zone. For example, non-officers at the branch level elect one representative to represent them at the area committee. In addition, there is a Central Committee of the Staff Association consisting of zonal representatives. Every month the association meets with the representative of the bank at the branch, area, and zone levels. The bank is represented by the managers at the respective levels. For example, the branch manager holds monthly meetings with representatives of the association at the branch level. In these monthly meetings, the association and management raise issues of mutual interest and resolve them through discussion and dialogue. Minutes of such meetings are recorded and sent to the next-level committees and to the bank's representative. Issues unresolved at the lower level are discussed by the higher-level committee. Every two months the Central Committee meets with representatives of the bank at head office. The bank is represented by the deputy managing director, general managers, and deputy general managers. These meeting are used to work out unresolved issues at the lower levels and to deal with issues that affect the whole organization. During this time, the Central Committee also holds a one-on-one meeting with the managing director. All these venues give the staff an opportunity to raise their concerns and grievances with the management and to reach solutions through bilateral discussions.

This unique institutional innovation in labor management has allowed the bank to bypass the militant and highly political trade unions in Bangladesh, whose influence goes beyond the standard industrial relations and into the political arena. A major problem faced by the state-owned commercial banks is undue influence of the trade unions. A task force headed by the deputy governor of the central bank in 1997 reported that some commercial banks had as many as six unions and none had less than three. When there is more than one union, the Registrar of Trade Unions selects a collective bargaining agent (CBA) for a period of two years through a secret ballot. The task force further reported that in eight big commercial banks at least 30% of employees do not work at all, as they were involved with trade unions.[16] The chairman of the task force summarized the problem with trade unionism in the country in an op-ed piece in the English-language newspaper *The Daily Star.*[17]

The Daily Star also published an investigative report on how state-owned banks are held hostage by the CBA:[18]

> CBAs are affiliated with major political parties and have very good connections with political leaders and influential ministers. --- Normally 80 per cent of transfers are done on the "request" of CBA leaders, --- 30 per cent of workers, holding different posts in the employee unions, do not perform their official duties. --- Each contractor is compelled to give 2 per cent of the bill amount

involved in any work order as toll to the workers' union. --- CBAs have established a parallel management in every NCB, which created a major barrier for improving the activities of the banks. --- Even with regard to promotion and transfer of officials, which is not under their purviews, they intervene and coerce the management. In such cases, they take bribe ranging from Tk 5,000 to Tk 20,000 from the official concerned.

The Staff Association provides staff with a voice in the management of the bank. It helps resolve conflicts in a congenial manner without the type of political intervention and corruption referred to in the report.[19] The staff play a crucial role in the opening and operation of the branches.

When the bank decides to open a new branch, the manager designate is sent to the target village with the assignment of preparing a socioeconomic report highlighting the area's geography, demography, economic structure, transport and communication networks, and political structure. This allows the manager to be familiar with his or her area of operation. The report is then sent to the head office for approval. Once the report is approved, the manager organizes a public meeting in the area, inviting all classes of people. In the meeting the manager introduces the visiting staff from the area and zonal offices and explains the purpose, rules, and program of the bank. The manager also makes it clear that it is up to the people of the area to decide whether or not to allow Grameen Bank to start operation. Once permission is granted to establish a branch, the staff invite interested persons who qualify for a loan to form a group of five people of similar economic conditions.[20] Once the branch is established, its staff try to increase its business slowly and carefully. The bank is now more than twenty-five years old, and the key question is how it has affected the borrowers, their families, and the greater community through its activities.

Since the core business of Grameen Bank is disbursement of credit, the most important challenge is to isolate the impact of credit from all other influences that affect the borrowers. Indeed, there is controversy as to whether the effect of credit can be determined at all.[21] Ideally, the way to assess the impact of credit is to observe households with and without credit and measure the impact of credit, holding all other effects constant. In real life, of course, this is not feasible. Another alternative would be to find a group of people who are essentially the same in every aspect and randomly assign them to two subgroups: with credit (treatment group) and without credit (control group). Since the people theoretically are the same in every aspect, any difference in their behavior could be attributed to the effect of credit. Even though random assignment to groups with or without credit is methodologically appealing, it is very difficult to implement in practice. A bank for the poor such as Grameen would find it hard to justify giving credit randomly to a group of poor people and declining credit to others for methodological convenience.

Most of the studies reported in this book compare a group receiving credit with a similar group without credit. The group selected to receive credit is not chosen randomly; rather, they have to meet certain conditions, such as land ownership below a cutoff point. Once the researchers identify the group with credit, they look for a group who qualify to receive credit by the same criterion but chose not to. The use of such nonexperimental data between participants and nonparticipants suffers from selection bias, however, as it may be difficult to find a control group that is identical to the group receiving credit. If the treatment group and the control group are not exactly the same, any difference between them could be erroneously attributed to the effect of credit. With the heavy penetration in Bangladesh of NGO-led credit disbursement as well as Grameen Bank, it is questionable whether one could find an ideal control group: individuals who are in the same economic condition as the members but have not joined the NGOs or the bank. Even if a control group could be effectively identified, people who participate may self-select themselves into these programs; that is, they participate essentially because they have the entrepreneurial ability to take advantage of credit and have the financial discipline and resources to make regular installment payments. Failure to correct for such bias will lead analysts to overestimate the effect of credit by conflating it with the entrepreneurial ability of the borrower.

Another complication with this method of testing arises because institutions do not place their programs randomly. If a program is placed in a relatively rich area with good infrastructure, the effect of intervention through credit will be lumped with access to better facilities.[22] Alternatively, if the program is placed where there are more poor people, as is the case with Grameen Bank, then comparing program participants with the control group without adjusting for this discrepancy will underestimate the impact of program participation.[23] As Pitt and Khandker argue,[24]

> Comparison of the two sets of villages as in a treatment/control framework would lead to a downward bias in the estimated effect of the program on household income and wealth (and other outcomes associated with income and wealth) and could even erroneously suggest that credit programs reduce income and wealth if the positive effect of the credit program on the difference between "treatment" and "control" villages did not exceed the negative village effect that induced the nonrandom placement.

Another potential source of bias is unmeasured village effects. If the village is close to an urban area, then the choice of location may affect the demand for credit as well as the attitudes and behaviors of the households. Another unresolved issue is the fungibility of credit. If the borrowers use credit from several sources, it will be difficult to identify which source is responsible for the alleged effects. However, if the households are credit constrained, needing more credit than is available through the program, then the problem of fungibility can be avoided. Most existing studies do not account for this issue.[25]

The first serious evaluation of Grameen Bank was conducted in 1988 by Mahbub Hossain, now the head of the Social Science Division of International Rice Research Institute. At the time, he was a staff member of the Bangladesh Institute of Development Studies. His study entailed comparing groups with credit from Grameen

Bank with control groups and did not correct for the biases mentioned above. Hossain found that Grameen Bank enhanced access to credit by people who were left out by such institutional sources as commercial banks. The bank was successful in reaching the poor: only 4.2% of the members had more than a half-acre of land, the cutoff point for being defined as poor. The most dramatic effect of the bank, according to Hossain, has been the accumulation of credit by the poor. He found that the amount of working capital employed by the borrowers increased three times during the survey period of twenty-seven months. Moreover, the borrowers were able to increase their income by investing the credit from the bank in income-earning activities. Hossain further showed that the growth of income was greatest for the absolutely landless.[26] Not surprisingly, most of the impacts were deemed positive.

Hossain's oft-cited study was part of a larger study of the impact of Grameen Bank conducted by the Bangladesh Institute of Development Studies.[27] Other researchers of the institute examined additional aspects of the effect of Grameen Bank's efforts. Rushidan Islam examined the impact of the bank on women's income, employment, consumption, fertility, and decision-making power, and found that credit from the bank had a positive impact on these important aspects of female life. Another researcher, Atiur Rahman, found that the local power structure was not a hindrance in targeting the rural poor for meaningful rural development. In another study, he found that the housing loan enabled members to make a vital investment that increased their productive capacity and improved their social status.

The most rigorous evaluation of Grameen Bank was conducted by the World Bank.[28] This was part of a larger project that evaluated the impact of Grameen Bank, BRAC (Bangladesh Rural Advancement Committee, an NGO), and BRDB (Bangladesh Rural Development Board, a government-sponsored microcredit program). The World Bank study was able to correct for differences in individual ability and village-level characteristics as well as nonrandom program placement by using features of the credit delivery design. Since participation in the program of Grameen Bank was determined by individual, household, microcredit programs, and village-level characteristics, and was not exogenous, the evaluation resorted to a quasi-experimental design using the program's own restriction—land ownership of less than half an acre—to exogenously determine program participation. The borrowers could get money from many sources, including microfinance institutions (MFIs) such as Grameen Bank, and since money is fungible, it would have been difficult to attribute the impacts to a particular source. The World Bank study, without specific testing, assumed that households were credit constrained and provided a number of justifications in support of this assumption, which allowed the researchers to assess the impact of borrowing from the bank as opposed to other sources of credit.[29] The authors used "a double-difference" approach: between eligible and ineligible households and between program and non-program villages. This approach allowed the researchers to identify the impact of credit from MFIs after controlling for various household characteristics.[30] For assessing impact, the World Bank study defined program participation as the cumulative amount of borrowing over the five-year period before the survey was conducted.[31]

The World Bank surveyed 1798 households in seventy-two program villages and fifteen control villages for the period 1991–1993.[32] The households in the program villages borrowed from Grameen Bank, BRAC, or BRDB. The study found that a 10% increase in credit to women borrowers raises household per-capita weekly expenditure by 0.43%.[33] For all three programs, the impact of borrowing on consumption by women is higher than for men: an additional 1 taka of credit provided to women adds 0.18 taka to total annual household expenditure, compared with 0.11 taka for men.[34] A 10% increase in borrowing from Grameen Bank increases the net worth (value of assets minus the value of loans outstanding) by 0.14% and 0.15% for female and male borrowers, respectively.[35] A 1% increase in credit to women increases the probability of school enrollment by 1.9% for girls and 2.4% for boys, whereas credit to men only increased the probability of school enrollment for boys by 2.8%.[36] Credit provided to women also improved the nutritional status of the children. A 10% increase in credit increased arm circumference in girls by 6.3%, with a somewhat smaller effect on the arm circumference of boys. In addition, a 10% increase in credit to females was found to increase the height of girls by 0.36 cm annually and of boys by 0.50 cm.[37] Credit given to men, on the other hand, did not have any effect on the nutritional status of the children regardless of their gender.

Surprisingly, the World Bank study found that credit to women reduced contraceptive use. The study explains this anomaly by suggesting that women in the credit group were already using contraceptives more than the control group. Helen Todd, who wrote an interesting book about long-term borrowers of Grameen Bank in Tangail titled *Women in the Center,* found an opposing explanation for the low or insignificant effect of credit on contraceptive usage. Todd reports that women in her control group used more contraception than the Grameen Bank borrowers.[38] Her explanation was that the control group consisted of older widows who were not asked about contraceptive use. Further, the control group consisted of younger women with much higher contraceptive use, while Grameen groups consisted of older women with husbands who were convinced of the benefit of larger family size.

Other studies found that the credit program of Grameen Bank promotes increased contraceptive use.[39] However, these studies do not control for the self-selection and nonrandom program placement biases mentioned earlier. In a later paper, Pitt, Khandker, and McKernan (1999) show that when these biases are corrected for, the rise in contraceptive use due to credit vanishes.[40] Still others suggest that the differences in the results are a reflection of the way participation is specified: the World Bank study measured program participation by the cumulative amount of loans in the last five years, whereas others measured participation using a question on whether the respondent belonged to a program and how long she has belonged.[41]

The ambiguous relationship between access to credit and fertility found in the empirical literature is also present in theory. First, credit increases the value of time spent by women on market-related activities, and this increases their income. An increase in income increases the demand for children, as increased income makes it possible for a family to have more children. This causal relationship is known as the "income effect." Second, the increased market value of women's time makes it costly for them to spend it raising children. In other words, having and raising children becomes an expensive proposition, and as a result, women will desire fewer children. This is called the "substitution effect." Third, cash income in the hands of women increases their bargaining strength in the household, allowing women to gain control of the decision to have children and possibly causing them to opt for fewer children as a result.[42] The consciousness-raising efforts of the bank by means of the "Sixteen Decisions" can also lead to reduced fertility, as decision 6 affirms, "We shall plan to keep our families small." In addition, the bank worker discusses the benefits of small families in center meetings. The pronouncements of the "Sixteen Decisions" and consciousness-raising efforts by the bank worker could thus lead to a changed norm of family size. Whether increased credit will affect fertility depends on the relative strengths of these various effects: some suggest that access to credit will increase the number of children, while others point to the opposite effect.

The primary objective of Grameen Bank is to reduce the poverty of its members. This reduction is supposed to occur as a result of the members using the borrowing and saving function of the bank to increase their income and thus reduce their vulnerability. Grameen Bank specifically targets the poor and expects that they will use the credit in productive investments that will raise their income, thereby reducing poverty. It follows that the most important evidence of the bank's success is whether or not it is reducing the poverty of its members.

Mahbub Hossain's survey revealed that 92% of Grameen borrowers demonstrated an increase in income, an effect he attributed to increased accumulation of capital and increased opportunity for productive employment made possible by membership in the bank.[43] Further, he reported that the average income of the bank members was significantly higher than that of nonparticipants—43% higher in the control villages and 28% higher in the project villages. To ascertain

the impact of poverty alleviation, Hossain calculated the food poverty line by computing the cost of a consumption bundle providing
an intake of 2112 calories and 58 grams of protein. The amount was
adjusted upward to account for non-food expenditure, resulting in
two poverty lines: a moderate poverty line of 3500 taka per capita
per year, and an extreme poverty line of 2975 taka per capita per
year.[44] Based on the poverty line, Hossain reports that 84% of target-
group nonparticipants—people with less than half an acre of land
who are not members of the bank—in project villages and 80% of
nonparticipants in control villages are poor, compared with 61% of
the bank members. The members also fared better in the extreme-
poverty category: 48% of them were living in extreme poverty,
compared with 75% for both control groups.[45]

The World Bank study found that membership in the bank has
increased consumption on the part of the borrowers and reduced poverty. A 10% increase in borrowing from Grameen Bank increases
expenditures of households by 0.4% when women borrow and by
0.2% when men borrow. Moreover, the study found that every 100
taka lent to a women borrower increased household consumption by
18 taka, while the same amount lent to men increased it by 11 taka.[46]
Using the same method mentioned earlier, the World Bank study
computed both a moderate and an extreme poverty line for the study
year.[47] About 21% of Grameen bank borrowers moved out of poverty
within a span of 4.2 years of membership. The study concludes that
5% of Grameen Bank borrowers left poverty status each year by borrowing from the bank.[48] Khandker (1998) further found that a 10%
increase in borrowing from Grameen Bank reduced the probability of
being below the poverty line by 0.3% for males and 0.2% for females.

The alleviation of poverty reported in the World Bank study
was challenged by Morduch (1999). He suggested that the optimis-
tic result was due to a failure to take into account the problem of
mistargeting—specifically, including people who have more than
half an acre of land at the time of membership in the bank. When Morduch excluded around 30% of the sample who did not qualify according to the land ownership criteria and used a simpler estimation

strategy, he found no increase in income due to membership in the bank. However, he did find that participation in Grameen Bank reduces variability of consumption and labor supply and, therefore, reduces vulnerability of the members. Menon (2003) also found that membership reduces variability of consumption across seasons. For a female participant, one year of membership reduced the change in per-capita consumption due to a shock (i.e., an unanticipated catastrophic occurrence such as a flood, crop failure, or husband's death) by 6%. Pitt (1999) provided a rejoinder to Morduch's criticism. His counter-argument was that the criterion for membership is defined in term of cultivatable land; what constitutes cultivatability, however, is ambiguous, as many households own land that is barely cultivatable or uncultivatable.[49] Pitt (1999) suggests that what appears to be mistargeting is actually due to adjustments the credit programs were making for varying land quality, as "mistargeted" households had land of lower value at the time of the survey.[50] This finding suggests that the land criterion could be loosened to take into account qualitative differences in the land. Another reason for not strictly interpreting the land criterion is that for a large household, per-capita landholding may be low. Pitt shows that earlier results showing positive benefits of credit on poverty hold up even under a looser eligibility standard of more than half an acre. In fact, the gender effect is strengthened, increasing returns from money lent to women from 18% to 20% under the weaker criterion for land ownership.[51]

The results reported above are based on data on borrowers in a given period of time. Based on a panel data set for 229 households, meaning that the information on these households was gathered over a period of time, Amin, Rai, and Topa (2003) show that microcredit programs such as Grameen Bank are successful in reaching the poor: a 24% decrease in consumption increases the probability of joining a microcredit program by 6–7%.[52]

Grameen Bank has set up an internal poverty audit to track the changes in the economic status of its borrowers. The bank uses the following ten indicators to assess whether members are moving out of poverty:[53]

- The members and their families are living in a tin-roofed house or in a house worth at least 25,000 taka, and the family members sleep on cots or a bedstead instead of the floor.
- The members drink pure water from tube-wells, boiled water, or arsenic-free water purified by the use of alum, purifying tablets, or pitcher filters.
- All of the members' children who are physically and mentally fit and are above the age of six either attend or have finished primary school.
- The member's minimum weekly installment is 200 taka.
- All family members use a hygienic and sanitary latrine.
- The family members have sufficient clothing to meet daily needs. Further, the family has winter clothes such as *kanthas* (light wraps made out of used clothing), wrappers, sweaters, quilts, and blankets to protect them from the cold, and they also have nets to protect them from mosquito bites.
- The family has additional sources of income, such as a vegetable garden or fruit-bearing tree, to fall back on when they need additional income.
- The borrower maintains an average annual balance of 5000 taka in her savings account.
- The borrower has the ability to feed her family members three square meals a day throughout the year; essentially, the family faces no food insecurity.
- All family members are conscious about their health. They have the ability to take immediate action for proper treatment and can pay medical expenses in the event of illness of any member of the family.

If borrowers meet the conditions in the list, they are defined as having moved out of poverty. Using the ten indicators, the bank conducts an annual survey of the poverty status of its borrowers, and the results are published in its annual report.[54] So far, the assessment has been done internally, which means that the branch staff conducts the survey, and results are checked by the audit department for errors and misreporting. The final report consists of the audited statements from the branches that have been aggregated to show the changes in the poverty status of all borrowers. Further, it specifies the numbers of borrowers who moved out of poverty, who are still in poverty, and who have fallen back into poverty. These figures are reported in annual as well in cumulative terms.

Following is a summary indicating the percentage of borrowers moving out of poverty on the basis of the bank's ten indicators:

Year	Percent above the Poverty Line
1997	15.1
1998	20.4
1999	24.1
2000	40.0
2001	42.0
2002	46.5
2003	51.1
2004	55.0
2005	58.4

Source: Monitoring and Evaluation Department, Grameen Bank.

The survey on the poverty status of borrowers is used to assess and reward the performance of branch, area, and zone staff. In the future, the bank plans to use an independent research organization to validate the survey instead of using its internal audit department. Aubert, de Janvry, and Sadoulet (2004) of the University of California at Berkeley suggest in a recent paper that monetary incentives to staff linked to repayment will undermine the poverty alleviation goal of pro-poor MFIs, as this would induce the staff to target the non-poor and the poor close to the poverty line. They argue in favor of a random audit to verify the poverty status of the borrowers managed by a worker and propose that such an audit will allow pro-poor MFIs to achieve the dual objective of sustainability and inclusion of the very poor.[55] Grameen Bank is doing more than what these researchers suggest: it is conducting a full, annual, and audited survey of the borrowers under the supervision of a worker and tying elimination of the borrower's poverty to the staff incentives structure. The annual survey on the poverty status of borrowers is another means of creating awareness among the staff about the ultimate objective of their work—poverty alleviation of the members.

Most of the studies cited so far, with the exception of the Amin, Rai, and Topa paper, have dealt with short-term impacts, the analysis of which is based on data from one period. To ascertain the real and sustainable impact of the bank on poverty, one needs a diachronic study that analyzes data for households over different periods. This method of collecting panel data is better because it can determine if the beneficial effects of Grameen Bank may be the result of redistribution of income—from the rich to the poor and, among the poor, from nonparticipant households to participants—rather than a permanent reduction in poverty. To determine whether the programs and their benefits are sustainable, the World Bank resurveyed the same households in 1999.[56] The study found that participants' moderate poverty was reduced by 8.5 percentage points over seven years, while extreme poverty dropped by 18.2 points.[57] As before, the study found that the effects are greater for females than for males, and that the impact of credit changes over time; in fact, the gain in consumption due to credit diminished over time, especially for women. Using the same data set, Khandker (2004) found that participants became less vulnerable, especially to floods, as a result of long-term access to microcredit.[58]

Helen Todd conducted an important study that evaluated the long-term impact of Grameen Bank on poverty and many other dimensions of life. She used a unique research design, collecting in-depth information on forty borrower households and twenty-four households in a control group for one year. The borrowers had borrowed at least eight times (in close to ten years of membership in the Bank); with this sample, long-term impacts of the bank operation could be studied.[59] Todd calculated the value of the poverty line based on a daily intake of 1800 calories per day, similar to the extreme-poverty line used by Hossain and Khandker. She found that 57% of the borrowers crossed the poverty line, compared with only 18% of the control group, during ten years of membership with the bank. In addition, 42.5% of the borrowers were still poor, compared with 82% of the non-borrowers. Among the poor, 27.5% of the borrowers were moderately poor and the rest were extremely poor. When she used the higher poverty line of 2112 calories per day, the numbers changed between Grameen borrowers and the control group, but the sharp distinction between the two groups did not.[60]

Even though the stated goal of the bank is to alleviate poverty, researchers have explored the noneconomic benefits of Grameen's operation, such as the effects on domestic violence, empowerment of women, and the education and health of the borrowers. These effects are directly related to increased income and to the provision of non-credit services such as training, information dissemination about health and hygiene, and the social charter—the "Sixteen Decisions." Most of these studies show that Grameen has positively affected these social aspects of the borrowers.[61] Hashemi, Schuler, and Riley (1996) created an index of empowerment in the form of a weighted average of individual empowerment indicators. These indicators measure the ability of the women to move freely, to make small and larger independent purchases, to participate in family decisions, and other measures. Hashemi and co-authors found not only that participation in Grameen Bank empowers women, but that some of the indicators of empowerment improve with the duration of membership. Schuler, Hashemi, Riley, and Akhtar (1996) found that Grameen Bank borrowers are better treated by their husbands; violence against them is reduced because of their economic role as borrowers.

Credit programs such as Grameen have also been found to have a positive impact on women's health. A study by a Bangladeshi NGO, UBINIG, states that a woman tends to report illness only after a condition has become severe; her reluctance is due to lack of money, lack of time for her husband to accompany her to the health center, and the general perception that women are born to suffer. Nanda (1999), using the World Bank data set and similar techniques to control for the biases mentioned earlier, found that participation in a credit program has a positive impact on a woman's decision to seek formal health care. According to Nanda, increased control over resources by the women, made possible through participation in credit programs, creates higher demand for formal health care.

Faridi (2003) takes a different tack to identify the effect of microcredit on women.[62] Motivated by results suggesting that women spend differently than men and that they spend money on food, durable goods for daily needs, and items used mainly by them, she uses expenditures on these items as a measure of women's performance in microcredit programs. The idea is that if microcredit is beneficial to women, then an appreciable increase in these expenditures should be noticeable. As we discussed before, a major problem of assessing the impact of credit is that women who participate in credit programs are generally more entrepreneurial. Unlike the Pitt and Khandker study, Faridi (2003) specifically estimates the unobserved characteristics of the women participants using a matching function informed by the condition of the marriage market. Again, the idea is that women who are more skilled will do well in the marriage market. These unobserved characteristics are then used to explain the benefit of participation by women in microcredit programs. Faridi found that microcredit programs benefit women by increasing expenditures on items and assets preferred by them.

Pitt, Khandker, and Cartwright (2003), using the 1999 World Bank survey data, find that

> credit program participation leads to women taking a greater role in household decision making, having greater access to financial and economic resources, having greater social networks, having greater bargaining power vis-à-vis their husbands, and having greater freedom of mobility. Female credit also tended to increase spousal communication in general about family planning and parenting concerns.[63]

These positive findings about the empowering effect of credit from Grameen Bank have not gone unchallenged. Goetz and Sen Gupta (1996) and Ackerly (1995) report that a significant number of women do not control the full use of the loan; instead they "pipe-line" the money to their husbands. Rahman (1999) reports similar findings, and he adds that women bear the burden of debt in their household. Given the complex nature of social interaction within the household and the myriad survival strategies used by the women, it is not clear if a complex and multidimensional concept such as empowerment can be captured simply by examining control over loan use. The challenge is masterfully captured by Todd: "Empowerment is a process. And this process by which women move from the margins to the center of economic management is complex and long-term. It is often underground; it involves the politics of bedroom and *bari* and can be seen by the outsider only in terms of outcomes."[64]

So far, we have reported research that examines the effect of participation in Grameen Bank on households rather than on individual members of households. This type of research is motivated by practical as well as theoretical issues. It is quite expensive and time-consuming to gather data about income and consumption for each member of the household as well as identifying how resources are allocated among them. Moreover, the theoretical model of households that forms the basis of this research assumes that resources are allocated to maximize household income; in these models, income or distribution of power among the members of the household does not matter. Given the dominance of patriarchy in Bangladesh, one should expect that the textbook model of a household—in which one member, a "benign dictator," such as the eldest male, controls all household resources—might hold true.

Increasingly, skepticism has been expressed about the applicability of these models in both rich and poor countries. New research shows that this type of household model has been rejected based on data from both developed and developing countries.[65] The differences in the use of increased income by males and females, widely documented by studies from many developing countries, represent another refutation of the unitary household model. Quisumbing and de la Briere (2000) and Hallman (2000), using data from a multi-country study sponsored by the International Food Policy Research Institute (IFPRI), report that in Bangladesh, despite the norm of the husband controlling most of the resources, the unitary model of household does not hold true.[66]

In poor countries, relationships among household members are characterized by patriarchy, gender disparity, and asymmetrical power relations. The "unitary model" of household has to be revised and upgraded for it to be used in poor countries. Moreover, data must be collected for all household members before one can evaluate who benefits and by how much.

The limitations of the unitary model of household have prompted economists to come up with alternative household models known as bargaining models. These models stipulate that resource allocation within the household is the result of bargaining between the members, with some threat point or breakdown position. A breakdown position is the level of welfare that a member of the household receives if no agreement can be reached. In case of a household, collapsed bargaining can be taken to mean divorce or separation. However, in the context of Bangladesh and South Asia in general, where divorces are relatively rare, the breakdown of bargaining between spouses is characterized by noncooperative behavior within marriages.[67] The bargaining models seem suited to analyze the effect of participation in credit programs: credit brought in by the women should change their bargaining strength and breakdown position. The need to identify what happens to the members of the household, and how their position within the household changes with the infusion of credit, is reinforced by the fact that only one member of the household is allowed to participate. There is a high probability that it is the female who will join a credit program.

Another means of identifying the empowering effect of microcredit is to examine if and how it improved the bargaining position of the female members within the household. Osmani (1998) used an extended version of the bargaining model to test if credit improved the female borrower's bargaining position. The traditional bargaining model was extended by Sen (1990) to account for the particular situations of traditional patriarchal societies. Sen argued that the outcome of bargaining in these societies depends on individual's perceived self-interest and perceived contribution, in addition to their breakdown position. Women in traditional societies are known to sacrifice their self-interest for the sake of family, but they do not feel that they are making an important contribution to the family, as most of their work does not lead to monetary return. Osmani (1998) finds that membership in Grameen Bank has enhanced women's perceived contribution and breakdown position: 3% of the borrowers feel that the husband contributes more to the family, compared with 23% among non-borrowers, and female borrowers personally own significantly higher amounts of both land and non-land assets compared with the non-borrower's wives. Osmani does not find any evidence of improvement in the perceived self-interest of the women: borrowers and non-borrowers alike feel that unequal access to food within the family between men and women is fair. She concludes that an improvement in bargaining position and perceived contribution has resulted in greater empowerment of women.

Helen Todd also found that the bargaining position of Grameen borrowers in her sample improved as a result of participation in the bank. Like Osmani, she found that the women borrowers have a clear perception of their contribution to the household.[68] In fact, she reports that "quite frequently they overestimate the size of their contribution."[69] Further, she found that borrowers who have retained control over loan use and have built up assets have seen an improvement in their breakdown position. She also finds that the women's improved breakdown position in many cases came at the expense of a weakened breakdown position of the husbands.

> What also makes the position of GB women so different is that the breakdown position of GB husbands is often less rosy than that of their wives. Like other poor men in the village, if the

marriage broke down a GB husband could get another wife, perhaps even a small dowry. His meal would be cooked and his *lunggi* washed. But if he divorced a center member, he would be hard put to get another GB wife. And there would go the loans, the assets in her name. . . . The benefits of cooperation are strong on both sides, but, on balance, stronger for him than for her.[70]

Ligon (2001) uses an extension of the bargaining model of households to explain why women "pipeline" or hand over their loans to their husbands.[71] He specifically explores what will happen to the agreed-upon bargaining outcome if one member's situation changes and he or she wants to renegotiate. For example, if the wife's economic situation improves after the marriage, she might demand a larger share of the household resources. Such renegotiation after the fact is not unusual. In fact, it is not uncommon for husbands to make demands for extra dowry payments after the marriage. Rao (1997)[72] found that a major cause of wife beating in South India is the shortfall between expected and actual dowry payments. Ligon extends the bargaining models to take into account such changes. Further, he includes income uncertainty to make the model more realistic and shows that pipelining the loan to the husband so that he undertakes all of the risk can improve the woman's bargaining position. Alternatively, loan use by women exclusively, so that they assume the full risk, makes their income less dependable and weakens their bargaining position vis-à-vis the husband. It also lessens their physical well-being as they are forced to consume less to be able to repay the loan.

Van Tassel (2004) also uses a dynamic bargaining model to explain the rationale for women handing over their loans to their husbands. In his model, however, instead of the members receiving cash exogenously as in Ligon, the income is generated by the decision of the members. The Van Tassel model indicates that it is efficient for the women to pipeline the loan to their husbands to avoid inefficient allocation of resources.[73] Unlike the case mentioned by Todd, where the husband's project yields higher return, Van Tassel's model shows women benefiting by transferring the loan to the men even if the woman's project yields the same return as the man's. By transferring the loan, the woman essentially guarantees that her husband will pay for the loan, allowing her to maintain the credit line.

As mentioned before, in addition to credit, the bank provides non-credit services such as information to improve health, literacy, leadership skills, and social empowerment. Some of these non-credit services are provided to encourage and support the "Sixteen Decisions"—the social charter of the bank. Many commentators believe that these social programs are extremely valuable, and that the success of the credit program depends on the effective implementation of these services. McKernan (2002) provides interesting evidence of the benefits of non-credit services, also known as "social intermediation," provided by credit programs such as Grameen Bank. Her work is the first formal and scientific attempt to measure the benefit of these non-credit services. McKernan uses an innovative strategy. First, she estimates the total effect of participation in a microcredit program on the profitability of self-employment of the borrowers. Then she estimates the same effect conditional on the productive capital. The idea is that the major impact of participation is the use of credit for the build-up of productive capital. The difference between the two measures captures the non-credit effects, because the financial intermediation by the bank allows the borrowers to build productive capital, and social intermediation leads to a build-up of human capital. Also, she uses capital instead of credit to capture the effect of non-credit services leading to the build-up of productive capital because, as mentioned earlier, credit will be used to add to capital.[74] McKernan uses the World Bank data and similar methodology to correct for biases inherent in a simple comparison of groups in a program with a control group.[75] The results show that participation in Grameen Bank increases total profit by 226 percent, and that a significant portion of this increase is due to non-credit factors. Further, she shows that households with fewer assets benefit more from the non-credit factors. In other words, relatively poorer households benefit more from these non-credit services.

Since the bank operates throughout the country with large numbers of borrowers, it should affect economic transactions in the whole economy. One study attempted to compute the impact of Grameen Bank on Bangladesh's GDP. Dr. Mohiuddin Alamgir, who was the director of the Policy and Planning Division of the United Nations International Fund for Agricultural Development between 1983 and 1995, claimed that Grameen Bank raised the gross domestic product of Bangladesh by as much as 1.10–1.50% between 1994 and 1996. Dr. Alamgir identified two sources through which the bank's operation contributes to the aggregate income of the country. One source is the bank itself; this consists of net interest receipts and profit of the bank, as well as wages and salaries paid to the bank employees. The other source is the activities that are stimulated, directly or indirectly, from the bank's credit operation. A careful reading of the study suggests that the claim might be an overestimation because of methodological errors and the assumption of an unusually high rate of return (60%) from bank-funded activities. Even if one adjusts the numbers downward to correct for these errors, however, the contribution of the bank to the economy is significant. Grameen's more important contribution lies in its impact on improving social welfare and reducing poverty, which might ultimately have the greatest effect on GDP in the long run.

Despite the reported success and positive benefits to borrowers and to the country, it is still appropriate to ask if the bank is cost-effective. The cost to the borrowers is the interest rate they have to pay on the loan from the bank. In addition, they must bear the cost of buying the share of the bank, which does not yet pay any dividends, as well as keeping compulsory savings with the bank without open access under the classical Grameen model. Mark Schreiner (2003), a researcher for the Center for Social Development at Washington University in St. Louis, used data on the elements of the costs mentioned above for the period 1983–1997 and arrived at a figure of $20 per person for annual membership in Grameen Bank. Even though he did not explicitly measure the benefits, Schreiner concluded that the benefits surely exceeded the costs and that Grameen Bank was probably a worthwhile social investment. [76]

Another issue related to cost-effectiveness is whether or not the subsidy received by Grameen Bank is justifiable. To appropriately address this issue, the sources of subsidy must first be identified and then the total amount of the subsidy computed. These calculations help to answer the question of whether society as a whole could do better by spending the direct and indirect subsidy on other poverty alleviation initiatives. Grameen Bank received direct and indirect subsidies from international donors, the Bangladesh government, and borrowers. In the formative years, donors provided grants and low-interest loans as a form of direct subsidy; during the mid-1990s the bulk of the funding came from the government and the sale of bonds to the commercial market. The funding from the government was at a concessional rate, and even the funds raised through the sale of bonds were at a below-market interest rate. Moreover, the profit of the bank was tax-exempt. The bank received indirect subsidies by selling shares to the borrowers without paying any dividends. By adding all of these direct and indirect subsidies, Jonathan Morduch of New York University concluded that, in 1996 alone, the total subsidies to Grameen Bank amounted to about US$26–30 million. This grand total corresponds to Schreiner's (2003) aforementioned $20 subsidy cost per person-year of membership in Grameen for the period 1983–1997.

Shahidur Khandker (1998) of the World Bank took the justification of Grameen's subsidy one step further by comparing the subsidy that Grameen received with the benefits of the bank. To calculate the benefits, he multiplied the average loan outstanding by the increase in consumption caused by the loan from the bank. We reported earlier that the increase in consumption was estimated at 18% for females and 11% for males. Using the relevant figures, Khandker concludes, "For Grameen Bank the cost-benefit ratios are 0.91 for female borrowing and 1.48 for male borrowing. This means that society pays Tk 0.91 for every Tk 1 of consumption generated by borrowing by women and Tk. 1.48 for every Tk 1 of consumption generated by borrowing by men from Grameen."[77] Further, Khandker shows that Grameen's cost-benefit ratio is better relative to other poverty alleviation schemes, such as Food-for-Work (Tk 1.7–2.6) and Vulnerable Group Development (Tk 1.5–1.7), and infrastructure projects such as building paved roads in an undeveloped village and electrifying a village (Tk 1.38). Another means of testing the cost-effectiveness of Grameen Bank is to examine its poverty alleviation impact—the bank's ultimate mission. In another paper, Khandker (1996) reports that it costs about $10 to lend to a new member, and since it takes about ten years for a member to move out of poverty, the cost of poverty alleviation is a mere $100. He concludes, "This is a very small price for poverty reduction."[78]

The most important question related to subsidies is whether they are justified and whether they are "smart." In a recent paper, Jonathan Morduch defined "smart subsidy" as follows:[79] "The idea of "smart subsidy" springs from the premise that subsidies are neither inherently useful nor inherently flawed. Rather, their effectiveness depends on design and implementation. Smart subsidies maximize social benefits while minimizing distortions and mistargeting."

Clearly, the way a subsidy was measured is not without problems. The extended discussion of the impacts and benefits of Grameen Bank programs in the preceding pages should provide ample evidence that the subsidy to Grameen Bank in its formative years was more than justified, and that they were "smart" subsidies.[80]

In this chapter, we have provided a brief history and evolution of the bank. We have described the various loan products of the bank and its organizational structure. More important, we have surveyed the various impacts of the bank. This background information will provide a context for understanding Grameen II. In the next chapter, we will look at the main ingredients of Grameen II and discuss how it differs from the classical Grameen model described in this chapter.

APPENDIX 2A: THE "SIXTEEN DECISIONS" OF GRAMEEN BANK

1. We shall follow and advance the four principles of Grameen Bank—Discipline, Unity, Courage, and Hard Work—in all walks of our lives.

2. Prosperity we shall bring to our families.

3. We shall not live in dilapidated houses. We shall repair our houses and work towards constructing new houses at the earliest.

4. We shall grow vegetables all the year round. We shall eat plenty of them and sell the surplus.

5. During the planting season, we shall plant as many seedlings as possible.

6. We shall plan to keep our families small. We shall minimize our expenditures. We shall look after our health.

7. We shall educate our children and ensure that they can earn to pay for their education.

8. We shall always keep our children and the environment clean.

9. We shall build and use pit-latrines.

10. We shall drink water from tube-wells. If it is not available, we shall boil water or use alum.

11. We shall not take any dowry at our sons' weddings, neither shall we give any dowry at our daughter's wedding. We shall keep our center free from the curse of dowry. We shall not practice child marriage.

12. We shall not inflict any injustice on anyone, neither shall we allow anyone to do so.

13. We shall collectively undertake bigger investments for higher incomes.

14. We shall always be ready to help each other. If anyone is in difficulty, we shall all help him or her.

15. If we come to know of any breach of discipline in any center, we shall all go there and help restore discipline.

16. We shall take part in all social activities collectively.

NOTES

1. Economists refer to these interactions as interlinking of markets. In this case, the market for credit to buy raw materials was linked with the market for products (bamboo stools). Other examples of such interlinking occur when the poor, landless workers borrow money to buy food during the lean employment period in between crop seasons. The landless workers then promise to work for the money lender in the next crop season to payoff the debt. In this case, the market for credit is interlinked with the market for labor. It is not unusual for the landless workers to commit the future labor of their children in addition to their own services. As one can easily guess, these types of interaction can be quite exploitive.
2. Grameen provides only collateral-free credit, the permission in the ordinance notwithstanding.
3. Government of the People's Republic of Bangladesh, *The Grameen Bank Ordinance,* Ordinance no. XLVI, 1983.
4. Muhammad Yunus, *Banker to the Poor: Micro-lending and the Battle against World Poverty* (New York: Public Affairs, 1999), p. 61.
5. Yunus, *Banker to the Poor,* p. 61.
6. Group organization around an activity is subject to what economist call *covariance risk*; a disease could affect all the goats owned by a group, and they all could lose their livestock.
7. For a full exposition of these decisions, see Alex Counts, *Give Us Credit* (New York: Times Books/Random House, 1996), pp. 347–348. For a graphical illustration of the "Sixteen Decisions," see Appendix 2A.
8. Much has been written and discussed about the group responsibility, and it has been interpreted as being tantamount to a joint liability contract where members are liable for each other's loans in the sense that if anyone defaults, the whole group will be held responsible and may be denied further loans. All theoretical models assume joint liability, and most commentators believe that it this feature of the model that led to the impressive results. In later chapters we will describe the conditions under which joint liability was used in loan contracts in Grameen Bank. Suffice it to say that the reality, however, is completely different from what is postulated in the theoretical models. For a survey of theoretical models of group lending, see Beatriz Armendariz de Aghion and J. Morduch, *The Economics of Microfinance* (Cambridge, MA: MIT Press, 2005), Chapter 4.
9. Public Thumbs Up for Grameen One," *Financial Express* July 24, 2005 (available at http://www.aims-bangladesh.com/press/2005.07.24_fe.html).

10. Rehman Sobhan, *A Macro Policy for Poverty Eradication through Structural Change*, World Institute for Development Economics Research Discussion Paper no. 2005/03, 2005.

11. Jamal Uddin, "Bangladesh Bank Advises Grameen Bank to Reduce Interest Rates and Distribute Dividends," *Daily Itefaq* (in Bangla), July 7, 2004.

12. Asif Dowla, "Micro Leasing: The Grameen Bank Experience," *Journal of Microfinance* 6(2), 2004, pp. 137–160.

13. Muhammad Yunus, "Expanding Microcredit Outreach to Reach the Millennium Development Goal: Some Issues for Attention," Paper presented at the International Seminar on Attacking Poverty with Microcredit organized by PKSF in Dhaka, January 8–9, 2003.

14. Michael Woolcock, "Social Theory, Development Policy, and Poverty Alleviation: A Comparative-Historical Analysis of Group-Based Banking in Developing Economies," unpublished Ph. D. dissertation, Brown University, Dept. of Sociology, 1999, p. 120.

15. For a list if tasks performed by a typical bank worker on a normal day, see Yunus, *Banker to the Poor*, pp. 104–105.

16. Reuters, *BD May Ban Trade Unions in Banks* (available at http://www.paksearch.com/br98/Feb/28/BDMAYBAN.htm).

17. K. Ibrahim Khaled, "Need for Trade Union Reform," *Daily Star Web Edition* 4(244), January 31, 2004 (available at: http://www.thedailystar.net/2004/01/31/d401311501104.htm).

18. Quoted in Khaled, "Need for Trade Union Reform."

19. For more historical background on the formation of the Staff Association, see David Bornstein, *The Price of a Dream* (New York: Simon & Schuster, 1996).

20. The process of opening a new branch has changed under Grameen II. We will explain the difference in a later chapter.

21. David Hulme, *Impact Assessment Methodologies for Microfinance: A Review* (IDPM, University of Manchester, 1999).

22. For a more detailed explanation of these biases, see Mark Pitt and S. Khandker, "The Impact of Group-Based Credit Programs on Poor Households in Bangladesh: Does the Gender of the Participants Matter?" *Journal of Political Economy* 106(5), 1998, p. 965. For an exhaustive discussion of the issues related to impact assessment, see R. L. Meyer, *Track Record of Financial Institutions in Assisting the Poor in Asia*, Asian Development Bank Institute Research Paper no. 49, 2002.

23. Martin Ravallion and Quentin Wodon, "Banking on the Poor? Branch Location and Nonfarm Rural Development in Bangladesh," *Review of Development Economics* 4(2), 2000, pp. 121–139.

24. Pitt and Khandker, "Impact of Group-Based Credit," p. 965.
25. Pitt and Khandker suggest that capital is not fungible within the household when resources are allocated on the basis of interaction between different members with different preferences. They argue that the differential effect of credit across gender after controlling for self-selection and other sources of endogeny provides empirical support for their theoretical conjecture that funds are not fungible within the household. "Impact of Group-Based Credit," pp. 962–963.
26. Mahbub Hossain, *Credit for Alleviation of Rural Poverty: The Grameen Bank in Bangladesh,* International Food Policy Research Institute Research Report no. 65, 1988, p. 10.
27. A. Rahman, R. Rahman, M. Hossain, and S. Hossain, *Early Impact of Grameen: A Multi-Dimensional Analysis,* Bangladesh Institute of Development Studies (Dhaka: Grameen Trust, 2002).
28. The project was labeled Credit Program for the Poor. The first project led to a book and several articles in peer-reviewed journals.
29. Shahidur Khandker, *Fighting Poverty with Microcredit: Experience in Bangladesh* (New York: Oxford University Press for the World Bank), p. 42.
30. Elvira Kurmanalieva, H. Montgomery, and J. Weiss, "Microfinance and Poverty Reduction in Asia: What's the Evidence?" Paper presented at the Annual Conference on Microcredit and Poverty Reduction organized by the Asian Development Bank Institute in Tokyo, December 5, 2003.
31. Khandker, *Fighting Poverty,* p. 41.
32. The World Bank study reported results for all three programs together. Unless otherwise stated, the results reported apply to the two other programs in addition to Grameen Bank.
33. Khandker, *Fighting Poverty,* p. 46.
34. Pitt and Khandker, "Impact of Group-Based Credit," p. 980.
35. Khandker, *Fighting Poverty,* p. 47.
36. Khandker, *Fighting Poverty,* p. 49.
37. Mark M. Pitt, S. Khandker, O. H. Chowdhury, et al., "Credit Programs for the Poor and the Health Status of Children in Rural Bangladesh," *International Economic Review* 44(1), 2003, pp. 87–118.
38. Helen Todd, *Women at the Center: Grameen Bank Borrowers after One Decade* (Dhaka: University Press, 1996), p. 193.
39. Ruhul Amin, A. U. Ahmed, J. Chowdhury, et al., "Poor Women's Participation in Income-Generating Projects and Their Fertility Regulation in Rural Bangladesh," *World Development* 22(4), 1994, pp. 555–565; Ruhul Amin, R. B. Hill, and Y. Li, "Poor Women's

Participation in Credit-Based Self-Employment: The Impact on Their Empowerment, Fertility, Contraceptive Use, and Fertility Desire in Rural Bangladesh," *Pakistan Development Review* 34(2), 1995, pp. 93–119; Ruhul Amin, Y. Li, and A. U. Ahmed, "Women's Credit Programs and Family Planning in Rural Bangladesh," *International Family Planning Perspectives* 22, 1996, pp. 158–162; Sidney Ruth Schuler and S. M. Hashemi, "Credit Programs, Women's Empowerment, and Contraceptive Use in Rural Bangladesh," *Studies in Family Planning* 25(2), 1994, pp. 65–76; Sidney Ruth Schuler, S. M. Hashemi, and A. P. Riley, "The Influence of Women's Changing Roles and Status in Bangladesh's Fertility and Contraceptive Use," *World Development* 25(4), 1997, pp. 563–575.

40. Mark Pitt, S. Khandker, Signe-Mary McKernan, et al., "Credit Programs for the Poor and Reproductive Behavior in Low Income Countries: Are the Reported Causal Relationships the Result of Heterogeneity Bias?" *Demography* 36(1), 1999, pp. 1–21.

41. Fiona Steele, Sajeda Amin, and Ruchira T. Naved, "Savings/Credit Group Formation and Change in Contraception," *Demography* 38(2), 2001, pp. 267–282.

42. Pitt, Khandker, McKernan, et al, "Credit Programs for the Poor," pp. 4–5.

43. Hossain, "Credit for Alleviation," p. 66.

44. Extreme poverty line is drawn to satisfy 85 percent of the required calorie and protein needs.

45. Hossain, *Credit for Alleviation*, p. 68.

46. Khandker, *Fighting Poverty*, p. 55.

47. The extreme-poverty line was established as 80% of the moderate-poverty line; Khandker, *Fighting Poverty*.

48. Khandker, *Fighting Poverty*, p. 56.

49. The official criterion is that households owning more than half an acre of medium-quality cultivable land should be excluded from the program. One thing that gets missed in this discussion is that landownership is an entry condition. The policy does not suggest that someone who exceeds the threshold amount of land after acquiring membership should be driven out of the program. Any discussion of landholding by Grameen members that does not mention the year of membership is bound to conflate the "mistargeting" with a positive impact effect.

50. Mark Pitt, "Reply to Jonathan Morduch's 'Does Microfinance Really Help the Poor? New Evidence from Flagship Programs in

Bangladesh,'" Typescript, Brown University, Department of Economics, 1999, p. 3.

51. Nidhiya Menon, "Consumption Smoothing in Micro-Credit Programs," Typescript, Brandeis University, Department of Economics, 2003, p. 18; Pitt, "Reply to Jonathan Morduch," p. 7. Both explain the reasons why loosening the land criterion enhances the significance and magnitude of the result.

52. The authors argue that since their data set includes information about the household before membership in any microcredit program, they can ignore the issue of endogeny mentioned earlier; Sajeda Amin, A. Rai, and G. Topa, "Does Microcredit Reach the Poor and Vulnerable? Evidence in Northern Bangladesh," *Journal of Development Economics* 70, 2003, p. 60.

53. The indicators were changed somewhat over time to take account of changing poverty dynamics in the country.

54. Grameen Bank, *Annual Report–2003* (Dhaka: Grameen Bank), p. 29.

55. Cecile Aubert, Alain de Janvry, and Elisabeth Sadoulet, *Creating Incentives for Micro-Credit Agents to Lend to the Poor,* Working Paper Series 988, University of California at Berkley, Department of Agricultural and Resource Economics, 2004.

56. Shahidur Khandker, *Micro-Finance and Poverty: Evidence Using Panel Data from Bangladesh,* Policy Research Working Paper 2945 (Washington, DC: World Bank, 2003).

57. Khandker, *Micro-Finance and Poverty,* p. 17. The moderate-poverty line is constructed by calculating the cost of buying a bundle consisting of 2112 calories and adjusting this cost upward by another 30% to account for non-food expenditures. As before, the extreme-poverty line represents 80% of the moderate-poverty line.

58. Shahidur Khandker, "Flood and Coping Ability in Bangladesh," Table 10, Typescript, World Bank, 2004.

59. Todd, *Women at the Center,* p. 236.

60. Todd, *Women at the Center,* pp. 37–38

61. Sidney R. Schuler, S. Hashemi, and A. Riley, "The Influence of Women's Changing Roles and Status in Bangladesh's Fertility and Contraceptive Use," *World Development* 31(3), 1997, pp. 513–534; Sidney Schuler, Syed Hashemi, and Shamsul H. Badal, "Men's Violence against Women in Rural Bangladesh: Undermined or Exacerbated by Microcredit Programmes?" *Development in Practice* 8(2), 1998; Sidney R. Schuler, Syed M. Hashemi, Ann Riley, et al., "Credit Programs, Patriarchy and Men's Violence against Women in Rural Bangladesh," *Social Science and Medicine* 43(12), 1996; Priya

Nanda, "Women's Participation in Rural Credit Programmes in Bangladesh and Their Demand for Formal Health Care: Is There a Positive Impact?" *Health Economics* 8, 1999, pp. 415–428.

62. Rashid Faridi, "Microcredit Programs in Bangladesh: Assessing the Performance of Participating Women," Mimeo, Virginia Polytechnic Institute and State University, Department of Economics, 2003.

63. Mark Pitt, S. Khandker, and J. Cartwright, *Does Micro-Credit Empower Women? Evidence from Bangladesh*, Policy Research Paper 2998, World Bank, 2003.

64. Todd, *Women at the Center*, p. 91.

65. John Strauss, Germano Mwabu, and Kathleen Beegle, "Intrahousehold Allocations: A Review of Theories and Empirical Evidence," *Journal of African Economics* 9, 2000, pp. 83–143.

66. Agnes Quisumbing and B. de la Briere, *Women's Assets and Intrahousehold Allocation in Rural Bangladesh: Testing Measures of Bargaining Power*, International Food Policy Research Institute, Food Consumption and Nutrition Division Discussion Paper no. 86, 2000; Kelly Hallman, *Mother-Father Resource Control, Marriage Payments, and Girl-Boy Health in Rural Bangladesh*, International Food Policy Research Institute, Food Consumption and Nutrition Division Discussion Paper no. 93, 2000.

67. Siwan Anderson and Mukesh Eswaran, *What Determines Female Autonomy? Evidence from Bangladesh*, Bureau for Research in Economic Analysis of Development, Working Paper no. 101, 2005.

68. As mentioned earlier, Helen Todd used a much smaller sample and collected date for a year. Unlike Osmani, she does not use empirical tests to measure the impact of credit on bargaining power. Her conclusion is based on observation of the household over a long period of time.

69. Todd, *Women at the Center*, p. 212.

70. Todd, *Women at the Center*, p. 213.

71. Ethan Ligon, *Dynamic Bargaining in Households (With an Application to Bangladesh)*, Working paper, University of California at Berkley, 2001 (available at http://are.berkeley.edu/~ligon/Papers/intra-household.pdf).

72. Vijayendra Rao, "Wife Beating in Rural South India: A Qualitative and Econometric Analysis," *Social Science and Medicine* 44(8), 1997, pp. 1169–1180.

73. Eric Van Tassel, "Household Bargaining and Microfinance," *Journal of Development Economics* 74, 2004, pp. 465–466.

74. Signe-Mary McKernan, "The Impact of Micro-Credit Programs on Self Employment Profits: Do Non-Credit Program Aspects Matter?" *Review of Economics and Statistics* 84(1), 2002, pp. 93–115.
75. A comparison of results shows that not correcting for these biases will overestimate the effects of participation on profits by 200%. McKernan, "Impact of Micro-Credit Programs," pp. 33.
76. Mark Schriener, "A Cost-Effectiveness Analysis of the Grameen Bank of Bangladesh," *Development Policy Review* 21(3), 2003, pp. 357–382.
77. Khandker, *Fighting Poverty*, p. 136.
78. Shahidur Khandker, "Grameen Bank: Impact, Costs, and Program Sustainability," *Asian Development Review* 14(1), 1996, pp. 97–130.
79. Jonathan Morduch, "Smart Subsidy for Sustainable Microfinance," *Finance for the Poor* 4(4), 2005.
80. Since 1998, the bank has not received any donor funds, and in recent years it has borrowed at market rate from the commercial market. Now it is completely dependent on its own source of funding.

Loan Products under Grameen II

S hahnur is a male member of Grameen Bank. A few years ago, the attraction of higher income overseas prompted Shahnur to leave for Libya without paying off a loan from the bank. Shahnur thought that rather than abiding by the strict conditions of his loan, he would try to become rich by earning a higher income in Libya. Shahnur's dream did not come true; he was defrauded by a manpower agent who took his money but did not give him the promised job. Dejected and heartbroken, he returned home. In the meantime, he went into arrears on his loan from the bank. Under the classical Grameen model, Shahnur would have become another entry in the financial statement of the bank. Since he could not have rescheduled the loan or stretched the installment payments, his loan would have been written off and he would have been declared a defaulter.

Grameen II offered a lifeline to Shahnur. He used his group fund to adjust the loan amount, signed a contract, and paid off the remainder on schedule. Although he had not given up his dream of getting out of poverty, Shahnur decided to stay in the country and try again. This time, he decided to build a chicken coop and start a poultry business. With much trepidation, he asked for a loan to buy chicks for his business. He was not sure if the bank would trust him with another loan. He was shocked when the manager approved a loan of 10,000 taka. Shahnur chose to go slow this time and borrowed only 5,000 taka.

The basic goal of Grameen I was to prove to a skeptical world that the poor are creditworthy and that, given credit, they will make every effort to pay back the money on time. However, the poor in Bangladesh—and, for that matter, all over the world—face tremendous uncertainty and vulnerability, which inhibit their ability to pay back on time. The poor's vulnerability is captured by the predicament of Shahnur. Shahnur was lucky in the sense that the crisis he faced was man-made: he still had his health, and he could take advantage of the second chance given by the bank. Most poor people must deal with natural crises, such as disease, flooding, and river bank erosion, that destroys their assets and resources, and in many cases leaves them in poor health and penniless. Despite these obstacles, however, microfinance practitioners have found that the poor will always pay back once their situation improves. The conviction that the poor will always pay back is the operating principle of Grameen II.

A hallmark of Grameen I was the group fund, the purpose of which was to act as a mini-bank for the group. Five percent of each loan plus a fixed weekly amount was deposited into this fund. The borrowers, with the approval of group members, could borrow from the fund for many purposes, but they had to pay the loan back within agreed-upon time. While borrowers who dropped out of the group could claim their remaining balance after adjusting for the part of the loan that was outstanding, borrowers in good standing were allowed open access to the balance after ten years of membership as the accumulated funds were credited to their personal savings accounts.

Under Grameen II, the notion of group fund has been abandoned. Instead, borrowers are offered individual accounts. For each loan an individual borrower takes, 5% is deducted and credited to her own accounts. This deposit is divided into two components: 2.5% of the compulsory deduction is deposited in an open-access personal savings account, and the remaining 2.5% is deposited in a special savings account. If a borrower holds a loan, she now must deposit a weekly minimum amount into her personal savings account.

This is usually determined by the size of the loan: 5 taka per week for loans up to 15,000 taka and 50 taka a week for loans of 100,000 taka or more. Although the borrower can withdraw any amount from her personal savings account at any time, she cannot withdraw savings if she owns a bridge loan or has a flexible loan.

The amount deposited in an obligatory savings account cannot be withdrawn for the first three years under normal circumstances. After three years, members can withdraw any amount in excess of 2000 taka from this account, and funds from this account can be used to buy shares of Grameen Bank. If a borrower leaves the group, the principal and the interest accumulated in the account can be used to pay off any outstanding loan amount and the borrower can take the remainder. In the event of a natural disaster or crisis, the borrower can apply to withdraw funds from this account. The borrower earns 8.5% on the obligatory and personal savings account balances, and the interest is credited yearly. The interest rate earned on the obligatory and personal savings accounts is quite generous compared with the current rate of 4% paid by the commercial banks in Bangladesh. The differences in the collection of savings between the two models are explained in Figure 3.1.

Another important dimension of Grameen II is the introduction of the pension savings scheme. This is a contractual savings arrangement where the borrower is required to deposit a fixed amount regularly into an account. Under Grameen II, all borrowers with loans above 8000 taka must contribute a minimum of 50 taka each month to a pension deposit account for five or ten years. The interest rate is 10% for a five-year term and 12% for a ten-year term. Because of the interest paid on this plan, the amount nearly doubles after ten years. Any delay exceeding four months in making deposits to this plan will turn the account into a regular savings account with a reduced interest rate of 8.5%.

The prime loan product of Grameen II is known as the basic loan. In contrast to Grameen I, all loans, with the exception of housing and the newly introduced education loans, have been merged into the basic loan. This loan can last for three months up to three years. Instead of fixed installments as under Grameen I, installments can

MANDATORY SAVINGS - GRAMEEN I

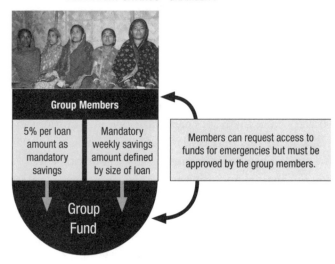

MANDATORY SAVINGS - GRAMEEN II

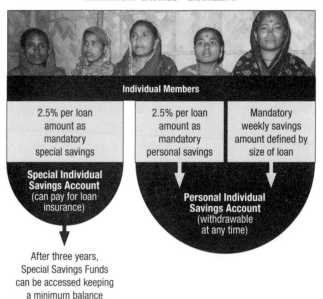

Figure 3.1   Savings under Grameen I and II.

vary according to the business environment of the borrower: high during the peak business period and low during the off-peak period, although the minimum payment for an installment is 1% of the loan. Currently, installment payments must be negotiated between the borrower and the bank prior to approval of the loan. Loans with duration less than a year can be repaid with one installment or per a schedule decided by the borrower. Loans that require more than one payment can be repaid through monthly installments. The borrower can also choose to pay every two or three months instead of using monthly installments, or in three or more equal large installments. Unlike the case with Grameen I, where loans were "staggered," all loans under Grameen II are disbursed to group members at the same time, provided they have repaid previous loans in full.

Another important change is that a member can now borrow the amount repaid in the first six months of the loan, adding the newly borrowed amount to the unpaid amount. In this way, loans can be topped up. Suppose a borrower takes a loan of 10,000 taka for one year. She pays weekly for twenty-six weeks, the first six months of the loan. Because she owns a retail business and needs more capital, she can take back the principal she has paid—5000 taka—as a new loan. Also, the loan period can be extended for another six months and the borrower can sign a new loan agreement with a repayment schedule that results in the same installment payment as with the initial 10,000 taka loan. This change is based on years of experience in which the bank determined that the credit needs of the borrowers do not necessarily follow the repayment schedules of loans. The bank found that when a borrower signs a loan contract for a year, she might need more money halfway through the loan to expand her business. Under Grameen II, she has to wait only six months to get a new loan to meet the credit need. Under Grameen I, the borrower had to wait for a full year before she could get another loan; by that time, the investment opportunity may have disappeared. The ability to borrow the amount repaid any time after six months is an acknowledgment of the dynamic nature of credit demand in rural Bangladesh. A borrower whose business does not need new infusion of capital—for example, to buy dairy cows—can stick to the schedule and pay off the full amount at the end of the year and receive another loan. The six-month cutoff period also serves as an early warning system for a loan. If a borrower faces problems making regular repayments in the first six months of the loan, the bank worker will be alerted that the borrower needs greater surveillance and counseling.

Grameen II has also altered the bank's loan ceiling policy. Instead of a common loan ceiling for all the borrowers of a branch, each borrower now has his or her own loan ceiling. This ceiling is customized based on the performance of the borrower, her group, her center, and the amount of deposits in her savings accounts. Under Grameen I, the presence of multiple loans enabled borrowers to increase their group's loan ceiling. Many times, however, borrowers increased their credit limit by using multiple loans without a concomitant increase in their investment capacity, resulting in an unsustainable burden of debt. Further, field-level experience with Grameen I indicated that once a borrower's individual loan ceiling was increased, others wanted their loan ceilings increased as well, even though they did not have the capacity to utilize large loans. Also, the borrower's husband often put pressure on the staff to increase the loan ceiling of his spouse. Grameen II has eliminated these problems by determining the borrower's loan ceiling endogenously and on the basis of individual performance.

There are two methods by which Grameen II determines a borrower's loan ceiling. Under the first criterion, the ceiling is based on the total amount of the savings accumulated by the borrower in "acceptable savings deposits." These include deposits in all savings accounts, such as the obligatory savings account, the Grameen pension scheme (GPS), fixed deposits, and other contractual savings. Excluded, however, are personal savings accounts and accounts that are maintained as a condition of owning a village phone. A borrower can borrow up to 150% of her total accumulated savings if she meets all of the conditions of previous loan. Under this criterion, the borrower can also borrow one and a half times her acceptable deposits after paying off an existing loan regularly for twenty-six weeks. However, the borrower cannot withdraw from these deposits. If the borrower reduces the loan outstanding by installment payments, then the difference between 150% of the deposits and the loan outstanding can be withdrawn.

Under the second criterion, the loan ceiling depends on the performance of the borrower, her group, and the center. If the borrower repays the loan without missing any installments and savings deposits, and attends all the weekly center meetings, her loan ceiling may be increased by 10%. If a borrower repays her loan in full despite missing some installments and occasionally being absent from the center meeting, her loan ceiling may be increased up to 5%. After measuring the borrower's status using both criteria, the bank approves the higher amount resulting from the two calculations as the loan ceiling.

The most important change to the classical Grameen model is that the group is no longer liable for individual loans, meaning that the group no longer has to provide a guarantee for the loan to its members. Researchers and practitioners alike hailed group liability or collective responsibility as the major reason for the high repayment rates experienced by Grameen Bank and other microfinance institutions.[1] To accommodate more groups, the bank has altered the seating arrangement in the center meeting. Under Grameen I, the members would sit in a row with the group chairperson sitting at the end of the row. Under Grameen II, group members sit together in a semicircle facing the bank worker (see Figure 3.2). This allows them to move around freely and to face each other easily.

The change in level of responsibility from group to individual does not mean that there is no longer a role for groups. In Grameen I, groups were used to simplify the collection of repayments, to reduce transaction costs of loan collection, and to support members in need. In some Grameen Bank branches the local staff made other borrowers in the group liable for a member's missed payment. Grameen I allowed other members of a group to pay for a member's missed payments, but restricted the practice by imposing a limit of a maximum period of four weeks. After twenty-five years of observing the negative aspects of groups, however, the bank decided to

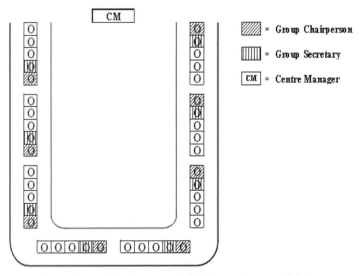

Note: Every Centre has Centre Chief & Deputy Centre Chief
who are Elected by the Group Chairperson.

Figure 3.2   New seating arrangement for center meeting.

invert the structure by rewarding an individual borrower for the
success of the group as a whole and blending the group responsibility. Previously, if everyone in the group performed well, there was
no reward, but if some members performed badly, the group had to
deal with the stigma. Now, groups are rewarded for their good performance. The founding principle of group lending—the use of the
group as a point of service—still applies. Center meetings of groups
are still being used to build social capital by promoting norms of
good behavior, networking to share information about health and
business opportunities, and building trust beyond the narrow
"radius of trust" that encompassed only family members.[2]

Lisa Larance's (2001) work aptly illustrates how the center meetings
are used to expand networks beyond weak, horizontal, and immediate-
family and kinship ties. Many of her respondents reported that the
center meetings enabled them to expand their social and information

networks to facilitate economic and non-economic transactions. Larance cites the example of a respondent who, because of her new networks, discovered and enrolled in the government's mass education program, which enabled her to learn how to read. Another member used the network to collect nutrient-rich rice water to feed a cow that she bought with a loan from the bank. In addition, 74% of Larance's respondents reported that the networks were used to make up for short-falls on loans. Members also reported using the networks to expand social exchanges. Respondents found that they could borrow clothes and jewelry from each other to wear on social occasions and could use the network to meet other social obligations, such as entertaining an unexpected guest or attending a marriage celebration. The networks eased mobility restrictions for women who were secluded within their neighborhoods (*bari*), where they interacted almost exclusively with the husband's kin. Increasing women's mobility beyond their *bari* to enable them to visit others and travel to a "public" place in the village challenged the well-established norm of *purdah*—a system of keeping women out of the sight of men other than their immediate family members. In addition, the network proved especially beneficial to women who were married patrilocally—away from their own village. Instead of going to their natal village for help, women could use the local network to seek assistance.

Members view groups as a reflection of accountability and permanence. The bank strongly believes that the center meeting of groups is an important forum for borrowers that continues to ensure the transparency of financial transactions. During the center meeting, for example, installments and savings deposits are collected in public, which prevents either the bank worker or the borrower from lying about the transaction. In these meetings, the group chairperson, a position that is regularly rotated to prevent distrust, collects repayments from members and hands them over to the bank worker, who makes the entry in the ledger book. This public collection precludes the possibility of misappropriation of funds by the staff and provides a sense of ownership to the members. In recent years, many staff members were, in fact, attacked on their way to the branch office with collected funds, and, as mentioned earlier, they often safeguarded these funds at the cost of serious physical injury to themselves.

Center meetings benefit the borrowers in other ways. Through regular attendance, borrowers are informed about the availability of scholarship funds, higher education loans for their offspring, and other important developments, such as innovations in the use of the loan fund, best practices adopted by other members, and even solutions to personal problems. Beginning with the month of June, prior to the onset of the floods, which are a common occurrence in Bangladesh, the center meeting is used to prepare the borrowers for flooding and post-flood rehabilitation. The center manager urges borrowers to save additional amounts so that these funds can be used to buy food during the flood and for post-flood rehabilitation. The borrowers are also advised to protect their in-kind savings—such as livestock and poultry—by immunizing them and are urged to stock up on squash, pumpkin, and other vegetables that can be stored for long periods to feed the family during the flood. The public repayment of installments still acts as an incentive to repay on time, with the added benefit of removing tension and shame from the process.

As mentioned earlier, Grameen II uses group responsibility in a positive way by rewarding each borrower in the group and center for their good behavior. Borrowers are rewarded in a number of ways. If the center's repayment rate is 100%, a member's ceiling may be increased up to 10%. If the center's repayment rate is less than 100% but a member's own group's repayment rate is 100%, then her ceiling may be raised by 5%. The borrower's loan ceiling may also be increased by 5% if the center has incomplete groups (groups with fewer than five members) as well as a 100% repayment record. If her own group's repayment rate is perfect but the center's repayment rate is less than 100%, then her ceiling may be increased up to 2.5%. One could argue that tying the credit limit to the performance of the group, center, and branch is a backhanded means of enforcing group liability. However, even if the group and the center are performing poorly, a borrower in good standing can increase her credit ceiling in accordance with the savings criteria mentioned earlier. This prevents an individual who is performing well from being held down by the less-than-stellar performance of others in the group, center, and branch. Also, by tying the loan ceiling to the performance of the borrower and her group, center, and branch, the bank can protect itself from pressures to increase the loan ceiling for everyone regardless of performance. Sanctioning larger loans to successful members has the added benefit of convincing others to repay on time, enabling a branch to become profitable quickly.

A borrower's loan ceiling may be lowered as well. If a borrower misses an installment, her loan ceiling will decrease by 2% for every missed installment thereafter. The bank also assigns the utmost importance to regular attendance at the weekly center meetings, based on the belief that absence without reasonable cause is an indicator of future problems with the borrower. While a borrower is expected to miss the occasional meeting, she can miss only two meetings in twenty-six weeks and, at most, four out of fifty-two possible meetings in a year without penalty. Pregnant borrowers are allowed to miss six meetings per year with prior approval of the zonal manager. For each day of absence exceeding the grace period, the loan ceiling is decreased by 50 taka per 1000 taka of loan. The total reduction, however, cannot exceed 500 taka, irrespective of the number of absences.

The borrower must also continue to pay her credit and savings installments on top of any penalty incurred for missed meetings. A borrower may make partial payments, such as paying the principal only rather than the full installment, which consists of principal and interest. If the interest amount (3 taka minimum per 1000 taka of loan amount) of an installment is not paid, the borrower's ceiling continues to decrease by 2% for every week of missed payments. In addition to the basic loan, a borrower can take a bridge loan at any time against her savings if the outstanding amount of her loan falls below 150% of the aforementioned "acceptable savings" figure.[3] For example, if a borrower has 10,000 taka in acceptable deposits and her outstanding loan balance is 12,000 taka, she will qualify for a bridge loan of 3000 taka, the difference between 150% of 10,000 taka and the loan balance of 12,000 taka. Although the borrower must repay the bridge loan within six months, she can take as many bridge loans as she wishes, provided that she has repaid her earlier bridge loans. In addition, as mentioned earlier, a borrower can borrow exactly the amount she has paid back during the first six months of the loan. This option makes the basic loan similar to a cash credit limit with a bank.

Experience showed that many borrowers were moving ahead in their businesses faster than others. The bank observed that members who had special advantages, such as proximity to the market, access to a larger market, and male family members experienced in running successful businesses, tended to demonstrate a rapid expansion in their investment capabilities. The bank decided to reward such borrowers with a variant of a basic loan with a much larger size, enabling individual borrowers to take advantage of their profitable investment opportunities. As mentioned in Chapter 2, in the mid-1980s the bank experimented with sanctioning larger loans to a group of borrowers known as collective loans. The idea was that as a group the borrowers would be able to manage the larger loan size and invest in profitable projects. It was thought that this would help them move out of poverty faster as well as create employment for others in the community. However, for reasons mentioned earlier, these group loans were not as successful as hoped, and the bank abandoned them. The larger loans instituted under Grameen II are motivated by similar concerns. This time, however, the loan is individual instead of collective, which allows the borrower to realize faster improvement in her economic condition and create employment for others without having to deal with group-related conflicts. Such a loan can be added to an existing basic loan without the usual loan ceiling, because the larger size of the loan is considered a temporary increase in the ceiling. This loan, appropriately labeled a "special investment project" or "micro-enterprise" loan, is a mixture of the leasing, *palli* phone (rural phone), and livestock loan under classical Grameen.[4] Small shops, village phones, power tillers, irrigation pumps, transport vehicles, and river craft for transportation and fishing are popular items financed under special investment or micro-enterprise loans. If such a loan is used for cow fattening, the maximum loan period is six months; a loan for phone service has a maximum period for repayment of two years. This difference in repayment time allows the borrower to synchronize repayment with the nature of the business. The livestock loan is typically used to fatten a cow for the Muslim celebration of *Qurbani.* The borrower uses the loan money to buy a cow, and it takes six months to fatten the cow to be sold for the *Qurbani* celebration. Many of the items funded by micro-enterprise loans, such as trucks, minivans, mechanized boats, and cellular phones can be insured by private insurance companies. The animal or other resource is insured by the bank, and for this coverage the borrower pays 5% of the loan amount as a premium.

A primary use of the special investment loan is to finance a unique and important project: the *palli* phone (village phone) project. Its objective is to establish village pay phones (VPPs) in rural areas of the country. Bangladesh has one of lowest teledensity rates (i.e., fixed and mobile phone connections per 100 inhabitants) in the world—only 1.32% in 2002, compared with 5.20% in India and 9.58% in Sri Lanka. The specified rate is a national average. The teledensity rate in the rural areas, where 80% of the population live, is even worse, estimated at only 0.19% in 2000.[5] Moreover, the waiting time for a landline phone connection is more than two years, and a new installation costs $450—one of the highest prices in the world. Most of the existing phones are used in the cities and owned by men. Cellular phones were introduced in Bangladesh in the early 1990s, with a monopoly provider selling a set at a cost of $2000. A cellular phone was a status symbol that only the very rich could afford. Once the government decided to open up the sector for competition, Grameen Phone, a for-profit company, was awarded a license for GSM cellular phones. Until recently, Grameen Phone was owned by a consortium made up of four partners: Telenor Mobile Communication of Norway (51%); Grameen Telecom (35%), a not-for-profit company and a sister organization of Grameen

Bank; Marubeni of Japan (9.5%); and Gonophone Development Company (4.5%). Grameen Telecom now owns a 38% share of Grameen Phone, with Telenor Mobile Communication of Norway owning the remaining 62%.

Under the *palli* phone project, a phone set is usually given to a female member, whose social status is at the bottom in a male-dominated society. The borrower buys the airtime from Grameen Telecom, which buys airtime at a 50% bulk discount from Grameen Phone. The borrower is chosen by the bank, and Grameen Telecom sets up and trains the phone operator. Grameen Phone charges Grameen Telecom for the total amount of all village phone subscriptions; Grameen Telecom in turn generates a bill for the airtime plus other charges such as line rent for each subscriber, and Grameen Bank collects the amount due from the borrowers. A 15% surcharge is added to the bill to cover handling costs incurred by Grameen Telecom and Grameen Bank. In reality, the discount on the rate received by Grameen Telecom reflects the savings received by Grameen Phone in distribution, billing, collection, and other costs as well as a discount for the bulk purchase of airtime by Grameen Telecom. Moreover, the high airtime usage of VPP reduces the transaction cost of phone connection by Grameen Phone to the VPP operator.[6] Even though VPP accounts for only 3.85% of all Grameen Phone users, it contributes 15.5% of all its airtime revenues. In other words, the additional cost to Grameen Phone of providing the phone connection to a VPP is close to zero. The borrower charges the customer the market rate for each minute of the phone call: 4 taka per minute for off-peak hours and 6 taka for the peak period, while she pays 1.24 taka for off-peak and 2.24 taka for peak period usage to Grameen Telecom. The borrower's net income is the difference between the total revenue she makes by selling airtime to the customer at the commercial rate and her billed amount minus the service charge. The average monthly bill for a VPP is approximately 5200 taka; the net monthly profit is 4000 taka.[7]

The VPP scheme works in stages. Before the borrower is allowed to buy the phone outright, she has to prove her ability to run the business for at least a month. The chosen operator has to be a member in good standing of the bank for at least two years. She must also be literate or have children who can read and write and understand the English system of digits. During this provisionary period, the respective branch maintains ownership of the phone set and the borrower pays 75% of her net income as a commission to the branch. The borrower also has to open a *palli* phone (rural phone) savings account, where the income from the phone business will be deposited. He or she must allow the relevant branch manager to deduct the bill from this account.

After successful completion of the provisionary period, which is one to two months, the borrower buys the phone set from Grameen Telecom under the lease financing program of Grameen Bank with a maximum lease duration of two years. The bank maintains ownership of the phone set until the loan is repaid fully. The borrower has to open a GPS account with a monthly installment of 200 taka. If the bill exceeds 5000 taka per month, she has to keep an average amount equivalent to two months of bills in the *palli* phone savings account. In addition, the borrower must maintain a weekly register that records the daily sale of phone services. The bank worker collects 75% of the revenue from the sale of phone services in the weekly meeting and deposits the amount in the savings account. The branch manager deducts the billed amount and other charges from the *palli* phone account.

The phone operator is responsible for providing services to her customers for both incoming and outgoing calls, collecting call charges, and ensuring proper maintenance of the handset. Making a phone call is simple: a customer visits the VPP center, which is usually the house of the phone owner, or "telephone lady," as she is called, and makes the call. When a customer gets a call from outside, the telephone lady takes the phone to his or her house for an extra fee. Alternatively, the caller makes the call at a predetermined time when the customer is waiting at the phone center.[8] In other words, these phone ladies "act as human pay phones in places where there are no land lines and no one has seen a telephone or made a phone call."[9] Currently, there are 192,000 VPPs in operation, financed through loans from Grameen Bank, providing telecommunication facilities to more than 60,000 thousand villages and to 65 million people living in the rural areas of Bangladesh.[10]

Access to cellular phones has been beneficial to both users and the operators. More important, the presence of VPP has reduced "information poverty," defined as "a situation in which an inadequate telecommunications infrastructure leads to limitations on the choices available to individuals because high costs of communication make it too costly to seek out information about alternative courses of action."[11] Research suggests that ownership of these phones has increased the income and social standing of the mostly female borrowers (Aminuzzaman, Baldersheim, and Jamil, 2003). Users have benefited greatly from the presence of VPPs in their villages. Survey research shows that the VPP program has saved time and money,[12] provided information about market prices and market trends, and reduced the risk of remittance transfers from the urban areas of the country as well from the Middle East. In addition, the phones help people better prepare for natural disasters, enable more efficient use of time, and enhance social relations by making it possible to stay in touch with family members who have moved to urban areas or out of the country (Aminuzzaman, Baldersheim, and Jamil, 2003; Richardson, Ramirez, and Haq, 2000). By placing one of the most important and up-to-date technologies in the hands of the poor, the bank has demolished the well-ingrained myths listed in Table 3.1

The operators and owners of VPP benefit immensely from their phone business. First, it has increased their income considerably (Bayes, 2001; Richardson, Ramirez, and Haq, 2000).[13] The owners have used the increased income to buy food; spend on business, clothing, and health care; and fund the education of their children.[14] Further, the operators have used VPP income to buy fixed assets such as land; build and renovate houses; invest in livestock, poultry, and fisheries, and buy shops and businesses, furniture, and fixtures (Sobhan, Kaleque, and Rahman, 2002).[15]

Table 3.1   Bringing Telecom to the Rural Poor: Myths and Facts

Myth	Fact
Phones cost too much.	Costs of communications have been declining as part of a broader trend in IT.
Phones have to be subsidized if they are to serve the poor.	The poor often pay a higher price for making calls by having to travel long distances to reach a phone (costing them more time and money).
Phones follow wealth. After a country becomes richer, people can afford more phones.	Wealth follows phones. The ITU estimates that Bangladesh, with per-capita annual income of US$275, could raise its GNP by an annual US$6000 with one additional phone.
One should aid the poor, not profit from them.	Phones are profitable and thus prove their usefulness, irrespective of whether they are used by the rich or the poor.
Phones serve secondary needs. The focus should be on the primary needs of the poor.	If the poor are empowered or enriched through having phones, they can assert their own requirements and better meet their primary needs.

Source: Grameen Phone, Annual Report 1998.

Box 3.1 provides a specific case study showing the positive impact of VPP on the life of the first Grameen "phone lady."

In addition to benefiting the users and operators of these phones, the cellular phone network has become an important management tool for the bank. Every branch manager now has a cellular phone. Grameen Telecom provided each branch manager of Grameen Bank with a free phone set, 200 taka worth of free airtime, and a waiver of connection fees. This was a reward for the managers' service in collecting the bills on behalf of the company. The bank pays for another 400 taka worth of airtime for the branch managers. Area managers and program officers also receive free phone sets from Grameen Telecom, and the bank pays for 1000 taka and 500 taka worth of airtime for these staff members, respectively. The free phones from Grameen Telecom and the subsidy for airtime usage by the bank have allowed

Box 3.1   Laily Begum: The First Grameen "Phone Lady"

Laily Begum began her life as the first phone lady by calling then Prime Minister Shiekh Hasina in March 1997. Now Laily is an important member of the community, and her ownership of the phone has brought her prestige and economic solvency. Her previous life, however, was not that pleasant. Her husband, Atikullah, was a day laborer, and she earned extra income by sewing blankets and doing embroidery work for other people. With their combined income, they had enough for two square meals a day.

She noticed that her landless neighbors had improved their living standards by joining Grameen Bank, and she wanted to improve economic conditions for her family as well. She was fortunate enough to join the bank on September 15, 1992, as a replacement for a member who dropped out. Her first loan was for 4000 taka to buy a milch cow and some chickens. By selling the calves of the milch cow she made a profit and used the money to set up a tea stall business for her husband. She took out five more loans from the bank and sought other means to make more money for her family.

She learned that the bank was planning to give cellular phones to its members to start the village pay phone business. She knew nothing about cellular phones or how to use them. Besides, the whole thing seemed implausible to her. She had heard that only rich people could use such expensive gadgets. The poor people of the village have a hard time affording food for their families, she thought; where would they get the money to pay for phone calls, and whom would they call? When the center manager discussed the VPP program in the weekly meeting, Laily expressed interest in having one. She discussed the idea with her neighbors and relatives, who were skeptical and voiced comments such as "Grameen has told you this for nothing. Why will the Grameen authority give this costly and valuable thing to illiterate people?" Laily felt encouraged when the officers from Grameen Bank and Grameen Telecom visited her house, and even her neighbors began to get excited about the possibility of a new technology coming to their village.

All speculation ended when Laily got the phone on March 26, 1997. It was the most memorable day in her life as she became the first person in her village as well as in the bank to receive a phone and talk to the prime minister. After finishing the phone call with the prime minister at the bank's premises, Laily and her husband started walking to their house. On the way home, some people tried to touch the phone and wanted to make sure that it could be used to talk to others. By the time they reached home, twelve to fourteen people had used the phone and they had earned 100 taka.

Atikullah now operates the VPP business in a booth built and owned by the family. On average, they service a total of 600 minutes of phone calls per week, 100 minutes of which are for the more lucrative overseas calls. For outgoing calls they have to follow the schedule provided by Grameen Telecom, whereas for incoming call they can choose the rate. The following table provides a detailed breakdown of the income, expenditure, and profit figures from Laily's phone business.

Box 3.1   Laily Begum: The First Grameen "Phone Lady" (Continued)

Year (1)	Income from Outgoing and Incoming Calls (Taka) (2)	Bill from Grameen Telecom (3)	Operating Costs (Electricity and Battery) (4)	Total Costs (5 = 3 + 4)	Net Income (Taka) (6 = 2 – 5)	Net Income ($) (7 = [2 – 5]/$)
1997	108,725	66,586	2500	69,086	39,639	678
1998	105,332	60,708	2500	63,208	42,124	720
1999	80,458	46,216	2500	48,716	31,742	543
2000	85,342	47,063	2500	49,563	35,779	612
2001	120,681	70,057	2500	72,557	48,124	823
2002	138,752	77,139	6400	83,539	55,213	944
2003	131,981	78,332	7200	85,532	46,449	794
2004	119,511	71,698	7500	79,198	40,313	689

Intially, Laily was earning 20,000 to 26,000 taka per month from her VPP business. With the increase in competition from landline and other mobile phones in the area, her net income dropped, but she was still earning a reasonable amount from the phone business, could easily pay the weekly installment of 160 taka, and was able to build sizable savings. On November 1, 1999, Laily paid off the loan for the phone in full.

Prior to owning the phone business, Laily lived in a mud house. Now she lives in a brick house with two rooms and a veranda. In the veranda are two additional rooms, one for dining and another for sitting. She owns another house that is rented out to a doctor for a monthly rent of 1500 taka. On the roadside, Laily has built five rooms for rent. Atikullah uses one room as the VPP both. The other spaces are rented out as two grocery shops, a laundry, and a pharmacy. Laily's children are going to school, and she can even afford to hire a private tutor for them. When she joined the bank, her assets consisted of homestead land, one house, one cot, utensils, and clothing, with a total value of 75,000 taka ($1282). The following table shows the current asset pool of Laily Begum.

Box 3.1   Laily Begum: The First Grameen "Phone Lady" (Continued)

Description	Quantity	Value (in taka, approx.)	Remarks
Homestead	8 katha	1,600,000	Present value of the land
Cultivatable land	1 acre	500,000	
House	2	215,000	Made of brick
Rented shops	5 rooms	150,000	
Refrigerator (8.5 cu ft)	1	29,000	
Television	1	7,300	Black and white
Tape recorder	1	2,000	
Steel wardrobe and showcase	1 of each	9,000	
Cot	2	4,000	
Chairs and tables	2 of each	1,000	
Chairs and tables	16 and 4, respectively	5,400	For use in the rental shops
Gold ornaments	300 g	50,000	
VPP phone set	1	22,000	
Utensils and ceiling fans		50,000	
Total		2,644,700 ($45,208)	

Laily Begum, nearly destitute only a few years ago, is now a respectable member of society—all because of her ownership of the VPP.

Source: Dipal Barua and Diane Diacon. *The Impact of the Grameen Bank Mobile Phone Programme on the Lives and Housing of Rural Women in Bangladesh.* Grameen Shakti and Building and Social Housing Foundation, 2003.

for the creation of a vast cellular phone network. The bank uses this network in a number of creative ways to improve the flow of information among its various hierarchies. For example, at the beginning of the work day, a staff member from the headquarters calls each zonal office to find out the amount of bad debt collected the previous day. The zonal office collects this information from the area office, which in turn receives the information from the branches through the cellular phone network. By the middle of the day, the staff in charge have the data on the amount of bad debt collected by each zone the previous day. At the end of the work day, the deputy managing director, who oversees the campaign to collect bad debts, examines the data and gains a clear picture of the daily collection trends. If there is a dip in the amount collected in a particular zone, he calls the zonal manager to find out why. Alternatively, he can call the zonal managers at night to get information about the status of the zone. As mentioned earlier, the managing director and the deputy managing director visit the zones at least once a month, usually on Saturday—an official holiday. During the long car ride to the zone, they use their cell phones as a mobile office and talk to other zonal managers on their route to learn the latest situation in the zones.

The cell phone network provides invaluable benefits in times of disasters. For example, during the flood of 2004 the zonal office maintained constant contact with the area and branch offices in the flood-affected areas through use of the phones. The cell phone was also useful in tracking down staff who visited members at great personal risk. The staff rented hand-paddled boats to visit centers and members living in areas that were covered in chest-deep water with strong currents, often in the dark of night. In some cases, the cell phone batteries lost their charge and the visiting staff had to find alternative means of charging the batteries and informing the office of their whereabouts. When the branch manager did not hear from traveling staff for an unduly long time, he or she called the phones of borrowers to check on the well-being of the staff as they went to the center meetings.

The phone network is also used to manage public relations. Occasionally, the press reports an erroneous story about the members and the bank, and the phone network is used to check the authenticity of the story and to provide quick rebuttal. In a recent episode, a national daily reported that a borrower had been forced to sell her newborn baby to repay her loan. Once the head office staff got a whiff of the story, they called the respective branch manager and asked her to conduct an inquiry about the incident. The branch manager went to the borrower's house, got the actual story, and reported it back to the head office within hours. The truth was that the female borrower was abandoned by her husband while she was pregnant, and her cousin from a nearby village promised to adopt the baby after it was born. The reporter told the borrower that if he reported the sale of the baby as the result of a debt burden, she would receive financial assistance from sympathetic readers. In addition to getting the story wrong, the reporter misquoted the amount of the outstanding balance. With the help of the phone network, the bank was able to set the record straight and avoid a public relations disaster.

Grameen Bank was also a pioneering organization in providing loans for housing. The bank considers a loan for housing as a production loan. This is because the house is used for production and because a well-designed house improves the productivity of the borrower by protecting her against the natural elements. Accordingly, the bank kept the interest rate low for these loans: 8% compared with 20% for ordinary loans. The bank, however, found that many borrowers were taking advantage of the generous terms for housing loans to buy and built rental property. Under Grameen II, any housing loan in excess of 15,000 taka is considered a micro-enterprise loan, for which the borrower has to pay the 20% interest rate.

A borrower is considered in arrears if (1) she fails to repay the contracted amount for a loan with a term of less than a year; (2) she fails to repay half of the contracted amount during the first six months (or twenty-six weeks) of a one-year loan; (3) she fails to repay the contracted amount (principal and interest) in the first six months for a loan with a term of more than one year; (4) she fails to repay the contractual amount on a housing loan or a special investment loan in the first twenty-six weeks; (5) she fails to repay a bridge loan on schedule; (6) she fails to pay the installments for a GPS, which are due every twenty-six weeks; or (7) she fails to repay installments for ten weeks at a stretch. Under classical Grameen, the bank would wait for a year before declaring a borrower in arrears for failing to meet the conditions stipulated in a credit contract. Now the borrower has to pass the quality control check in the first six months of the loan.

Even if a borrower has difficulty making repayment under Grameen II and ends up in arrears, however, all is not lost. In the old system, once a borrower was off track, it was hard to become regular in one's payments again, as the conditions were difficult to meet, especially for the poorest borrowers, given the precarious conditions in which they live. They could not continue to repay the same amount every week as they were, in most cases, having difficulty meeting their own basic needs. The rigid repayment schedule turned what were temporary problems with repaying installments into full-blown cases of default. After missing a few installments, borrowers tended to stop coming to the center meetings and lost all contact with the bank because they could not renegotiate the loan amount or the installment. In contrast, a borrower now can opt out of a basic loan in favor of a flexible loan. In Bengali this option is called a *chukti*, meaning "contract" or renegotiated loan; the borrower can renegotiate a new contract with a fresh repayment schedule and choose an installment amount consistent with her repayment capacity. The flexible loan allows the borrower to reduce the loan's installment size and thus extend the loan period. It is not, however, an independent loan. A flexible loan is only a temporary detour from the basic loan; it is simply a rescheduled basic loan with its own set of separate rules. The borrower can use money from her savings deposits to pay off the remaining balance on her account. She can also switch to a flexible loan without using the proceeds from her savings account. While on a flexible loan, the borrower may not withdraw from any of her savings accounts unless such withdrawal is used to pay off an outstanding loan. Unlike the basic loan, the full amount of the 5% deduction for mandatory savings is used to repay past-due interests or loans outstanding.

A member on a flexible loan can take up to three years to repay the loan amount. The member can borrow twice the amount repaid in the first six months or twenty-six weeks for the first time, provided she did not miss any previous installment payments. The borrower can take advantage of this facility, however, only after she has developed a perfect repayment record, which includes paying installments on schedule, attending center meetings faithfully, and depositing weekly savings regularly. If the borrower's repayment record is not perfect in the first six months, she can borrow only 175% of the amount repaid if she paid the installments and deposited savings regularly, 150% of the amount repaid if she paid the installments and attended the center meetings regularly, 125% of the amount repaid if she only paid the installments regularly, and 100% of the amount repaid if she is irregular in making repayment, in depositing savings, and in attending center meetings. The borrower has the opportunity to sign new contracts if she faces problems repaying even the flexible loan. A borrower on a flexible loan is not required to hold a Grameen pension scheme (GPS) account. She is, however, encouraged to open one after the successful completion of the first six months.

After taking advantage of the opportunity to borrow twice the amount repaid in the first six months of the loan, she can borrow only the exact same amount that she will be paying back in each subsequent six-month period. This option allows one to borrow the same amount or less, cycle after cycle, without increasing the loan size. When a flexible loan is fully repaid on schedule, the borrower will be eligible for the basic loan again. The bank could, however, opt to keep the borrower under observation for three months instead of switching her to the basic loan immediately. During the observation period, bank workers monitor the borrower's attendance at meetings and confirms that she is contributing at least 5 taka per week to her personal savings account. If it appears that the borrower is able and willing, then she will again be allowed a basic loan.

Once a borrower is back on the basic loan, her loan ceiling has to be readjusted. The new ceiling will be equal to the ceiling she enjoyed immediately before taking the option to exit into the flexible loan. In severe cases, where the borrower has used several loan contracts and required a long time to repay the flexible loans, the ceiling might be refixed at the entry-level loan ceiling. The reduction in the loan ceiling and other conditions are instituted to discourage borrowers from exercising the option of switching to a flexible loan. On the other hand, as the name suggests, the option is available to allow borrowers the flexibility of extra time to repay the loan while remaining in good standing with the bank. An analogy with highway traffic flow in the United States is appropriate here. A flexible loan serves as an exit ramp from the highway to a service road. Once the flexible loan has been repaid on time and the borrower has met all of the conditions of the loan, she is allowed back on the highway. However, she will have to drive at a slower speed (lower credit ceiling) and be confined to the slow lane until she builds up

Box 3.2   Borrowers in Trouble

Sahera Khatoon is a member of the bank in the Chapra Saramjani branch of the Nilfamari subzone. She moved to this area twenty years ago after losing her homestead to erosion caused by flooding of the Bramaputra River. When Grameen Bank started operating in this area, she became a member. She hoped that by taking advantage of bank membership, she would be able to improve her economic condition. She was a regular member for a while, making installment payments on time, but the illness of her son and husband forced her into arrears, and she lost contact with the bank. She had a hard time making ends meet, and after her husband recouped from the illness, he leased a rickshaw at a daily rate of 15 taka. When the flexible loan was introduced in her center, I met her, her husband, and her son in their house and explained the benefits of the flexible loan. After I reassured them that they would be able to borrow after paying twenty-six installments on time, they signed a contract for a flexible loan. In the meantime, her son was leasing another rickshaw. He said, "Sir, I will set aside 25 taka out of my income from rickshaw pulling daily that I share with my father, and we can pay our installment from that extra income. Because we will use the money we will receive after twenty-six weeks to buy our own rickshaw, we will not have any problem paying installment."

After paying installments for five weeks, she signed a contract for a weekly installment payment of 125 taka. After perfect adherence to the schedule of repaying the contractual amount for twenty-six weeks, she received a 6500 taka loan. With this money her husband, Nur Mohammad, bought a new rickshaw from Syedpur. Now that they own their own rickshaw, they do not have pay the rental fee. Currently, Sahera is paying an installment of 195 taka per week and she opened a GPS account with 100 deposits per month. The top-up loan has given Sahera a new lease on life. She now owns a new passenger rickshaw and a rickshaw van.

Source: Mohammad Abdul Mottalib, Branch Manager, Chapra Saramjani Branch, Nilfamari Subzone, published in *Uddog*, August 2002.

Box 3.2   Borrowers in Trouble (Continued)

> Monwara Begum became a member of Grameen Bank in March 1986. From 1986 to 1991 she had the best repayment record of her center as well as the branch. This distinction gave her the right to lay the foundation stone for the permanent office of the branch. Her name is still engraved on the plaque at the entrance of the office building.
>
> In a cruel twist of fate, in 1993, as a result of having to pay the medical expenses for her husband's incurable disease and the dowry for her daughter's marriage, she became irregular in her payments. She would hide to avoid contact with bank staff.
>
> After becoming the manager of this branch, I met with her and her husband. They were convinced that since she had not been paying her installments and deposit savings, the bank would refuse her another loan even if she entered into a contract to repay the loan. After much discussion and persuasion, she rejoined the center and started depositing savings and paying installments. On October 31 she signed a contract to repay 125 taka per week in loan installments and 5 taka per week in savings. After making twenty-six such installments, she was approved a new loan of 6000 taka. When she took the money in her hand, Monwara shed tears of joy. She could not believe this day had come.
>
> *Source:* Gorachandra Sarkar, Branch Manager, Shukurer Hat Mitapukur Branch, Rangpur Zone.

her credit history by means of perfect repayment and attendance records; then will be ready to advance to the faster lanes.

The ability to switch to a flexible loan offers an alternative route for borrowers who need it, without making them feel guilty about failing to fulfill the requirements of the basic loan. This is Grameen's way of acknowledging the perennial vulnerability of the poor in Bangladesh. Switching to a flexible loan reduces the borrower's installment payments. At the same time, however, it allows her to borrow the amount of the loan repaid after six months, giving her the opportunity to take advantage of new investment opportunities. The latter option lets her quickly return to her pre-crisis condition.

Researchers at the Bangladesh Institute of Development Studies (BIDS) have identified the major categories of crisis faced by the poor in Bangladesh:[16]

Natural disasters include crop damage, housing and similar damages due to tornado, floods etc., and finally, river erosion. Illness expenditure/loss includes both expenditure on member illness and livestock death through disease. Insecurity includes dacoity, theft, eviction from land, money cheating, land litigation, physical assault, physical threats, police harassment, court/thana [police station] expenses, rape and abandonment of women. Dowry includes expenses incurred on daughter's marriage. Lastly, life-cycle includes death of main earner.[17]

The study further found that illness and insecurity are the major and stable categories of crisis regularly affecting most of the poor. A recent study of chronic poverty in Bangladesh, based on multi-period data by Naila Kabeer of the Institute of Development Studies at Sussex, reports that the most frequently reported crisis for all households was illness and accident or death in the family.[18] Many Grameen borrowers, even better-off members of the group, face these shocks (see Box 3.2). Years of experience with poor borrowers has convinced the bank that default is caused by such crises. Granted, some defaults are intentional; some borrowers do not repay their loans even though telltale signs (for example, quality of the house, asset ownership, access to additional sources of income) suggest that they could do so. The bank realized, however, that most repayment difficulties are caused by circumstances beyond the borrower's control. A borrower may not be able to pay because her husband has fallen ill and the money slated for installment payments must be used to buy medicine.[19,20] Perhaps she was defrauded and lost her investment in a project whose proceeds were to be used for repaying the bank. If a borrower insists on making the repayment, at any cost, in such circumstances, she may have to sell her assets or withdraw her children from school in addition to facing the public shame of being branded a defaulter. Aggressive insistence by the bank on strict adherence to rigid rules might lead borrowers back to destitution, defeating its original mission. Even people who are better off than the poor, termed by poverty researchers as "tomorrow's poor," are not immune from crises that hamper their income and cause repayment problems.[21] The flexible loan is a way of giving the borrowers—the moderate poor, extreme poor, and tomorrow's poor—a fresh start.

While borrowers are always concerned about debt burdens, they are terrified at the possibility of leaving debt behind in the event of their death. Such concern stems from cultural and religious sanctions against unpaid debt. Grameen II relieved borrowers of this burden by giving them the option to insure their loans. The loan insurance program has evolved over time. Initially, to insure the loan borrowers had to deposit 2.5% of the loan amount outstanding on the last day of the calendar year. [22] The rate was later raised to 3% of loan outstanding to cover the shortfall in the insurance fund. The shortfall was caused by a death rate among borrowers higher than the rate of 5000 deaths a year assumed in the simulation. Interest payments on these accounts, at 12% per year, are used to finance the insurance fund. If the borrower should die any time during the following year, the fund pays off the entire outstanding amount. In addition, the amount deposited in the savings account along with 12% interest is returned to the family of the deceased.[23] Borrowers must deposit an extra amount if the loan outstanding on the last day of the following year exceeds the first year's amount. The scheme is extremely popular with the borrowers, especially now that borrowers' husbands are covered under the insurance program in Grameen II.[24] Until recently, if a borrower wanted her husband to be covered under the scheme, she had to pay 6% of the total outstanding loan amount at the end of the year; in the event of her husband's death, her entire loan was forgiven and the 6% plus accumulated interest was returned to her savings account. Helen Todd's research with long-term borrowers of Grameen Bank showed that death of a borrower's husband nearly always causes the widowed loanee, especially if she has no adult son, to slip back into poverty. In addition, an older widow is likely to die quickly and suffer from ill health due to a lack of access to resources. These facts, well known among borrowers, explain the desire among the female borrowers to cover their husbands under the loan insurance scheme. Unpublished research by an independent observer and internal research by the bank suggest that an important factor leading to member dropout is the problem of paying installments after the death of the husband. Out of concern for and loyalty to its female borrowers, the bank helps prevent these vulnerable widows from slipping into destitution through its "debt relief on death" program.

Unfortunately, the higher-than-expected death rate among husbands has created another shortfall in the insurance fund. As a result, the bank has had to change the policy on loan insurance program once again.[25] Under a new policy implemented on October 1, 2005, all borrowers must deposit 3% of the loan amount in the loan insurance savings account for every new loan instead of the loan amount outstanding at the end of the year. If the female borrower wants to cover her husband under the program, she has to deposit an additional 7% of the loan amount in the loan insurance savings account. Under the new policy, the borrower can use the 2.5% in obligatory savings deposits to make partial payment to the loan insurance account. Loan insurance is not obligatory for the members or the husbands. However, if a female borrower is on a special enterprise loan, both she and her husband must be covered by the loan insurance program.

Having laid out the basics of Grameen I and II, we are now in a position to review the main differences between the two models. Instead of several loan products as under Grameen I, there is now one prime loan product: the basic loan. The duration of the loan can vary from three months to three years, as opposed to the typical one-year loan under Grameen I. The installment size can also vary during the loan period and can be tailored to meet the needs of the borrower. Under Grameen I, loans were staggered, with two members receiving their loans first, then another two, and then typically the group chairperson. Now all members can receive loans at the same time. Moreover, instead of being disbursed at one time, loan amounts can be disbursed in tranches under Grameen II. Previously, a borrower could not receive a new loan without fully repaying a loan of same type. Under Grameen II, with the exception of special investment and housing loans, a member can borrow the amount repaid after six months without having to repay the original loan in full. A borrower can also repay the loan in a large, lump-sum amount, which was not allowed in Grameen I. A borrower under classical Grameen was branded a defaulter if she could not repay the full amount of a loan within fifty-two weeks. Now she will be labeled a defaulter if she cannot repay the due amount per schedule within six months or twenty-six weeks, and instead of defaulting, she has the temporary option of switching to a flexible loan contract. Under Grameen I, failure to repay the installment was the only way a borrower could become in arrears. Now a borrower can also become a defaulter if she fails to make deposits for four consecutive months in her GPS account.

The method of setting the loan ceiling has also changed under the new model. In Grameen I, a common loan ceiling existed for all borrowers of a branch. Under Grameen II, each borrower has her own ceiling, which depends on her performance and the performance of the group, center, and branch, as well as on the amount of her savings. Under Grameen I, there was no hard and fast rule about increasing or decreasing the loan ceiling; under Grameen II, the loan ceiling is affected by the size of savings deposits, frequency of attendance at center meetings, and the overall performance of the borrower, her group, her center, and the branch. As mentioned earlier, group fund savings have been eliminated under Grameen II. Another change is the amount of weekly savings. In Grameen I weekly savings were uniform, while under the current regime weekly savings are tied to the loan amounts.[26]

This chapter has explained the main elements of Grameen II and how they differ from classical Grameen. However, we have covered only the major elements, loan products. We will discuss other changes that came about with Grameen II in the next chapter.

NOTES

1. See note 8 of Chapter 2.
2. Asif Dowla, "In Credit We Trust: Building Social Capital by Grameen Bank in Bangladesh," *Journal of Socio-Economics* 35(1), 2006, pp. 102–122.
3. This is similar to home equity loans in the United States. A homeowner can borrow 80% of the difference between the assessed value of the home and the loan outstanding. For example, if a house has a market value of $100,000 and the principal and interest outstanding on the mortgage total $50,000, the homeowner will get a line of credit of 0.8 × $50,000 = $40,000.
4. Asif Dowla, "Micro Leasing: The Grameen Bank Experience," *Journal of Microfinance* 6(2), 2004, pp. 137–160.
5. B. d'Ansembourg and Ichiro Tambo, "GrameenPhone Revisited: Investors Reaching Out to the Poor," *DAC Journal* 5(3), 2004, pp. 15–55.
6. The average revenue per user (ARPU) of VPP subscribers is double that of the average Grameen Phone business user. *The Village Phone* (Grameen Phone Online, 2004) (available at http://www.grameenphone.com/modules.php?name=Content&pa=showpage&pid=3:11:1).
7. Rezwan Alauddin, *Connecting People in Rural Communities through ICT: Grameen Telecom Experience* (Asian Development Bank Institute, 2005) (available at http://www.adbi.org/files/2004.12.08.cpp.connecting.rural.ict.pdf).
8. Dipal C. Barua and Dian Diacon, *The Impact of the Grameen Bank Mobile Phone Programme on the Lives and Housing of Rural Women in Bangladesh* (Grameen Shakti and Building and Social Housing Foundation, 2003).
9. Muhammad Yunus, "Alleviating Poverty through Technology," *Science* 282(5388), 1998, pp. 409–410.
10. *Village Phone.*
11. S. Aminumzzaman, H. Baldersheim, and I. Jamil, "Talking Back! Empowerment and Mobile Phones in Rural Bangladesh: Study of the Village Phone Scheme of Grameen Bank," *Contemporary South Asia* 12(3), 2003, pp. 329.
12. A phone call that replaces a physical trip from a village to the capital city of Dhaka generates a consumer surplus of 2.64% to 9.8% of mean monthly household income. The cost of a trip to the city is about two to eight times the cost of a single phone call. This amounts to a savings of 132 to 490 taka for individual calls. Don R. Richardson, R. Ramirez, and M. Haq, *Grameen Telcom's Village Phone Programme in Rural Bangladesh: A Multi-Media Case Study* (Guelph, Ontario: TeleCommons Development Group, 2000).

13. A. Bayes, "Infrastructure and Rural Development: Insights from a Grameen Bank Village Phone Initiative in Bangladesh," *Agricultural Economics* 25, 2001, pp. 261–272.

14. Farooq Sobhan, M. H. Khaleque, and S. Rahman, *Factors Shaping Successful Public Private Partnerships in the ICT Sector in Bangladesh* (Bangladesh Enterprise Institute, 2002).

15. About 43% of VPP income is spent on food, 15% on business, 12.78% on clothing, 8.69% on health, 4.43% on education, and 4.33% on contributions to savings. About 37% of the operators purchased land from VPP income; 24% built or developed houses; 12% purchased shops or businesses; 7.14% invested in livestock, poultry, or fisheries; and 12% and 17% bought furniture and fixtures, respectively.

16. H. Z. Rahman, Mahbub Hossain, and Binayak Sen, *1987–1994: Dynamics of Rural Poverty in Bangladesh* (Dhaka: Bangladesh Institute of Development Studies, 1996).

17. Rahman, Hossain, and Sen, p. 108.

18. Naila Kabeer, *Snakes, Ladders and Traps: Changing Lives and Livelihoods in Rural Bangladesh (1994–2001),* Joint CPRP-IDS Working Paper (Brighton, UK: Institute of Development Studies, 2004).

19. Helzi Noponen and Paula Kantor, using panel data on 308 randomly selected members of SEWA, a renowned credit-granting NGO in India, found that illness is the major stress event faced by these households. Helzi Noponen and Paula Kantor, "Crisis, Setbacks and Chronic Problems: The Determinants of Economic Stress Events among Poor Households in India," *Journal of International Development* 16, 2004, pp. 529–545.

20. A recent study by several Harvard faculty members found that 50% of personal bankruptcy in the United States is caused by illness. See David U. Himmelstein, Elizabeth Warren, Deborah Thomas, et al., "Market Watch: Illness and Injury as Contributors to Bankruptcy," *Health Affairs* web exclusive (Feb. 2, 2005) (available at http://content.healthaffairs.org/cgi/reprint/hlthaff.w5.63v1).

21. H. Z. Rahman, "Bangladesh: Dynamics of Rural Poverty," Paper presented at the International Conference on Poverty: Emerging Challenges, organized by the Bangladesh Institute of Development Studies in association with Grameen Trust and LGED (Dhaka, February 9–11, 1998).

22. On December 31, 2002, 2.4 million borrowers had an average outstanding loan amount of 10,000 taka. At the rate of 2.5% premium the borrowers deposited 600 million taka in the insurance fund. At an interest rate of 8.5%, the interest income would have been 51 million taka, and this amount could fund an average loan balance of 10,200 taka.

23. At the beginning of the scheme the interest rate on the loan insurance deposit was 8.5%. It was changed to 12% to cover the shortfall in the insurance fund.
24. This is actually different from a standard insurance program; the borrowers are relieved of the full insured amount (actual loan outstanding instead of loan outstanding at the end of December 31 of the preceding year), and the deposit in the loan insurance savings account (now 3% of the loan outstanding at the end of December 31 of the preceding year) is returned to the borrower.
25. At the end of September 2005, 6541 female borrowers and 9574 husbands of female borrowers of the bank had died. The death rate of husbands is higher in the southern part of the country. A major contributing factor to the higher death rate among husbands is the high incidence of motor boat capsizing in the southern part of the country. The motor boat is the only means of transportation to major towns in the delta region of the country.
26. The weekly savings schedule is related to the loan amount: 5 taka for loans up to 15,000 taka, 10 taka for loans in the range of 15,001 to 25,000 taka, 15 taka for loans in the range of 25,001 to 50,000 taka, 25 taka for loans in the range of 50,001 taka to 100,000 taka, and 50 taka for loans exceeding 100,000 taka.

4

Savings Mobilization: From One Taka to 3000 Billion Taka

The most innovative aspect of Grameen II is the introduction of numerous savings products and a major emphasis on collecting savings from members and the general public. Before we discuss these products and the procedure for collecting savings, we must put savings in the proper cultural context. In Bangladesh the majority of the people live in rural areas, and household savings constitutes the largest component of total savings in the country. As a result, any discussion of savings in Bangladesh must be couched mainly in terms of savings in rural areas. Moreover, there is an urgent need to study rural savings in the absence of adequate formal banks in these areas. Several surveys have estimated the size of savings in these areas. As part of the Rural Finance Project of Bangladesh Bank (the central bank), Maloney and Ahmed (1988) conducted a survey of 300 households in rural Bangladesh. The survey shows that the poor save between 2% and 12% of their income, with the moderately poor saving an average of 12% to 14%. For the purpose of the survey, the authors defined savings as did the people themselves: cash savings. The survey found that buying land was cited as the most important reason for saving, followed by providing family security against unforeseen contingencies. The education and marriage of children along with the purchase of agricultural inputs were other factors found to influence savings.

R. I. Rahman (1998a) conducted a survey of 370 households in two villages to estimate the rural households' demand for liquid savings services. Save the Children (USA) commissioned this survey to assist in the provision of liquid saving services by a credit-granting NGO in the areas covered by their credit program. Savings was defined as the difference between estimated income and consumption expenditures of the household. The average saving rate was 9% (16.6% in one village and –5.5% in another village). However, a sizable portion of savings was directly invested in asset build-up, leaving a smaller percentage that the NGO could collect. Female respondents suggested that the purchase of various assets such as livestock and land, and the future needs of the family and children are the major incentives for saving. The survey also revealed some demand for long-term savings. However, most of the respondents were expecting their children to take care of them during old age, offsetting the need for retirement savings. R. I. Rahman (1998a) argued that cash savings would be higher and respondents would not feel the need to invest the savings in family enterprises if formal savings services were available to them. She also found that familiarity with financial institutions such as NGOs leads to much higher potential savings.

In an innovative study, Rutherford (2002) examined the financial transactions—individual acts of saving, lending, borrowing, and repaying—of forty-two households in villages and urban slums in Bangladesh for one year. The study entailed the creation of financial diaries for the households through twice-monthly visits with all financial transactions noted, no matter how small. The study found that of all of the financial transactions recorded, saving at home was conducted by all households. Further, the study reported that the savings balances were small relative to annual income, and that these balances were used to create small to medium lump sums for immediate use rather than long-term investment. The lump sums created out of savings were used, broadly speaking, for major events such as births, education, marriage, and deaths; to deal with emergencies involving health, theft, and natural and man-made calamities; or to take advantage of opportunities such as investments in productive assets, business, land, or consumer durables.

The brief surveys reported here provide an introduction to the salient feature of savings in rural Bangladesh. They show that households in Bangladesh rarely save for life cycle events such as retirement; instead, people expect their children to take care of them in old age (R. I. Rahman, 1998a). The savings, which are small relative to income, are used frequently to close the gap between consumption and uncertain income (Rutherford, 2002).

A few caveats about estimates of savings based on household surveys are in order. It is likely that the savings numbers reported in the survey are an underestimation, as people tend to undervalue their financial situation for fear that the researcher may pass the information on to tax authorities. Even if the respondents are truthful about their income, income is difficult to estimate, as a large percentage of poor people are self-employed. In addition, the survey was unable to capture the level of savings that would have resulted if microfinance institutions (MFIs) were available to collect savings. Wright (1998) and Kabeer (1998), on the other hand, suggest that once the means of depositing savings become available, poor people save a great deal. Moreover, a respondent's definition of income, consumption, and savings is not always consistent with the enumerator's definition, as noted by Maloney and Ahmed (1988):

> If a farmer buys tin (corrugated iron) for his roof it is consumption, according to normal economics. But the farmer certainly considers it also as a savings for emergency, and will always say that in time of crisis he can sell it. The farmer also considers it an investment in his local socioeconomic status, as without the appearance of some success in his life it is impossible for him to forge the social links to generate more prosperity. So, should researchers classify the tin as consumption, savings or investment?

Another important aspect of savings is gender-related differences in saving behavior. This very real aspect of savings tends to be ignored in the literature. Women do tend to save in cash as well as in kind, a fact that they hide from their husbands and other relatives in order to maintain their own private savings that their male relatives cannot touch. "Women actively seek to hedge against patriarchal risk in other ways as well. With the collusion of a young son a women may sell grain without her husband's knowledge and accumulate savings. There are cases of women surreptitiously purchasing land (usually outside of the village), or engaging in money-lending activities without their husband's knowledge."[1] Kabeer (1998) called these "clandestine savings." Naved (2000) reports that all of the women in some of her study villages maintain a secret saving store (*zolaitta*). Wright and Mutesasira (2001) noted that many of the Association for Social Advancement's members were using the associate member's savings account to store "secret" savings out of the sight and grasp of their husbands. Savings, in this case, is used as a form of women's everyday resistance to inequities in intra-household resource allocation (Agarwal, 1997). In much the same way, there is a long-standing tradition of women setting aside a morsel of rice (*mushtichaal*) when they cook the main meal of the day. Rice saved in this way is used to tide over days when rice is in short supply, an example of women serving as main conduit for providing food security for the family.

The studies reviewed so far deal with cash savings. Savings, however, can also exist in the form of "stock" or commodities such as livestock or jewelry. Unfortunately, even though stocks are easy to measure, we are not aware of any attempts to measure in-kind or stock savings in Bangladesh. Like all financial institutions, Grameen Bank is primarily involved in collecting cash savings.

While savings collection was one of the core elements of Grameen, it was not the main objective. The earliest branches of the bank had booths for savings collection; later these were removed to facilitate credit disbursement, which had by then become the primary mission. Under Grameen I, borrowers had to start depositing savings daily the first week after formation of the group. During this week, group members learned about the various aspects of the bank's rules, regulations, and products. At the end of the week, members had accumulated 7 taka each in the group fund. The group received formal recognition at the end of the training period once each member had passed an oral test. Once the group was recognized, the two neediest members would receive credit while the others continued to save weekly until it was their turn to receive credit.[2] Under Grameen II, however, new members deposit 5 taka daily in their personal savings account until the group becomes formally recognized by the bank. The difference now is that all members can receive credit simultaneously after the group's formal recognition. Moreover, the members now deposit a variable amount that depends on the size of the loan along with 2.5% of all loans in their personal savings accounts. The bank has also been aggressively collecting savings from the general public. These accounts pay 8.5% interest and the account owners can access them at will. Table 4.1 reports the amounts of savings collected by the bank in recent years.

At the start of Grameen, there was concern that collecting voluntary savings, which was easier than credit disbursement and collect-

Table 4.1   Yearly Balances on Savings Accounts

	Balance (Million Taka)			
Year	Members	Non-members*	Total	Total (Million $)**
2000	202.8	682.2	845.0	12.62
2001	1479.0	867.2	2346.2	35.02
2002	1889.7	1049.8	2939.5	43.87
2003	2277.8	1910.1	4187.9	62.51
2004	2780.7	3413.3	6194.0	92.45
2005	3645.3	5188.2	8833.5	131.84

*The higher savings by nonmembers is partly accounted for by the deposits of many of Grameen's sister organizations, such as Grameen Shakti and Grameen Krishi. Many smaller credit-granting NGOs also deposit their excess savings with Grameen Bank
**$1 = 67 taka.

Source: Monitoring and Evaluation Department, Grameen Bank.

ing repayments, would prompt staff to lose sight of the bank's main mission: alleviating poverty through credit.[3] Most of the savings were accumulated in the group fund, which was obligatory. In contrast, Grameen II instituted voluntary and easy access to savings as an important element of the new model, a crucial difference from the earlier savings regime. While there are still some obligatory savings requirements, they are not as onerous as those for the group fund of Grameen I. In fact, savings capability is positively linked to loan size under Grameen II, allowing the loan ceiling to increase with an increase in savings deposits. Higher savings can to lead to better access to credit via the bridge loan discussed in Chapter 3. A borrower, under the basic loan, can borrow the difference between her outstanding loan and 150% of her acceptable savings deposits. The acceptable savings deposit includes items such as the Grameen pension scheme (GPS), special savings accounts, fixed deposits, and other contractual savings deposits, with the exception of personal savings and security deposits against the village phone.

The success and popularity of GPS provided the necessary impetus for collecting voluntary savings. Commercial banks in Bangladesh introduced DPS (deposit pension scheme, a type of contractual saving) several years ago, and it enjoyed early success. Under the plan, the borrower deposits a fixed amount every month for five to ten years and receives a lump sum at the end of the period. The borrower receives a cumulative interest rate that is compounded every year. In fact, many Grameen staff as well as members opened DPS accounts with commercial banks. During monthly visits by the managing director of the bank, the field staff and the members urged the bank to introduce a similar scheme in the bank. These requests were not initially heeded because the management thought such a plan would be too complicated and the costs of collecting savings might be prohibitive. During the process of redesigning the bank, the leadership initiated a discussion about introducing a DPS type of scheme. The conclusion was that, in addition to meeting the demand of the staff and the borrowers and providing a vehicle for the borrowers to save for retirement, such a scheme would provide a secure source of funding for the bank. The bad experience of using the discount window of the central bank to meet the liquidity crisis after the flood of 1998 convinced the bank that it had to depend on its own resources as much as possible to fund regular operations as well as emergencies caused by natural disasters.[4] However, the major hindrance to the introduction of GPS was the bank's quest to keep income from such deposits tax-free for its members, in contrast to DPS, the income from which was taxable. The bank had spent two years seeking to be granted tax-free status by the Ministry of Finance. When the ministry finally granted the bank permission, however, it allowed for the collection of deposits only from members, effectively excluding staff and the general public. The staff asked the managing director, Professor Yunus, to seek permission from the ministry to allow them to save with their own institution. This permission was granted after three months, and the bank finally introduced the GPS scheme for members who could save 100 taka per month. Instituting the GPS scheme involved a lively internal debate about whether members would have the capacity to save taka 100 per month and whether the cost of collecting such deposits would justify the benefits. The biggest skeptic was Professor Yunus himself. He conceded that the popularity of and the large deposits to GPS were a huge surprise for him.[5]

The bank introduced GPS in February 2000. Under the scheme, a borrower deposits a fixed amount every month for five or ten years. The accumulated principal and interest—at a generous rate of 12% for the ten-year version and 10% for the five-year version—is released to her as a lump sum or as monthly income. After the initial success with GPS, a simulation was conducted by the staff to approximate the total deposit (100 × 2.4 million[6] taka) that would be available if each member deposited 100 taka per month. Some staff members questioned how the bank would pay off the depositors when these schemes matured. Others did not believe that the bank would be able to pay off the maturing deposits at all. The simulation took into account the different maturing dates as well as the possibility that a matured plan might not be cashed in right away or all on one day. The bank staff also reasoned it was likely that some members would roll over the GPS for another five- or ten-year term after its maturation. The results of the simulation with these various contingencies taken into account convinced the bank that introducing GPS would be cost-effective. Figure 4.1 shows the trend of GPS collection over the years.

A requirement was added that to be member of Grameen Bank, one must have a GPS. Such a requirement would protect the bank from excessive fund outflow from maturing GPS accounts. Members were also given the option of contributing more than 100 taka per month for GPS, as well as the ability to open multiple GPS accounts, the latter of which was opposed by some staff on the grounds that the poor would not have enough surplus funds to maintain several savings accounts requiring contractual monthly deposits. Once these issues were sorted out, questions arose as to what to do for new members, who were generally not as well off as established members and thus might not be able to bear the burden of installment of payments as well as a compulsory contribution to GPS. As a result, the obligatory contribution of 100 taka per month

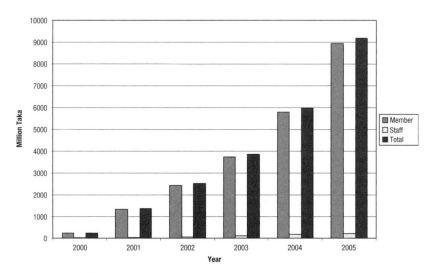

Figure 4.1   GPS collection over time from members and staff.

was reduced to a minimum of 50 taka per month for members borrowing 5000 taka or less. This reduction led to the introduction of "Red GPS" and "Green GPS"—"Red" representing the required amount of taka (50) and "Green" representing an amount exceeding the minimum. Later, the amount of a loan requiring GPS contributions was raised to 8000 taka. In some branches of the bank an extra 10 taka is added to the borrower's weekly installment to meet this requirement, and the borrower can also give written permission to transfer this amount from her personal savings account every month. The advantage of the GPS scheme is that the amount deposited will double in ten years; and even if the borrower leaves the bank, she can still maintain her GPS with the bank.

The bank's main motivation for requiring mandatory GPS for a loan exceeding a certain amount is that it enables borrowers to save a lump sum that can serve in the future as a pension. Providing a pension for borrowers in such a way raises several questions about the true need for this type of mandatory savings. First of all, why can't the borrower be trusted to make arrangements for his or her own retirement, or even continue to earn a living by working longer? While an alternative to pension planning is to continue taking loans and working, given the realities in rural Bangladesh, working to pay living costs at an old age is not a feasible option. Evidence suggests that people age faster in the rural areas from excessive labor during their working life, malnutrition, inadequate health care, frequent childbirths for women, and the hardships of dealing with recurrent natural disasters. Given the restrictions on women's mobility in the rural areas, women especially will be unable to work to support themselves in their old age. Research suggests that several years of successful membership in the bank leads to a build-up of assets that can be used in retirement. Then why develop a separate, mandatory pension scheme to pay for retirement? The reason is that some of these assets may not be income bearing. For example, a borrower may purchase a house by using a loan from the bank, but the house cannot be used to generate income. Ownership of property such as land may also be transferred to children as an inheritance. A mandatory pension plan such as GPS ensures that the elderly will have usable income in the future, allowing them to survive without the need to work or be dependent on their children.

Traditionally, children in Bangladesh provide old-age security to their parents. This option is, however, becoming less viable due to the increasing break-up of joint families in rural areas, causing an even greater need for pension plans like GPS.[7] A survey of respondents from a project involving destitutes as well as the bank's case studies of struggling members suggest that the abandonment of elderly parents by children is on the rise. A significant number of R. I. Rahman's (1998a) respondents were uncertain about their fate during old age and did not know how they would support themselves. Further, she reports that only 20% of households expressed a desire to enter into a long-term savings scheme lasting, on average, ten years. These findings suggest that borrowers have to protect themselves from destitution in old age using their own means; it is appropriate, therefore, to provide a mechanism such as GPS. The huge success of GPS (see Figure 4.1) proves that borrowers are increasingly coming to this realization.

Another source of support on which the elderly of Bangladesh rely is transfers from sons, relatives, extended family, and the community.[8] This option, however, is even less likely to provide sufficient income given the breakdown of community norms and increased financial needs of the family. Bangladesh now has a public pension system for older people. The government introduced an old-age allowance scheme in 1997–1998. Under the plan, a monthly allowance of 180 taka is given to the ten poorest (five men and five women) and oldest members of each ward of the union, the lowest administrative unit. Recently, the government introduced another social assistance program for women who become widowed or are abandoned by their husbands. Under this program, five women from each ward of the union receive 180 taka per month. Studies show that even though these programs were well received, they cover only a fraction of deserving cases (Begum, 2003).[9] By providing the opportunity to finance retirement through

GPS, the bank is filling an important void left by the community and the government.

Making adequate arrangements for old age is especially important for women, in part because women tend to live longer than men. Even if men and women had the same mortality rate, in Bangladesh a woman will most likely outlive her husband due to the wide age difference at the time of marriage. Because of a lack of a social support network and broader public or private insurance and pension schemes, women have to depend on their husbands for old-age support. Those without husbands and those who lose husbands through death become extremely vulnerable because, as women, their economic and social status is closely tied to marriage. Rahman (2000) found that widowed women have worse health compared with their currently married peers.[10] In another study, Rahman (1997) showed that widowed women also have a higher mortality rate than their currently married peers. These statistics reflect the poverty that befalls women upon the death of their husbands.[11] While older males can use income from land ownership for retirement, women rarely own land. Women may own some land under inheritance law after the death of their husbands, but it is difficult for an older woman to use the land as a source of income without help from her sons and male relatives. Helen Todd (1996) showed that the death of a husband nearly always causes the widowed loanee, especially if she has no adult son, to slip back into poverty. Savings via GPS, however, serves as a safety net against poverty and ill health for aged women. Staff report that the female borrowers are opening extra GPS accounts that they want kept secret from their husbands. This report of secret savings in GPS accounts by female borrowers is corroborated by unpublished field research by Stuart Rutherford and is related to gendered aspects of savings mentioned earlier.

So far, we have explored how GPS can act as a safety net for borrowers in their old age. A related question is why GPS is mandatory for loans exceeding a certain limit. If GPS were voluntary, it is highly unlikely that many borrowers would sign up, because they would not see the need for retirement savings and would rather depend on fate or the hope that their children and extended family will take care of them. Modern research by behavioral economists in advanced countries indicates that it is hard for most people to save on their own. Even though it may be rational for an individual to plan for retirement, many are unable to stick to their plan of saving regularly. Moreover, when the time comes to save, people tend to procrastinate and postpone saving for another day. Behavioral economists have labeled this divergence between plan and reality "time inconsistency." A related concept is "hyperbolic discounting," which proposes that individuals prefer income that will arrive sooner over income that will accrue in the distant future. According to behavioral economists, individuals tend to be impatient with consumption in the near future and relatively patient with consumption in the distant future. One means of avoiding the problem of time inconsistency is to pre-commit oneself. Signing up for GPS is a method of pre-commitment that allows borrowers to save for the long term and forces them to stick with the plan.[12] Shefrin and Thaler (1992) suggest that people use distinct "mental accounts" to separate various sources of income and to decide what fraction of income to save. They suggest that people save a large fraction of their income from assets and future income, whereas current income is consumed quickly. This saving pattern suggests that individuals must exercise a high degree of self-control to save out of current income.[13]

In an innovative study three economists, Dean Karlan, Nava Ashraf, and Wesley Yin, put these ideas to the test.[14] In a field experiment they offered a randomly chosen subset of 710 clients of Green Bank of Carga, a small rural bank in the Philippines, the option to open savings accounts with commitment features that restricted withdrawals. The clients could decide to restrict the withdrawal until a certain date or until a certain amount was accumulated in the accounts. In addition, the clients were encouraged to set a written goal for their savings. To ascertain the pure demand for commitment savings, the clients were not compensated with a higher interest rate. The economists found that after six months the treatment group (clients chosen randomly and offered the option to open a savings account) increased savings by 47% more than the control group (clients who were not offered the option to open a savings account randomly), and those who opened accounts increased savings by 130.7% more than the control group. The increase in savings continued after the six-month period: savings increased by 82.5% after twelve months. Further, the economists found that women who exhibit hyperbolic discounting are more likely to accept an offer of commitment savings products. The increased balances in these accounts were created out of new savings rather than by shifting savings from other accounts, which suggests that commitment devices such as the specified savings account could lead to additional savings without depleting other types of savings.

The survey by R. I. Rahman (1998a) indicates that rather than being rational,[15] many poor individuals are unsure about what will happen to them in old age and are rather fatalistic about it: 30.1% of male and 26.7% of female respondents did not know how they would support themselves in old age. The poor also face the problem of time inconsistency—they cannot follow through with their plans. Their inability to follow the plan when the time comes is not mainly the result of procrastination, as stipulated in the behavior economic literature. Rather, the poor's income is subject to various demands that take precedence over saving for retirement. First and foremost is the need for day-to-day survival. The poor have to choose whether to save or to buy medicine for sick children or parents, pay the children's school fees, or buy seeds for next year's crop. Even if they are lucky enough to pay for these needs without violating their plan for savings, they may face demands to lend to extended family members, friends, or neighbors. If they have some money left for savings after these pressing demands, they must take time from their daily schedule to go to the bank, which might well be a few hours' walk away, to make their deposits. Even if such a woman is able to get to the bank, she may not be able to obtain the necessary application form to open a DPS account because of her poor economic condition and her gender.[16] A woman may not even be able to make this trip, in which case she may have to wait for her husband or son to make the deposit at the bank.

The GPS solves all of these problems. It provides a commitment device for borrowers to save regularly for retirement while protecting funds from competing family needs. It gives the poor a perfect alibi to resist social demands on their money. It makes savings for retirement an "optimum default" option by making it a requirement for a loan. It makes it easy for the poor to make deposits at center meetings instead of going to the bank, and most of all, it provides them a vehicle for saving risk-free[17] with a credible, brand-name institution. Moreover, because savings in GPS is a public act, the borrowers can use a collective mechanism to maintain self-control.[18] By providing an opportunity to save for retirement, the bank is in essence guaranteeing a level of income for its borrowers when they will be too weak to work, thereby protecting them from having to depend on children and family to maintain a reasonable standard of living. Table 4.2 provides data about GPS collection over the years.

Emboldened by the success of GPS, the bank introduced other saving plans to be offered to members and nonmembers alike. A popular scheme is fixed deposits, which are similar to term

Table 4.2   GPS Collection over Time

Year	Balance (Million Taka)			Total (Million $)*
	Members	**Staff**	**Total**	
2000	243.4	14.5	257.9	3.85
2001	1330.7	46.2	1376.9	20.55
2002	2448.7	82.2	2530.9	37.77
2003	3735.2	129.9	3865.1	57.69
2004	5796.6	177.2	5973.8	89.16
2005	8958.1	225.7	9183.8	137.07

*$1 = 67 taka

Source: Grameen Bank, Monitoring and Evaluation Department

deposits or certificates of deposit. The minimum amount for this account is 1000 taka, and a member can open an account (which should amount to a multiple of 1000 taka) at any time of the month. The deposit can be held for one to three years, and the interest rate varies with the length of time: 8.75% for one year, 9.25% for two years, and 9.5% for three years. A member can own several of these accounts. This savings scheme also allows automatic renewal of the accounts. Members can withdraw funds before maturity of the account, but the interest paid on premature withdrawal will depend on the time of withdrawal. For example, a three-year fixed deposit closed in the second year will receive the interest rate for the second year (i.e., 9.25% instead of 9.5%). If the funds are withdrawn before one year, the member will receive no interest. The bank believes that these deposits will be used by borrowers to pay for their children's education and marriages and to acquire various types of assets. This plan is also popular with nonmembers, because it enjoys tax-free status and because Grameen's wide network in the rural areas allows them to deposit with the bank easily. Grameen's high reputation and familiar name represent an additional draw for nonmembers. The fixed deposit scheme allows borrowers to build a lump sum of funds that can be used to finance larger investment projects; these nest eggs can reduce their vulnerability. By making this option available, the bank provides a commitment device for nonmembers to save for their own retirement.

Another scheme is known as "double in seven years." This scheme is related to the fixed deposit scheme. The difference is that the amount deposited doubles after seven years. The effective interest rate for this type of deposit is slightly higher than 10%. The amount deposited must be a multiple of 1000 taka, and the minimum deposit is 1000 taka. Borrowers can also withdraw funds before the scheme matures. The following schedule shows the amounts borrowers will receive if they deposit 1000 taka and withdraw funds before their full maturity:

Duration	Principal and Interest at the End of the Period
After one year	1087 taka
After two years	1193 taka
After three years	1312 taka
After four years	1450 taka
After five years	1610 taka
After six years	1795 taka
After seven years	2000 taka

The fixed deposit and "double in seven years" schemes enable members and nonmembers alike to save for large anticipated expenses such as higher education for children or a daughter's marriage. These schemes allow members to save in the form of money rather than riskier physical assets such as livestock. Such physical assets are subject to risks such as death or theft of the animal, whereas money kept in fixed deposit accounts is relatively risk-free and is therefore a more secure guarantee for the future.[19] Table 4.3 provides data about savings collection in these two instruments.

Another savings product introduced under Grameen II is the monthly income plan. Under this program, a borrower can deposit a minimum of 20,000 taka and then a multiple of 10,000 taka into an account, which can be for a five- or ten-year duration. The difference between this and the other schemes is that instead of waiting to receive the principal and the accumulated interest, the borrower receives interest monthly. For example, if someone deposits the minimum amount of 20,000 taka, she will receive 160 taka as monthly income in the five-year scheme and 170 taka in the ten-year scheme. The annual rate of interest turns out to be 10.04% and 10.67% for the five- and ten-year schemes, respectively. The plan can be renewed by the depositor or automatically by the bank, and it can be closed at any time. However, if the plan is discontinued before a year, the profits distributed to that

Table 4.3   Yearly Balances on Fixed Deposit and "Double in Seven Years" Savings Schemes

| Year | Balance (Million Taka) on Fixed Deposits | | | |
	Members	Nonmembers	Total	Total (Million $)*
2002	21.2	111.6	132.8	1.98
2003	33.5	165.5	199.0	2.97
2004	48.6	444.7	493.3	7.36
2005	64.0	633.7	697.7	10.41

| Year | Balance (Million Taka) on "Double in Seven Years" Savings Scheme | | | |
	Members	Nonmembers	Total	Total (Million $)*
2002	249.0	339.1	588.1	8.78
2003	448.9	890.7	1339.6	19.99
2004	743.9	2156.9	2900.8	43.25
2005	1030.1	4123.8	5153.9	76.92

*$1 = 67 taka

Source: Grameen Bank, Evaluation and Monitoring Department.

point will be subtracted from the principal amount so that the borrower will receive zero profit. If the plan is abandoned after one year but before the five- or ten-year maturity, the following schedule is used to determine profit:

Maturity	Rate of Profit (Simple Interest)
More than a year but less than three years	7.0%
More than three years but less than five years	8.0%
More than five years but less than ten years	8.5%

Table 4.4   Yearly Balances for Monthly Profit Savings Scheme

Year	Balance (Million Taka)			Total (Million $)*
	Members	Nonmembers	Total	
2002	0.43	5.76	6.19	0.92
2003	1.34	21.42	22.76	0.34
2004	2.97	68.33	71.30	1.06
2005	4.66	127.02	131.68	1.96

*$1 = 67 taka

Source: Grameen Bank, Evaluation and Monitoring Department.

Table 4.4 provides information about the collection of savings under the monthly profit scheme.

At the founding of Grameen Bank in 1979, the savings requirement was 1 taka per week. The total savings of Grameen Bank will soon exceed 30 billion taka. The introduction of Grameen II has led to radical changes in emphasis on and types of savings collections. Initially, as a precondition for a loan, one had to begin saving during the process of group formation. However, these weekly savings were deposited in a group fund that was not freely accessible. Members could borrow from the group fund with the approval of the group, and until 1995 they had to pay a 5% tax known as Group Tax 2 on loans from the group fund. The annual reports of Grameen Bank document the various uses of these savings, which include even repayment of loans with proceeds from the group fund. This particular use led analysts to suggest that the group fund acted as a form of insurance; however, the members had to return these savings to the fund and could get access to the accumulated balance only if they dropped out.[20]

The rapid increase in the mobilization of voluntary deposits is the most radical departure of Grameen II. Practitioners and academics criticized the bank for not paying attention to savings mobilization. A well-known critic went so far as to label the Grameen model a "left-hand theory of finance." Surveys show that only one-sixth of the people in the world are left-handed, and this critic believed that the number of people willing to save exceeded the number of people willing to borrow in a ratio similar to that of right-handers to left-handers. Another critic labeled Grameen's lack of attention to savings as the "forgotten half" of finance. A recent academic work by Pankaj Jain and Mick Moore, of the Institute of Development Studies in Sussex, notes, "We are dealing with microcredit, not microfinance. Neither the Grameen Bank nor similar organizations have been able to develop a large business in deposit mobilization. It is at least arguable that they *never* will, because they have become locked into a particular strategy— essentially one of dispersing a limited range of loan packages against what some would regard as (limited) forced savings" (emphasis added).[21] The success of Grameen has proven, however, that those who criticized its lack of attention to savings were wrong.

Grameen has found that the potential for savings is huge in Bangladesh, even at the "bottom of the pyramid." The contractual savings plans have enabled the poor to break free from the trap of low savings. Savings in large amounts by group members have prompted others in the group and even nonmembers to save more. In many branches, savings exceed loans by a wide margin. As mentioned before, during the 1998 flood the bank borrowed from the central bank and the commercial market to deal with a shortage of funds to make new loans. In addition, Grameen suspended payments for the borrowers. During the flood of 2004, however, the bank and its borrowers used different means to deal with the disruption of economic activities that accompanied the flood. Borrowers used their savings to withstand the flood and the bank used the cushion of large amounts of internal savings to deal with the two stages of the flood—the first in July and the second in September 2004. Many areas were affected by both waves, which were caused by excessive monsoon rains and the resulting flooding of major rivers. The bank had urged borrowers to deposit extra amounts in their personal savings account and to take the necessary steps to protect their in-kind savings in livestock and poultry before the onset of the flood season. During the flood, bank workers went to the borrowers' homes and emergency shelters to hand-deliver their personal savings, in many cases using a boat, as the roads were submerged under waist-high water.

Table 4.5 Savings Deposit and Withdrawal History in the Branches Most Affected by Flooding in 2004

Branch	Zone	July Deposit	July Withdrawal	August Deposit	August Withdrawal	September Deposit	September Withdrawal	October Deposit	October Withdrawal
Hasail Banri Tangabari	Naryanganj	447,000	466,000	739,000	845,000	747,000	698,000	802,000	327,000
Konkosher Lowhajang	–	895,000	1,220,000	1,212,000	897,000	1,261,000	889,000	1,057,000	278,000
Bajgao Lowhajang	–	476,000	776,000	509,000	357,000	659,000	197,000	582,000	189,000
Bhaggakool Srinagar	–	1,591,000	2,226,000	1,525,000	856,000	1,579,000	944,000	1,598,000	576,000
Diyabari Harirampur	Dhaka	813,000	1,401,000	1,082,000	1,046,000	953,000	1,177,000	1,024,000	819,000
Mohadevpur Shibaloi	–	606,000	751,000	3,507,000	3,265,000	901,000	859,000	862,000	57,000
Paschim Jaflong	Sylhet	427,000	719,000	876,000	559,000	392,000	153,000	913,000	638,000
Rongerchar Sunanganj	–	458,000	586,000	824,000	595,000	777,000	565,000	608,000	423,000
Gobindaganj Chatak	Sylhet	722,000	930,000	1,097,000	899,000	928,000	817,000	939,000	737,000
Dhakin Doarabazar	–	740,000	891,000	1,004,000	866,000	951,000	973,000	5,159,000	5,008,000

Table 4.5 Savings Deposit and Withdrawal History in the Branches Most Affected by Flooding in 2004 (Continued)

Branch	Zone	July Deposit	July Withdrawal	August Deposit	August Withdrawal	September Deposit	September Withdrawal	October Deposit	October Withdrawal
Bhadra Nagarpur	Tangail	495,000	660,000	680,000	570,000	556,000	415,000	720,000	545,000
Goyahata Nagarpur	–	503,000	618,000	759,000	659,000	548,000	189,000	537,000	375,000
Garisher Nadia	Faridpur	226,000	1,302,000	870,000	749,000	1,061,000	530,000	913,000	838,000
Jajira	–	368,00	434,000	512,000	336,000	534,000	472,000	600,000	401,000
Char Bhadrashan	–	670,000	768,000	914,000	616,000	867,000	616,000	956,000	785,000
Belagasa Islampur	Jamalpur	273,000	576,000	442,000	292,000	372,000	245,000	323,000	205,000
Gunaritala Madariganj	Jamalpur	496,000	532,000	822,000	542,000	732,000	685,000	671,000	421,000
Mahmudpur Melandah	Jamalpur	236,000	422,000	567,000	361,000	525,000	350,000	579,000	451,000
Jafarganj (North) Dabiddar	Comilla	1,153,000	1,783,000	1,384,000	1,165,000	1,403,000	1,011,000	1,543,000	1,162,000
Nabipur (West) Muradnagar	Comilla	838,000	2,378,000	1,964,000	1,642,000	2,187,000	2,091,000	2,298,000	1,745,000

Table 4.5 Savings Deposit and Withdrawal History in the Branches Most Affected by Flooding in 2004 (Continued)

Branch	Zone	July		August		September		October	
		Deposit	Withdrawal	Deposit	Withdrawal	Deposit	Withdrawal	Deposit	Withdrawal
Boroshalgar (North) Dabiddar	Comilla	287,000	1,192,000	1,106,000	1,046,000	1,002,000	880,000	1,333,000	1,161,000
Bangora (East) Muradnagar	Comilla	258,000	1,098,000	1,031,000	1,062,000	1,117,000	777,000	1,158,000	758,000
Srikail Muradnagar	Comilla	314,000	811,000	678,000	519,000	801,000	797,000	733,000	623,000
Gandail Gazipur	Bogra	103,000	967,000	1,421,000	1,337,000	1,359,000	815,000	1,430,000	1,085,000
Chongasa Sirajganj	Bogra	514,000	1,198,000	1,358,000	857,000	1,177,000	1,047,000	1,330,000	1,131,000
Dhunat	Bogra	619,000	1,392,000	1,122,000	903,000	1,122,000	991,000	1,792,000	1,490,000
Paachgachi Kurigram	Rangpur	404,000	501,000	531,000	532,000	563,000	331,000	477,000	382,000
Thanahot Chilmari	Rangpur	368,000	474,000	468,000	468,000	325,000	206,000	395,000	388,000

Table 4.5 reports the withdrawal and deposit history for personal savings accounts in the branches most affected by flooding. A close examination of the data reveals an interesting pattern: large net withdrawals in July, the first month of the flood, followed by net deposits in the succeeding months. The withdrawal of savings in the first month is understandable, as borrowers needed money to buy food and provisions on an emergency basis. Net deposits in the post-flood season are a bit puzzling, as one would think that the borrowers would need funds more than ever during this period to rebuild their houses and businesses. One explanation for these documented deposits is the preference for security. During the flood, the borrowers had to move out of their homes to a shelter, returning home only after the flood was over. Since their homes had been damaged by the flood, the borrowers preferred depositing cash savings in the bank; this seemed a safer option than keeping them in an insecure house. Some NGOs also reported an increase in savings deposits during the flood of 1998. Again, this behavior was motivated by security concerns. The clients of SafeSave, an urban NGO, behaved the same way during the 1998 and 2004 floods: as the floodwaters rose, they borrowed and saved more than usual to protect themselves in case the situation got even worse.[22]

While the security of bank deposits was one of the reasons for an increase in net deposits after the flood, the bank's flood rehabilitation plan was the main reason for the resumption of net deposits by Grameen borrowers. In accordance with the plan, borrowers were given food on credit and fresh loans to resume normal business after the flood. In the hardest-hit areas, the head office released funds from the central Rehabilitation Fund to issue new loans to rebuild houses damaged by the flood. Further, the bank organized health camps to provide free medical checkups to its members, and in many cases even to nonmembers. The borrowers did, however, have to pay for the cost of the medicine. In other words, the bank took care of the most urgent needs of its borrowers: food, shelter, and health care after the flood. An important question is why borrowers do not use their savings rather than the bank's resources to pay for these needs. A background paper on the poverty alleviation impacts of microfinance commissioned for the World Bank's World Development Report (2000/2001) explored this issue.[23] The report notes that "while the clients placed great importance on cash savings, many clients were reluctant to part with them when faced with a shock or economic stress event. They expressed a preference for borrowing over using saving when faced with an unexpected need for a lump sum of cash." The study, which was based on field reports from Uganda, the Philippines, Bangladesh, and Bolivia, further notes that when faced with a crisis, borrowers prefer to use other options such as borrowing from friends and relatives and local money lenders before depleting their cash savings to deal with the crisis. Lower-than-expected savings withdrawals were also observed at BRAC and BURO-Tangail (two credit-granting NGOs in Bangladesh) during the 1998 flood. After a massive cyclone in 1991, Action Aid, an international NGO, used donor funds to deposit 500 taka in the savings account of each of the 25,000 members enrolled in its microcredit program in the Bhola district, in the southern part of the country. Action Aid allowed members the option to withdraw money from these accounts any time, for any reason. Very few members withdrew in full, however, and a majority retained the funds to protect themselves in case the situation got worse.[24]

Other researchers reported the same trend based on information they gathered from other countries. Fafchamps and Lund (2003) found that in the rural Philippines, when faced with an emergency need for cash, people reduce consumption, mobilize labor, or borrow or take gifts from friends and relatives rather than use the savings they have on hand.[25] Noponen and Kantor (2004) report that members of SEWA, an NGO in India, tend to borrow from the money lenders rather than use savings in response to a shock.[26] The Grameen borrowers' behavior was thus not an anomaly. They used their savings to deal with urgent needs at the onset of the flood, and once the bank's disaster plan had kicked in, they went back to the old mode of financial intermediation—using savings to build up assets over the longer term and credit to smooth consumption and to fund lumpy investment. Their behavior is consistent with the behavioral finance prediction that people use "mental accounts" to differentiate between borrowed money and personal savings and to determine what fractions of these accounts they want to spend (Shefrin and Thaler, 1992).

One might argue that the increase in saving through GPS and other contractual savings schemes comes at the expense of other forms of savings, resulting in a net change of zero in the borrower's aggregate savings. In other words, borrowers are likely to continue to save the same amount as before the introduction of these savings instruments; only the composition of their savings has changed. No formal study has yet been done to test this possibility. However, anecdotal evidence and an unpublished field-level study by Stuart Rutherford suggest that borrowers are holding more than one GPS account, even though they are required only to hold a single GPS account subject to weekly deposits of 50 taka for a loan exceeding 8000 taka. The same study does suggest that there has been a decline in the average balance of personal savings accounts since the introduction of GPS. The net effect on aggregate savings is hard to discern, however, because this study also suggests that in addition to saving with the bank, borrowers keep cash at home and participate in informal group savings arrangements.

Savings mobilization among members and nonmembers is the most important change instituted under Grameen II. The current importance of savings mobilization is highlighted by how a new branch opening is handled under Grameen II. In addition to organizing a public meeting explaining the functioning of Grameen's credit side, staff are also now required to hold a special meeting to explain various savings products to the borrowers and, more important, to the general public. At this meeting with nonmembers, held before the meeting with the target group, deposits are collected to generate start-up funds for the new branch. This mode of initiating a new branch is dramatically different from Grameen I, where funds from the head office were borrowed at the rate of 12% per year to create a revolving fund for running a new branch.

Moreover, under Grameen I, it took a branch five years, on average, to pay back the funds borrowed from the head office and to become profitable. Under Grameen II, new branches are encouraged to be self-reliant from day 1. The branches can no longer borrow funds from the head office to undertake on-lending activities. New branches have to fund their loan operations with the money collected from depositors (members and nonmembers) or loans from the zonal office, which must be repaid within six months. The older branches that do not owe any money to the head office and have more savings than credit are recognized for their achievement in the annual competition among staff and with other branches.

Even though the Ministry of Finance did not permit the bank to allow nonmembers to open GPS accounts, Grameen is in a unique position among microfinance institutions operating in Bangladesh. The formal status and statutory right of the bank allows it to collect savings from nonmembers in other accounts such as fixed deposit, "double in seven years," and monthly income savings schemes. Table 4.6 gives data on the amounts collected from nonmembers upon the opening of selected new branches established after the implementation of Grameen II.

The huge success of saving plans for members and nonmembers alike has interesting policy implications. It suggests not only that poor people save, but that they save in large quantities. In the past, the absence of financial institutions in close proximity forced the poor to save via commodities and informal means. The presence of a formal institution like the Grameen Bank, with high credibility and a reputation for its pro-poor stance, prompted the poor to save with the bank in large sums. Grameen also has an added advantage over formal financial institutions: instead of the borrowers going to the bank to deposit their savings, the bank comes to them to collect their savings, thus eliminating transportation costs and making it easier for the poor to save. The nonmembers, however, have to deposit their savings at the local branches of the bank.

The phenomenal success of GPS suggests that there is a huge need for a commitment mechanism to encourage the poor to save

Table 4.6   Opening-Day Collection of Deposits and Savings in Selected New Branches

Branch	Zone	Date	Number of Deposit Accounts	Amount Deposited
Alanga Kalihati	Tangail	10/26/03	253	5,656,941
Arankhola Madhupur	Tangail	9/29/03	205	1,486,828
Dabottor Atgharia	Bogra	5/26/03	367	6,518,635
Majgao Boraigram	Rajshahi	5/23/03	1042	1,324,479
Hatkalupara Atrai	Rajshahi	5/23/03	280	8,656,458
Niamatpur	Rajshahi	5/23/03	653	3,819,561
Ramchandrapur (North) Muradnagar	Comilla	9/10/03	305	8,000,243
Ghatnal Matlab	Comilla	2/29/04	217	2,647,059
Akubpur Muradnagar	Comilla	5/29/03	258	2,512,160
Mohammadpur Chatkhil	Noakhali	2/14/04	373	4,210,000

for life cycle needs such as retirement. Rutherford (2004) summarizes the experience with GPS clearly:

> By contrast, the GPS caused a big stir. It was immediately welcomed by many members. Others were wary at first but soon came to appreciate the facility. Some members joined expressly to be able to open a GPS, which is available only to members and staff. Others have multiple GPSs, or hold GPSs that are much bigger than required for borrowing. A few hold GPSs as "proxies" for non-member family and neighbours. Many older members prefer a GPS to their loans: the frenzy of loans with their rapid turnover is fine when you're building up your life,

but as you approach old age a GPS is a more restful way to leverage the few taka that you can spare from your cash-flow each week or month.

A borrower's husband interviewed for this study noted, "Our main ambitions are for our children's futures, and this GPS seems a better way to deal with their future schooling and marriage costs. Grameen should have done this years ago."[27]

The success of GPS most likely is due to the specific labeling of funds. Modern behavioral economics suggests that unlabeled money will be spent freely. Currently, in terms of the amount of savings, GPS accounts dominate other contractual savings schemes. Taking a tip from the behavioral economics research, the bank should assign strategic names to other contractual savings schemes—such as Hajj account, education account, and marriage account—to increase deposits in these accounts.

This chapter has dealt with various savings-related products and has explained how these various products were introduced under Grameen II. In Chapter 3 and this chapter, we have explained the key elements of loan and savings products under Grameen II. In the next chapter, we will discuss the circumstances that led to the emergence of Grameen II. In particular, we will provide a detailed narrative as to why and how changes to both the loan and the savings products were instituted to the classical Grameen model.

NOTES

1. M. Cain, S. R. Khanam, and S. Nahar, "Class, Patriarchy, and the Structure of Women's Work in Rural Bangladesh," *Population and Development Review* 5(3), 1979, p. 433.
2. Other NGOs require applicants to save for several weeks before they become eligible for loan.
3. Previously, branch offices of the bank had special booths for collecting savings. Once credit disbursement became the main function of the bank, the booths were dismantled.
4. An initial assessment suggested that the bank would need $100 million to replenish the funds lost by allowing the flood-affected borrowers to use up their group fund deposits (*Financial Times,* October 1, 1998). However, the bank was able to borrow only $20.37 million from the central bank at the commercial rate of 10% and another $40.75 million from commercial banks by issuing three-year bonds at 10% interest. Muhammad Yunus, *Grameen Bank at a Glance* (Dhaka: Grameen Bank, 2004).
5. Muhammad Yunus, interview with Asif Dowla, January 9, 2003.
6. The number of borrowers in February 2000.
7. Demographers refer to this as nuclearization. Research suggests that a joint family usually does not last more than four generations.
8. The authors report that credit given to women reduces the transfers received. Signe-Mary McKernan, M. Pitt, and D. Moskowitz, *Use of the Formal and Informal Financial Sectors: Does Gender Matter? Empirical Evidence from Rural Bangladesh,* Policy Research Working Paper no. 3491 (World Bank, January 2005).
9. S. Begum, "Pension and Social Security in Bangladesh," mimeo (Dhaka: Bangladesh Institute of Development Studies, 2003).
10. Omar Rahman, "Living Arrangements and the Health of Older Persons in Less Developed Countries: Evidence from Rural Bangladesh," paper presented at the technical meeting on "Population Ageing and Living Arrangements of Older Persons: Critical Issues and Policy Responses," Population Division, Department of Economic and Social Affairs, United Nations Secretariat, New York, February 8–10, 2000.
11. Omar Rahman, "The Effect of Spouses on the Mortality of Older People in Rural Bangladesh," *Health Transition Review* 7, 1997, pp. 1–12.
12. The primary reason for lack of savings by Americans appears to be lack of self-control. Most of the savings of Americans are tied up in "forced savings" (e.g., accumulating value in a home by paying mortgage, and participation in pension plans). S. Mullainathan and R.

Thaler, "Behavioral Economics," Mimeo no. 00-27 (Cambridge, MA: MIT, Department of Economics, 2000).

13. Economists are suggesting automatic enrollment in a tax-sheltered saving plan as a means of increasing individual savings for retirement in the United States. William G. Gale, J. M. Iwry, and P. R. Orszag, "The Automatic 401(k): A Simple Way to Strengthen Retirement Savings," *Tax Notes* 106(10), 2005, pp. 1027–1214.

14. Nava Ashraf, Dean Karlan, and Wesley Yin, "Tying Odysseus to the Mast: Evidence from a Community Savings Product in the Philippines," working paper (Princeton, NJ: Princeton University, 2004).

15. Ester Duflo, William Gale, Jeffrey Liebman, and Emmanuel Saez of the Brookings Institution, with the cooperation of H&R Block—the largest tax preparer in the country—conducted a large, randomized field experiment to investigate the savings behavior of low- and middle-income Americans. The experiment was built around the Express Individual Retirement Account (IRA) provided by H&R Block. The Express IRA allows clients to save a part of their anticipated tax refund in the IRA. The experiment entailed randomly matching the clients' IRA contributions. The control group's contribution was unmatched whereas two other groups' contributions were matched at 20% and 50%, respectively. The results show that savings behavior is not consistent with the model of a fully informed and fully rational saver. The study concluded that "the combination of a clear and understandable match for saving, easily accessible savings vehicles, the opportunity to use part of an income tax refund to save, and professional assistance could generate a significant increase in retirement saving participation and contributions, even among middle- and low-income households." See Esther Duflo, William G. Gale, Jeffery Liebman, et al., "Savings Incentives for Low- and Middle-Income Families: Evidence from a Field Experiment with H&R Block," Retirement Security Project, Working Paper 2005-05 (Washington, DC: Brookings Institution,2005), p. 28.

16. This was the reason mentioned by a respondent to a researcher doing field-level work in Bangladesh.

17. Some of the informal pre-commitment devices such as using a "money guard," putting the money in a lockbox, joining a rotating savings and credit association (ROSCA), or just keeping the money with someone outside of the family entail considerable risk. The "money guard" could expropriate the money or underpay. A lockbox such as earthen clay pot can be easily broken or stolen. The ROSCA could fail and may not have enough participants so that it can be repeated and enable them to save the predetermined amount. Wright and Mutesasira, using data from

Uganda, report that 99% of respondents saving in the informal sector report losing some of their savings. They conclude that "the formal sector, for those lucky enough to have access to it, is safer both in terms of likelihood of losing any savings and in terms of the relative loss (amount lost to amount saved). Those with no option but to save in the informal sector are almost bound to lose some money—probably around one quarter of what they save there." Graham Wright and Leonard Mutesasira, "The Relative Risk to Poor People's Savings," *Journal of Small Enterprise Development* 12(3), 2001, p. 3.

18. Similar behavioral arguments have been used to explain why people participate in rotating savings and credit associations (ROSCAS). See Mary Kay Gugerty, "You Can't Save Alone: Testing Theories of Rotating Savings and Credit Associations in Kenya," mimeo (University of Washington, 2003). Most of her respondents report that they join ROSCAs to "get the strength to save." See also Stefan Ambec and Nicholas Triech, *Roscas as Financial Agreements to Cope with Social Pressure*, Working Paper no. 103 (Center for Studies in Economics and Finance, 2003).

19. The average inflation rate was 5.5% for the years 2003–2005. International Monetary Fund, *Bangladesh: Poverty Reduction Strategy Paper*, IMF Country Report No. 05/410 (Washington, DC: IMF, 2005).

20. Mansoora Rashid and Robert M. Townsend, *Targeting Credit and Insurance: Efficiency, Mechanism Design, and Program Evaluation*, Discussion Paper no. 47 (World Bank, Education and Social Policy Department, 1994); Jonathan Morduch, "Between the State and the Market: Can Informal Insurance Patch the Safety Net?" *World Bank Research Observer* 14(2), 1999, pp. 187–207.

21. P. Jain and M. Moore, *What Makes Microcredit Programmes Effective? Fashionable Fallacies and Workable Realities*, Working Paper no. 177 (Sussex, UK: Institute of Development Studies, 2003).

22. Stuart Rutherford, e-mail communication with author, January 7, 2005.

23. Jennifer Sebstad and Monique Cohen, *Microfinance, Risk, and Poverty* (Washington, DC: World Bank, 2001).

24. Rutherford, e-mail communication with author.

25. Marcel Fafchamps and Susan Lund, "Risk-Sharing Networks in Rural Philippines," *Journal of Development Economics* 71, 2003, pp. 261–287.

26. Helzi Noponen and Paula Kantor, "Crisis, Setbacks and Chronic Problems: The Determinants of Economic Stress Events among Poor Households in India," *Journal of International Development* 16, 2004, pp. 529–545.

27. Stuart Rutherford, "Grameen II at the End of 2003: A 'Grounded View' of How Grameen's New Initiative is Progressing in Villages," typescript (Dhaka: MicroSave, 2004).

5

Archeology of Grameen II

In 1998 Bangladesh faced the worst flood in its history. Two-thirds of the country was inundated for eleven weeks starting in mid-July. "It is not just another flood; it is THE FLOOD, which all Bangladeshis will remember for generations to come," declared Muhammad Yunus, the managing director of Grameen Bank in an op-ed piece in the local newspaper *The Daily Star.* The flood affected around 30 million people and caused over 1000 deaths along with extensive damage to infrastructure. Two rice crops were also lost due to the flood, creating a serious food shortage for the affected population. In addition, the disruption in economic activity decreased the rate of growth of the GDP.[1] Grameen Bank, being the largest microfinance institution at the time, did not escape damage. The flood affected 71% of the branches, 58% of the centers, and 52% of the members. With their houses under water or otherwise damaged by the flood, borrowers had to halt all economic activities during the period. The center meetings were suspended, and in some cases branch offices were submerged and the staff had to find alternative shelters. One hundred and fifty-four of the bank's members died as a result of the flood. In addition, many members lost family members while still others suffered damage to or loss of their homes.

Natural disasters such as floods are common in Bangladesh, a reality with which most institutions in the nation must learn how to deal. Grameen Bank is no exception. However, because of the underdeveloped financial market, the bank cannot insure against floods.[2] The bank faced its earliest repayment problem in 1987, when half of the borrowers in Rangpur zone lost assets such as livestock, many found their homes damaged or destroyed, and 170 members lost their lives.[3] In response, the bank created a disaster fund in each center to deal with flood and post-flood costs in the affected areas. The bank created this fund using the food aid it received from international relief organizations. Instead of distributing these items for free, the bank gave the food to the borrowers under the condition that they return the value of the food in cash when their economic conditions improved. The money thus collected was deposited in a savings account to supply the disaster funds for each center in the flood-affected areas. The interest income from the account is used to pay for the various expenses related to disasters.

The Rangpur zone was struck again by flood in 1988 and then again in 1991. The 1988 flood was even worse than the one in 1987, as it damaged standing crops that were a major source of income for borrowers and their customers. The initial response of the bank was to suspend repayments for several weeks for those affected. The situation in the Rangpur zone deteriorated so much that whereas it had once been deemed the best-performing zone for the bank, it now had to be put in an "intensive care unit."[4] The zonal manager was replaced and the new manager was given a free hand to bend or even ignore Grameen rules to rehabilitate the zone. As we will see later, similar action on a larger scale led to the emergence of Grameen II. The experiences of dealing with these floods and other natural disasters, such as a tidal wave in 1991 that affected the Chittagong zone, led to the creation of a disaster management plan for the institution as a whole. The salient features of the plan are to (1) give top priority to ensuring the safety of the borrowers by visiting them in their homes and emergency shelters, and distributing alum, water purification tablets, and oral rehydration solution; (2) authorize local managers to declare their centers disaster center, which entails suspending repayments and allowing borrowers access to their group funds; (3) provide emergency food aid with the stipulation captured in the slogan "We will take during the bad times and repay when the good times roll in."

After the massive flood of 1998, the bank declared 42% of its centers "disaster centers," suspending normal activities such as the collection of installments. The immediate objective of the bank was to ensure the safety of its borrowers and to help them rehabilitate themselves. To that end, the bank provided interest-free cash as well as in-kind assistance from the central disaster fund. More important, the bank allowed the members to use up to 90%, and in some cases up to 100%, of their savings from the group fund. The bank also issued fresh loans to borrowers who were five to ten installments short of repaying their earlier loans. Borrowers who had repaid half or more of their loans became eligible for new loans from the bank to equal to the amount repaid. The latter group also received a one-year extension of their repayment schedule.

Many of the borrowers' houses that had been damaged by the flood were originally built using the housing loan from the bank. These members received a 5000 taka supplementary loan for use in repairing their homes. Members without a housing loan were given 2500 taka to fix their homes. To relieve the economic burden, the bank stopped collecting repayment until January 1999, effectively suspending payments for five months. Despite the good intentions behind these measures, they adversely affected the borrowers and the institution as a whole. First of all, issuing new loans for housing, fresh loans for resuming economic activity, and loans from the group fund to deal with emergency needs during the flood and post-flood period increased the debt burden of the borrowers. It is not clear if all this inflow of funds was sufficient to meet the day-to-day needs of the borrowers, especially given the fact that they could not earn any income for almost three months. Khandker (2004) reports that the wages of the average adult male fell by 10% in agricultural and 13% in non-agricultural sectors due to reduced demand in the labor market. The average household surveyed lost 90% of such assets as crops, livestock, and poultry. Studies also indicated that many borrowers had to borrow from the local money lenders at a high interest rate to meet the shortfall.[5]

Researchers from the International Food Policy Research Institute collected data covering 750 households for three periods: November–December 1998 (three months after the flood), April–May 1999, and

November–December 1999. The data was analyzed to determine the impact of the flood on household assets, consumption, health, and nutrition. The study found that the sample households coped with the flood by reducing expenditures, selling assets, and borrowing. Borrowing from non-institutional sources was the main means used by these household to cope with the flood.[6] The study further revealed that household debt rose to an average of 1.5 months' worth of consumption. The borrowed funds were used mainly to pay for food expenditures. Grameen borrowers most likely used similar coping mechanisms to deal with the flood, such as borrowing from non-institutional sources as well as from the bank.[7] After the flood of 1998, Grameen borrowers were suddenly faced with the burden of paying old and new loans as well as paying off the group fund loans they had taken during the flood. The bleak debt situation was aptly captured by the founder of the bank, Professor Yunus:

> Soon borrowers started to feel the burden of accumulated loans. They found the new installment sizes exceeded their capacity to repay. They gradually started to stay away from weekly center meetings. Grameen Bank repayment started to show quick decline. We tried to improve the situation, but it did not produce desired results. Impact of the post-flood repayment crisis was compounded by its overlap with a recovery problem from an earlier crisis. In 1995, a large number of our borrowers stayed away from center meeting and stopped paying loan installments. . . . At the end we resolved the problem by creating some opening in our rules, but Grameen's repayment rate had gone down in the mean time. Many borrowers continued to abstain from repaying their loans even after the matter was resolved.[8]

The crisis was exacerbated by the program design of classical Grameen, which did not have the inherent flexibility to cope with huge natural disasters such as the flood of 1998. After the flood, the bank gave new loans to members to resume income-earning opportunities, rescheduling old loans at the same time. Many borrowers continued to service new loans without realizing that they were becoming irregular in the repayment of old loans. When the problem was eventually identified, the debt burden of many members had become unserviceable. Under these circumstances, many borrowers stopped coming to the bank and their growing debt burden discouraged them from making payments on their loans.

The flood and the recovery efforts affected the institution itself. The suspension of repayment and the eventual decline in the repayment rate, along with the issuance of new loans and depletion of the group fund, meant that the bank needed fresh funds to continue to operate at the pre-flood level. To meet the funding requirements, the bank had to borrow a total of $20.37 million from the central bank at a 10% interest rate, as well as another $40.75 million from commercial banks by issuing bonds of three-year duration under government guarantee of a 10% interest rate.[9]

Perhaps the biggest impact of the flood on the institution arrived a year later, around the middle of 1999. At that time, the bank was faced with a situation where pockets of operation—Mymensingh, Tangail, Jamalpur, Habiganj, Rangpur—faced problems of large-scale defaults. Although the majority of the borrowers were in good standing, a sizable number were in arrears. Among these areas and zones, some of the branches faced acute problems: the repayment rate dropped, borrowers stopped attending the center meetings, and the staff were demoralized. What was most interesting was that some of the centers where all borrowers were making regular payments were geographically next to centers where few members were attending weekly meetings and many were in arrears. The fact that both types of centers had been equally affected by the flood and yet were performing at such different levels created an inconsistency that convinced the leadership that something more fundamental was at work. Apparently, the flood only brought forth problems that had been simmering for a long time under the surface. The leaders grew convinced that a complete overhaul of the system was necessary.

Prior to the restructuring of Grameen II, the bank had tinkered with its well-honed system but had never felt the need for fundamental restructuring. After the organized defaults in several zones in 1995, however, the bank created a special cell ("problem cell") in the head office to monitor and solve localized problems before they became widespread. Dipal Barua, co-author of this book, was responsible for managing the cell and was its founding manager. The problem cell received regular reports of localized problems, some of which it managed to solve and others of which local staff solved on their own. Staff members were encouraged to publish their experiences in the in-house journal *Uddog* so that others could learn how to deal with and solve similar problems. The bank has always encouraged staff to share their experiences, whether through writing directly to the managing director or through the branch manager's monthly reports. Grameen Bank was born and developed through what Susan Holcombe (1999) calls the "learning process approach." This approach is a trial-and-error process, and it took many years for the bank to evolve into its fixed, core model of operation (Grameen I). Most of the changes and adaptations, however, occurred chiefly "at the margins,"[10] involving peripheral matters without signaling a need to change the core model. As part of the process of continual improvement, some of the ideas for dealing with specific problems were tried out in a branch or a center, and the experience was then disseminated through formal and informal channels. Those who faced similar problems were then able to use the lessons learned by others that had been published in *Uddog*.

Many of these ideas and innovations produced good results. The following are examples of such innovations that worked at various times:

- In the case of the leasing loan, the system of peak and off-peak installment payment was introduced. The borrower could pay a minimum amount during the off-peak season, which was made up for with higher payments during the peak period. Moreover, borrowers could customize their repayment schedules to synchronize them with the business cycle.[11]
- In the case of livestock leasing, the borrower could pay off the principal and interest with one payment at the end of the contract period without a pre-payment penalty.[12]
- *Samahar:* According to this system, all loans that had the same interest rate, such as a general loan and various types of seasonal loans, were consolidated into one amount, and

the borrower had to repay the total outstanding amount in equal installments. The last few installments counted for the accumulated interest on the loan. After making installment payments for a year, borrowers were given fresh loans equal to the amount repaid in a year.

- In the Faridpur zone, the bank tried bimonthly meetings and repayments. The experiment was abandoned when the staff found that the installment payments were becoming burdensome for the borrowers, and two weeks was too long a period for the borrowers to resist succumbing to other demand for these funds.[13] The borrowers, especially the females, objected to the reduction in meeting times because weekly meetings were the only avenue for them to get out of the *bari* (homestead) and congregate and network with nonrelatives.[14]

Since problems such as these arose only occasionally and the innovations were locally generated, however, there was no attempt to expand the innovations. Moreover, the bank never felt the need to question the fundamental, core components of the Grameen system: one-year fixed installment loans, the group fund, group responsibility, and compulsory savings. The concern was that tinkering with the core of the system would shake up the institution itself, with worldwide implications for Grameen replications in other countries. As a result, there was never pressure to disturb the overall system, despite a great deal of interior tinkering.

The well-honed system of classical Grameen had its own inertia and resiliency, and the consensus was that this was why the limited innovations never took hold. For example, when the flexible loan was introduced with the provision that members could borrow the amount repaid within a certain time period, detractors pointed out how a similar system, *Samahar*, was tried earlier and did not seem to work because the borrowers did not pay the last few installments, which counted for interest payments. The leadership responded by suggesting that the context was totally different this time around—that a *Samahar*-like system did not work and could not have worked within the structure of the old system of Grameen. Besides, the installment payments now included principal as well as interest. In the process of implementing these minor and short-lived changes, the organization accumulated ideas and knowledge about fundamental changes that might be necessary.

Through trial and error, the leaders of Grameen began to put together the bits and pieces that now make up Grameen II, but it was the aftermath of the 1998 flood that provided the opportunity to integrate them into a new system. The difference during the post-flood time was that the leadership made deliberate attempts to change the mindset of the staff, convincing them, for example, to reconsider the straitjacket of a one-year fixed installment loan and their often unrelenting focus on the repayment rate only. The complete overhaul of a system that had evolved over decades, however, was expected to be time-consuming.

When adversity hit the bank in 1999, and efforts to solve the problems that the branches were experiencing seemed futile, it seemed an opportune moment to fall back on the accumulated knowledge of the bank and try some of the past innovations with new vigor. The crisis provided the bank with the opportunity to think and experiment outside of the box and beyond, as if the rules did not exist. Professor Yunus recalls,

> Now looking back I feel that it was lucky for us that Grameen was faced with a crisis. This crisis led us to create Grameen II, which has the built-in capacity to handle crises and disasters in a much better way than ever before. Under normal conditions, [Grameen II] is not only a powerful and efficient system, capable of providing custom-made financial services to support the economic and social upliftment of each individual borrower family, but also it frees micro-credit from the usual stresses and strains.[15]

Faced with the crisis, the bank marshaled its resources to solve the problem. Staff members in the head office were invited to submit their names to a pool of "volunteer area managers." This tactic is used by many organizations to deal with extraordinary problems, especially in the information technology (IT) divisions. When local staff cannot solve the problem of, say, a major virus infection in a computer network, outsiders are bought in to crack the problem. In IT industry parlance, these outsiders are call "firefighters." The volunteer area managers stayed in a branch for three to six months and essentially put out the "fire" in an area before it could engulf the whole zone. The zonal office continued to monitor the branch while the volunteer area manager sent information to the area office for better coordination. The task of such managers was to do anything and everything necessary to revive a branch.

The first task of a volunteer manager was to hold intensive meetings with the branch staff to identify the problems. The manager would then meet the family members and husbands of the borrowers, urging and motivating them to repay their loans. Further, the manager would prepare a list of borrowers who had stopped paying off their loans and/or attending center meetings, and would then brainstorm strategies to try to bring them back into the fold of the bank. The manager would also classify borrowers according to the amount due and attempt to encourage those with least amount owed to sign a "pledge to repay" contract with the bank.

During the flood of 1998, management noticed that the repayment problems had a geographical dimension: they were confined to zones in the middle and north of the country. At the height of the problem, the repayment rate in some centers in these zones dropped significantly, meaning that the underperforming centers were affecting the repayment performance of the whole zone. The head office realized that the zonal offices in these areas were unable to give extra help to the nonperforming centers and branches. In April 1999 the head office began identifying the weakest branches in each problem zone and decided to create two four-member special task forces to rehabilitate these branches. The chairman of the task force was a general manager or a deputy general manager, the task manager was from middle management, and the rest of the members were drawn from lower-level staff in the head office.

The mission of the special task forces was to rehabilitate the weakest branch. Toward this end, the responsibility of the branch was transferred to the task force in the head office. The task force was given complete freedom to do whatever was necessary to rehabilitate the branch in question, including splitting or abolishing centers and transferring staff who were underperforming. Task force members could also cancel a group or organize new groups. The members were required to visit the branch at least once a month; if necessary, the task force members could split the centers among themselves and manage the centers individually.

Positive feedback from the special task forces led to the establishment of nine more task forces. The underlying philosophy was to force staff in the head office, who had become detached from actual happenings in the field, to get involved in solving specific crises at hand. In essence, the task force was created as a reality check for the senior staff. Like the initial task forces, the new ones consisted of four staff members from different sections of the head office. To promote interaction, open channels of communication, transparency, and diversity of opinion, the members were from different departments of the head office (e.g., accounts, operations, audit and monitoring).

The chairs of most of the task forces were foot soldiers of the original Grameen. Most of these senior managers achieved higher positions in the organization after accumulating extensive field experience. They were instrumental in implementing and installing the foundation of the bank. The creation of task forces allowed them to reacquaint themselves with their roots and rebuild the bank they had founded.

Each task force, which was given the responsibility of running a branch in the worst-performing zones, was given carte blanche to start from scratch and to do whatever was needed to rebuild the branch. At first, the resiliency and inertia of the system and the presence of "groupthink" were evident in the task forces. Rather than starting over and adopting a holistic approach to improve the overall performance of the branch, the task forces concentrated on improving the repayment rate only. Management believed, however, that an overemphasis on maintaining repayment rate at the expense of other criteria of success had led to the crisis in the first place. Essentially, the staff were trying to sacrifice everything to maintain the repayment rate, which, according to management, was akin to examining the tongue of a patient to diagnose a disease; a trained doctor would develop a case history and examine the eyes, nose, and ears in addition to the tongue to make a worthwhile diagnosis. Leadership urged the staff to explore other measures of success, such as attendance at meetings and submission of deposits.

The task forces met every Monday to discuss the problems of their respective branches. Each meeting had a well-defined agenda, and a report of the meeting was sent to the problem cell for review. The cell then produced an executive summary of all reports, and the summary was circulated to members of all task forces so that they could see what others were doing in the field. In their regular weekly meeting, task force members would discuss the executive summary from previous meetings and consider what actions they could implement. The minutes of the task force were also circulated among staff not involved in the day-to-day operation of the task force so that they could see the various measures being instituted in an attempt to resolve the crisis. The widespread sharing of the minutes is analogous to doctors circulating the X-ray chart and related report of a patient so that everyone can see what is wrong and what is being done to solve the problem.

Management made it clear to the staff that task force meetings should get priority over other duties assigned to the members. In addition to the summaries of the meetings, assessments of the performance of each task force were disseminated. These reports included narratives and graphs showing the number and value of contracts, number of contracts per worker, rate of contractual loans, rate of savings collection, repayment rates, loans in default, and amount of uncollected interest and loans.

These task forces played an extremely important role in the rebuilding of the bank. While not all of their suggestions and innovations were codified into Grameen II, they created an open market for good ideas. Through deliberation, debate, and extended discussion, the winning ideas were incorporated into Grameen II. In effect, two separate management structures were working in one location: the task force and the local-level administration run by the area and the zonal offices. In many cases, the field staff members in charge of other distressed branches were more successful than the task force members in improving the performance of the struggling branches. This success put pressure on the task forces to find creative solutions to the problems faced by their respective branches.

The idea was that a friendly but fierce competition would lead to a successful outcome. The publishing and widespread sharing of successes and lessons of the task forces made this competition possible.

The task forces tried various strategies to revive their branches. Task force members collected as much information about their branch as possible. For example, they gleaned information about the branch from the monitoring cell, studied the branch's history of loan disbursement and repayment problems, gathered and studied branch mangers' monthly reports to the head office, collected reports of the branch's audit team, and determined if meetings were held according to schedule. The task forces then held extensive interviews with the previous branch managers to learn more about the history and source of the branch's problem. The task force members supplemented this information with field visits to the areas being studied, which involved talking to the staff, attending meetings, and gathering with borrowers and their family members. They also examined the service record of branch mangers to find out how long they had been with the branch, where they had previously worked, and their home districts. All of these details were then analyzed to identify factors at work that might have allowed a manager to shirk his or her duties and responsibilities. For example, one of the task forces learned that the previous manager had retired before being replaced by the current manager, and that the current manager had asked to be transferred as soon as he was assigned to the branch in question. Clearly, the previous manager had slacked off as he was preparing to retire, and the new manager never took ownership of the branch because he was planning to be transferred; these factors created a leadership vacuum with consequences for the branch itself.

An important assignment for the task force was to identify the causes of the specific problem in a branch. Anecdotal evidence suggests that the problems were caused by structural faults with the system that extended far beyond the flood and the concomitant difficulties. These problems had arisen in the absence of any natural calamity or organized protest, and their causes included such as too much loan disbursement and mismanagement by mangers and staff. The borrowers' lack of interaction with the bank was also revealed as a major cause of problems at the branches. The bank used to take pride in the fact that at least once a week staff were able to come face to face with their clients. When members stopped coming to the regular weekly meetings and staff began going to members' homes to collect installments, the public exhibition of loyalty to the bank and the transparency of interaction with the staff were lost. The task forces identified lack of attendance at weekly meetings as a major reason for the crisis. In the process of rebuilding the bank, many suggested that members should be informed that their attendance was being recorded. Hence, the bank renewed its attention to the attendance registry and used it to determine the size of future loans.[16] Staff were also asked to visit members in the evening before the meeting to remind them of the next day's meeting and were told not to visit the same center twice a day. The latter would encourage the members not to show up for the meeting on time. Some task forces also found that one person would use the group members as a proxy to get larger loans, and the group's default could be traced to this person.

Another flaw identified by the task forces was the inappropriate use of loan money. When loans are disbursed in large quantities, it is difficult to monitor their use. In theory, the group was supposed to monitor the use of loans, but this rarely happened due to collusive behavior on the part of borrowers. When demoralized staff had to rush from meeting to meeting, they were not motivated to monitor loan use as closely as they should have. To correct this problem, one of the task forces suggested issuing attestation certificates to authenticate the loan use. It was proposed that at least twelve certificates be used for a twelve-month loan.

After an exhaustive study of the causes of the crisis of 1999, the various task forces started working on steps to rebuild their respective branches. As mentioned earlier, the task forces had virtual freedom in their choice of remedies. At the same time, through consultation, debate, and discussions, the task forces were able to learn from each other. In some instances, a task force replicated a method that worked elsewhere, and in many cases tried to improve upon it. There were, however, some task forces that refused to adapt a method that was successful in other branches on the grounds that it would not work in their area of operation.

Regardless of how they chose to solve their respective problems, a major initiative for all of the task forces was to help borrowers find sources of income that could be used to pay off loans under contract. The task forces suggested that borrowers raise ducks, lease goats, and grow vegetables to generate such income. Some task forces suggested distributing chicks and egg-producing hens to the borrowers, while others suggested the distribution of tree saplings. Many of the borrower defaults were prompted by pressure from family members, especially husbands, who would convince their spouses not to pay based on the erroneous belief that non-repayment would benefit them. To rectify this situation, the task forces suggested involvement of the male members of the borrower's family in the approval and use of the loan. To that end, the task forces organized meetings with the male members of the family. The strategy was that by informing the husband and other male members about the rules and regulations of the bank, the use of the loan could be made a family enterprise. Task forces found that many of the center chiefs were in default themselves; as a result, they lacked the moral authority to ask others to repay. The task force suggested replacing these defaulter chiefs by members with perfect repayment rates.

Another important initiative suggested by the task force was to adopt a triage in classifying the loans, with loans of smaller size recouped first. Task forces prepared a list of members whose outstanding balance was between 500 and 1000 taka. Individual action plans were prepared for teaching these members how to turn themselves into regular loanees by repaying the amount due, which would be easier given the relatively small size of the loan. Similarly, those members who had repaid the principal but had become irregular by failing to pay the interest were also identified. The task force contacted these borrowers and urged them to sign contracts to repay the interest due. Since each borrower of this type had multiple loans, the task force suggested that the staff identify the smallest of the loans—livestock leasing, sanitary loan, rehab loans—and try to reduce the balance of such loans to zero.

In addition to the triage, task forces experimented with various borrower classifications so that they could come up with strategies to motivate them to rejoin the bank. One task force classified members and determined their loan ceiling based on following categories:

- A class: Never defaulted—loan ceiling 20,000 taka
- B class: Irregular but repaid within the 52-week time limit—loan ceiling 15,000 taka
- C class: Exceeded the 52-week limit
  - Repaid within 60 weeks—loan ceiling 13,000 taka
  - Repaid within 70 weeks—loan ceiling 12,000 taka
  - Repaid within 80 weeks—loan ceiling 11,000 taka
  - Repaid within 80 weeks and above—loan ceiling 10,000 taka

As mentioned earlier, the crisis had a geographical dimension. Three areas—Sherpur, in the Mymensingh zone, and Melandah and Jamalpur, in the Tangail zone—demonstrated severe repayment problems related to their geographic isolation. The Sherpur area office was 70 km from the zonal office in Mymensingh, and the most remote branch office was 135 km from the zonal office. Similarly, Melandha and Jamalpur were 120 km and 100 km, respectively, from the zonal office in Tangail; the farthest branches from the zonal offices were at distances of 157 km and 145 km, respectively. These three areas, which were surrounded by the Jamuna and Bramapurta rivers, were annually subjected to severe river bank erosion. The decline of jute trading, a major economic activity for the area, further weakened the economic base of these areas. To direct special attention to these perennial problem areas, the head office created a special zone called Jamalpur out of these areas and put it under the receivership of the problem cell managed by Dipal Barua, the co-author of this book. A project manager was then put in charge of handling the day-to-day operation of the zone, under the guidance of the head of the problem cell. Many of the newer, more innovative ideas for the construction of Grameen II were tried out in this special zone first. This played an important role in the development of the main elements of Grameen II.

Under classical Grameen, a borrower could access, in addition to a general loan, loans designed for housing, leasing, seasonal uses, and cattle rearing. As mentioned earlier, the decline in economic activity and the presence of multiple loans increased the debt burden of the borrowers. In many cases, borrowers did not realize that although they were making regular payments on their general loan, they were in arrears in other loans. In some cases, the members were paying installments for only one loan out of many that were overdue; accumulating interest on unpaid balances was leading them into an even larger debt burden. Many borrowers were mired in despair, fearing they would not be able to repay the bank because of the sheer size of their unpaid debts. To ease the burden of the borrowers and to improve the bank's overall repayment rate, the project manager of the special zone proposed consolidating all loans into one. The project manager also realized that loan consolidation would help motivate the borrowers to return to the fold and resume repayment.

The special zone management further proposed closing centers in two branches of each area that had the lowest repayment rates and transferring the staff to branches with shortages of employees. Members who were paying regularly from these centers were asked to pay their installments at an adjacent center. Instead of closing centers that were in different parts of the area of operation, it was suggested that staff close nearby centers, if necessary, and create new ones with members in good standing. The idea was that the success of the new center would motivate former members in arrears to rejoin the bank.

As a result of the restructuring and rebuilding of the weakest areas, the bank had a surplus of workers. To ensure that these excess workers were being used to their full potential, the bank created a special employee pool to be sent where there were worker shortages. This pool was used exclusively to aid in the recovery of old loans. Each recovery worker was given the responsibility to collect principal and interest from at least fifty members who had stopped payments.

Many branches under the special zone faced the problem of what to do with the money accumulated in group funds by borrowers who were in arrears. In the special zone, many centers were inoperative because of the economic impact of river bank erosion. As a result, the bank ended up in an awkward position in which many borrowers were unable to pay back their loans despite having sizable holdings in their group fund. The bank had allowed the staff to use the savings accumulated in the group fund to pay off the loans; the special zone, however, faced the problem of being unable to contact its members because many had left the area. As a result, staff members in this zone were unable to adjust the loan amount against the group fund. A few branches were relatively new and could not adjust the group fund because the members had not yet reached the threshold of ten years of membership. To correct this problem, the staff of the special zone proposed adjusting the group fund against the loan amount of members who had lost contact with the bank by sending three registered letters every two weeks to a member's home address. These letters stated that if the borrower did not repay the bank, the bank reserved the right to adjust his or her outstanding amount against the group fund. After the last letter, the bank would wait another two months and then adjust the loan, with the remaining members serving as witnesses. After the adjustment, the bank would send another letter to the member stating the amount due after the adjustment.

The special zone also proposed allowing members of more than five years to have access to their savings in the group fund. If the members did not need group funds to pay for their loans, the staff had to ensure that the money was transferred to an individual savings account. The staff members were asked to make sure that the lump-sum fund was not spent quickly, and to encourage the members to put the money in a time deposit so that they could use it for investment in income-earning projects.

Clearly, the major task of the staff was to instill repayment discipline and improve attendance among the borrowers. To that end, the task forces and the special zone staff proposed rewards for good borrowers. Borrowers who repaid loan installments, deposited savings on time, and attended meetings regularly received large leasing loans that would have an immediate impact on their income-earning capability. These loans showed irregular borrowers that responsible behavior would be rewarded. Instead of leasing loans, some task forces initially gave cellular phones to good borrowers under the arrangement that the income from the sale of phone services would be shared by the borrower and the branch. The borrowers valued the phones greatly due to their high income-earning potential; monthly gross income from a set could be as high as 100,000 taka ($1492) and the sales commission on these phones provided additional income for the branch. Regular commissions for successive periods served as another signal of good behavior by the borrower. Once the borrower established a credit history by paying commissions regularly, the phone was leased out to the borrower.

The rules for loan disbursement under Grameen I were rather rigid. There was a ceiling on the size of the loan for each branch, and bank workers could not reward good members with loans that exceeded the ceiling. The zone proposed giving loans against savings to encourage borrowers to rejoin the bank. This constituted another way to reward borrowers with perfect repayment records and sizable deposits in their savings accounts. The proposal suggested giving 150% of the deposited amount as a loan. However, the borrowers would not be allowed to withdraw the savings until the loan was completely repaid within a year. Moreover, borrowers who repaid loans on time for at least seven years were declared "golden members."

The task forces also suggested introducing the Grameen pension scheme (GPS) as an incentive for borrowers to come back to the bank and reschedule their loans, giving them the opportunity to save with high and safe returns. When one task force introduced GPS in its branch, 110 members opened GPS accounts on the first day with a total amount of 22,900 taka. The same task force also suggested taking deposits from nonmembers. Encouraged by the success of loan consolidation in the Jamalpur special zone, other task forces adopted the practice, using the draft contract form produced by Jamalpur special zone staff (see Appendix 5A).

The overarching issue for the task forces was how to bring borrowers in default back to the bank. Since its inception, Grameen's primary objective has been to "motivate, motivate, and motivate" borrowers to pay off their loans on time and not to default. In the face of large-scale default, it was clear that verbal motivation alone would not work. The task forces realized that borrowers needed something tangible to become sufficiently motivated to start repaying their loans. The Jamalpur special zone staff proposed that once borrowers repaid the agreed-upon installment for twenty-six weeks, they should be rewarded with a new loan equal to 60% of the principal repaid. Later they proposed offering a loan equal to the amount repaid by the first six months or twenty-six weeks. The borrowers were also allowed to choose an installment amount that fit their needs and repayment capacities. However, some suggested that borrowers might not find it lucrative enough to repay in this way, since they would be getting the same amount back at the end of six months and would most likely consider repaying the bank unnecessary. To create an incentive to repay, one task force suggested that borrowers be allowed to borrow twice the amount repaid in the first six months of the loan. Opponents, however, pointed out that once the borrower received twice the amount of payment, he or she might flee with the money, making the problem of default even worse.

Advocates of the policy countered that once borrowers dutifully repaid for the first six months to get twice the amount, they had already revealed their willingness to repay. This incentive, they believed, was much better at eliciting a willingness to repay than if the borrower were only allowed to borrow what she repaid in the first six months. Further, they pointed out that not all of the amount would be doubled, and that the doubling would not happen simultaneously, because not all borrowers would be able to abide by the conditions, such as not missing any installment payments in the first twenty-six weeks. Experience in the field suggested that the advocates of the policy were correct. Instead of running away with the money after receiving the large loan at the end of six months, borrowers apparently wanted to maintain this line of credit. While critics believed that up to 5% of borrowers could be expected to default on their rescheduled loans, advocates felt that it would not be prudent to punish 95% of borrowers for the sins of only 5%.

Debate continued over this policy. Most task forces liked the idea of allowing a member to borrow the amount repaid at six-month intervals, but no one wanted to double the amount. As a result, some task forces started experimenting with repaying borrowers the amount they had repaid after six months. Some of the borrowers who were on the fence began to repay their old loans, and the ability to borrow the amount repaid in six months satisfied their ongoing credit demands. One task force brave enough to reward borrowers with 1.5 times the amount repaid found that they responded quite enthusiastically. Still, most task forces were leery of doubling the entire amount repaid for fear that borrowers would flee.

Finally, one task force took the bold step of doubling the borrower's repaid amount. They found the result satisfactory, as the borrowers utilized the money successfully. Encouraged by this positive result, many other zones replicated the new system.

Despite this success, loaning double the amount after six months often led to a logistical problem: violation of the branch's loan ceiling. To combat this problem, one task force grudgingly accepted the practice of doubling the repaid amount, but put a ceiling on the total amount of 10,000 taka. Other problems that task forces encountered, such as breach of the terms of the contract, were solved by intensive monitoring of loan use. Task forces created schedules that tracked how many borrowers broke the contract, how many took credit for the second time, the amount each repaid, and the new amount disbursed. Field visits also revealed that the borrowers were not always crystal clear about the details of the contract. Task force members solved this problem by instructing branches to make sure that their clients thoroughly understood what they were getting into by explaining all aspects of the contract during home visits.

To ensure effective participation and execution of necessary changes, task forces also paid special attention to improving staff morale and performance. The operation of the task forces created, in effect, a parallel administrative structure that discouraged branches from believing they could bypass the bank's hierarchy, since it forced the branches to report problems to both the area office and the task force in the head office. To ensure that branch staff did not feel left out of the process, the branch manager and his or her second-in-command were assigned responsibility for "bad" centers. Task force members were also assigned responsibility for bad centers in addition to the right to approve loan proposals. The objective was to solve these centers' problems through cooperation and healthy competition between these parallel organizations. One task force suggested that the staff prepare an area office—approved work plan for each worker in the branch. The work plan assigned a target number of irregular borrowers that the worker had to persuade to sign a contract.

In an attempt to improve overall staff performance, one task force set about creating a detailed schedule for time use by the staff. The schedule included time allotted for informal meetings with members prior to the center meeting, time spent in center meetings (with the understanding that the worker had to run the meeting on time), and time spent meeting members in arrears after the meeting. In monitoring the time workers were spending, one task force proposed declaring one staff member "man of the month" in hopes of inspiring all workers to perform at their best. Even trainees were sent to the branches under the task force for a sort of "baptism by fire."

Through this process of trial and error and small-scale pilot testing, the main elements of Grameen II began to take shape. We have mentioned several changes that were suggested and tried out by the task forces. However, not all changes were adopted in Grameen II. Through deliberation, debate, and an open process of dissemination and critical evaluation of results, only the winning ideas survived to be incorporated into the new system. Once the replication and use of Grameen II became widespread within the organization, many of the experiences, rules, and scenarios of the re-creation process had to be formalized and written down. These writings resulted in the published *Nitimala* (rules), which Dipal Barua, then general manager and now deputy managing director, was instrumental in authoring. We will discuss these rules in depth in Chapter 6.

While the task forces spent the majority of their time evaluating the worth and efficacy of Grameen and its many components, they themselves were subject to a certain amount of scrutiny. Different types of information were collected to evaluate the performance of the task forces based on Grameen's goal at the time. Initially, evaluation was based on increasing the importance of attendance, savings collections, and other criteria. Around mid-2000, however, everything hinged on signing contracts with borrowers who owed the bank money, with a pledge to repay in a negotiated schedule. As task forces began to monitor the rate of contract signing more intensely, this came to be used as the main performance indicator rather than the repayment rate. After December 31, 2000, task forces were required to report plans for contracts, the feasible number of contracts, the preliminary rate of contracts, and the expected date at which the proportion of people approved with new contracts would reach 25%, 50%, 75%, and eventually 100%.

Starting in February 2001, information about the performance of the task forces began to be collected and appended to the executive summary of the weekly meeting. The tables indicating the number of signed contracts were sorted in descending order so that every task force could clearly see how it was performing relative to others. There were also special meetings of task forces with the managing director in which members and the managing director discussed the problems faced by the various task forces and how they solved them. The managing director and the deputy managing director also made regular field trips. In these meetings, the managing director shared with the task forces lessons learned from personal visits with borrowers and queried the various task forces about the steps taken by them. The members of the task forces had to defend their actions in the field. The meetings were characterized by open discussion and debate. Prior to each meeting, the managing director would receive the monitoring report produced by the problem cell to assist in questioning the various task forces about their successes as well as their failures.

The task forces provided a system of cooperative checks and balances that functioned much like the World Health Organization (WHO) during its quest to identify the cause of SARS. WHO assigned eleven research centers around the world to find the cause of the deadly flu; these centers collected samples, analyzed them, and posted the results on a website. Author and *New Yorker* columnist James Surowiecki describes the interactive process:

> Every day the labs took part in daily teleconferences, where they shared their work, discussed avenues for future investigation, and

debated current results. On a WHO web site, the labs posted electron-microscope photographs of viruses isolated from SARS victims (any one which might have been the cause of the disease), virus analyses and test results. The labs regularly traded virus samples, allowing them to both check on and learn from each other's work.[17]

As we have seen, the various task forces of Grameen Bank worked in a similar manner. They shared the information, learned from each other, and challenged each other's findings. Just as no one laboratory is credited with discovering the source of the SARS virus, no one person came up with the idea of Grameen II. Rather, Grameen II grew out of the collective efforts of staff, senior management, and borrowers.

Grameen II resulted from a number of fundamental changes in the elements of Grameen, including the flexible loan, the basic loan, and the six-month quality control check mentioned in this and in the previous chapter. Given this background on how the bank resolved the crisis with the effective participation of the staff and the management, it will be useful to tie this information to the core elements of Grameen II.

The flexible loan has a limit in that whatever amount a borrower repays, he or she can borrow twice the amount back at the six-month interval, and then every six months thereafter an amount equivalent to the amount repaid. This loan is analogous to a line of credit, in that there is a credit limit and the borrower has to pay off half the loan in six months in order to stay current. However, the staff had difficulty tracing borrowers, and even if they could find them, borrowers had no incentive to repay the loan. Borrowers felt that because they had defaulted, the bank would not give them another loan even if they were to repay the old loan. To dispel this sense of resignation and reach out to these borrowers, the staff established contact with many of the defaulters and urged them to restart their installment payments. The staff found, however, that while the borrowers would promise to come back and repay, they would not keep this promise. The bank then realized that personal contact with the borrowers was a necessary icebreaker; what they needed was something formal, like a written contract or, in Bengali, a *chukti.*

Thus, the idea of a *cukti rin*, a contractual loan, now called a flexible loan, was transformed from a principle to a reality.

In the latest incarnation of *chukti rin*, the bank used it to target the large number of borrowers who were in default rather than using it to solve small-scale localized problems. A zonal manager in Bogra used the slogan *chukti te mukti*, meaning "salvation in signing contracts," to entice defaulters to repay. The bank encouraged staff to sit down with borrowers, figure out how much they owed the bank, and then have them sign contracts outlining the repayment schedule. The contract, or *chukti*, specifies how much the borrower is to repay every week in installments, as well as the duration of the loan. More important, the contract involves a written promise of regular attendance at center meetings (see Appendix 5A). The bank decided to use the *chukti* again in Grameen II, in an attempt to get borrowers to repay bad debts (*ku-rin* in Bengali)—loans that have been written off. To differentiate this version of the flexible loan from the earlier concept that referred to a contractual agreement to repay loans in arrears, it was labeled "flexible loan 2" (*chukti rin* 2), with the first version labeled "flexible loan 1" (*chukti rin* 1).

Another outcome of the development of the flexible loan was the dismantling of the group fund, which was an important ingredient of Grameen I. It had become clear to the task forces that even irregular borrowers who had large sums of money in group funds were earning 8.5% interest on their deposits, whereas they were paying 20% on their outstanding loans. Now, to correct this imbalance, when the individual savings in a group fund are subtracted from loans outstanding, this adjustment drastically reduces the contractual amount and the weekly installment payments. This allows borrowers to switch from irregular to regular status in a short span of time. As we will see later, convincing the borrowers, and particularly the husbands of the female borrowers, to use the group fund to pay off outstanding loans was a difficult task.

The idea for six-month quality control check also arose through the implementation of the flexible loan. Six months was deemed long enough for the borrower to accumulate some money, and yet short enough for the institution to verify that he or she has used the money productively. A borrower who had to wait too long might become too disenchanted to pay back the loan. In the same respect, three months is too short a time for the institution to evaluate the potential of the borrower. Moreover, the accumulated repayment will not be significant enough to be enticing. The idea is that the cutoff period for doubling the amount should be such that borrowers are entitled to a large amount if they make repayments on their defaulted loans.

The bank also uses the six-month cutoff to evaluate the quality of the loan in a timely manner, rather than delaying evaluation and thus facing a problem at the end of the year. A borrower who fails to pass the six-month test of regular weekly payments and attendance in meetings is required to switch to a flexible loan. The six-month quality control check is beneficial for the bank in that it acts as an early warning system, preventing it from being surprised by borrower default at the end of the year. It also improves loan monitoring because the bank is able to identify a problem loan early rather than at the end of the loan period. The early check allows the bank to take corrective measures at the first sign of trouble, thus improving the transparency and efficiency of transactions.

The six-month quality control check benefits the borrower as well. If she is current on her repayment, she can borrow again to expand her business if she so desires. Alternatively, if her business is not running smoothly or she is facing other factors beyond her control that prevent her from making regular payments, she can switch to a contractual loan to avoid default.

The idea of the basic loan came considerably later. The paramount issue was how to bring defaulters, or irregular borrowers, into the fold of regular borrowers. The flexible loan was the avenue used to turn these irregular borrowers into regular borrowers. At the peak of trouble, which was localized in nature, 80% of the borrowers were perfect in their repayments, an accomplishment that the leadership decided to reward by offering the positive aspects of the flexible loan. For instance, the six-month quality control check was introduced for the regular borrowers: they could borrow the amount repaid at the end of six months. In the process of writing rules for Grameen II, questions were raised as to why the maturity of the loan had to be one year only. After much discussion, a wider range—three months to three years—

for the maturity of the loan was introduced. Later, a span of more than three years was also included in the rule book. Another innovation borrowed from the flexible loan is the lumping of all regular loans into one account appropriately named the "basic loan" (*sohoj rin*). From that point forward, the bank vocabulary was couched in terms of two loans: the basic loan and the flexible loan of Grameen II. Later the bank suggested that, theoretically, there was only one loan: the basic loan. Whenever the borrower defaults on this loan, she has a way out—a switch to a contractual loan with stringent conditions and penalties. The root structure, however, remains the basic loan.

Despite the reassurance that there is theoretically only one loan, staff paid more attention to the flexible loan. The challenge then became converting all outstanding loans to basic loans so that a branch's portfolio would consist of flexible and basic loans.[18] Achieving this feat was one of the important milestones of entering *ditio onko,* or Phase II.

In this chapter we have shown how the main elements of Grameen II grew out of a trial-and-error process supplemented by feedback from the field. Once the main elements of Grameen II started to take shape, the next step was to formalize them by writing rules and regulations, and to train the staff to implement them in the field and to persuade borrowers to go along with these radical changes.

APPENDIX 5A
Contract Form and Repayment Schedule for a Flexible Loan

Grameen Bank

_____ Branch   _____ Area
_____ Zone/Project   Date: _____

Agreement for *Chukti Rin*

1. I _____ Husband/Father's Name _____
   Loanee No. _____ Group No. _____ Center
   No. _____ declare, being appraised of all terms and conditions of
   Grameen Bank's "chukti rin," that I agree to repay the full contractual amount derived at
   by adding all outstanding loans and interest payments.
2. I agree to repay the principal and interest amount of any new loan accepted during the
   contractual period.
3. I will repay the principal and the interest of "chukti rin" according to conditions specified.
   If I fail to meet the conditions, then either by paying extra installments or paying one time
   I will repay the outstanding principal and interest within the agreed-upon period.
4. If I fail to repay the "chukti rin" as well as all other loans in principal and in interest
   according to the conditions, the branch manager can transfer money from my private savings or other savings accounts to pay for the unpaid principal and interest.
5. I will pay 5% of the loan amount as a group tax when I get a loan during the "chukti rin."
   I promise that if I fail to meet the condition of chukti rin, I will not withdraw any money
   from the group fund or other savings accounts.
6. To come under the domain of Grameen Bank's chukti rin program, I allow the branch manager to use proceeds from the group fund due to me to pay off unpaid principal and interest.
7. I give the branch manager the right to suspend withdrawal from my savings account if I
   fail to pay the installments.
8. The ownership of all businesses and assets funded by the loan belongs to the bank until
   the loan is repaid in full.
9. I am completely informed about the terms and conditions of the loan. I sign the contract
   today on _____ by agreeing to any future changes, extensions, and
   amendments to these conditions by the bank management.

Witness:

Witness Number 1–(Husband/Father. In the absence of a husband of a father, another member of the family approved by the branch manager)

Signature: _____

Name: _____

Relationship with the member:

_____

Signature: _____

Member's Name: _____

Loanee Number: _____

Group Number: _____.

Center Number: _____

Witness Number 2–(Center chief or group
chair or a member of the Center)

Signature: _____

Name: _____

Loanee Number: _____

Group Number: _____

Signature of the worker (with date):   Signature of the branch manager:

_____

Name (with date):   Name:

_____

Identity Number: _____Identity Number: _____

Rank: _____ Rank: _____

Grameen Bank

_____ Branch

Agreement for Chukti Rin

(Schedule of repayment)

| Date of contract: _____ |
| Contract number: _____ |

1. The amount of my loan is _____ taka.
2. I will completely repay my loan according to the following schedule in _____ weeks.

Month	Information about weekly installment	Comments	Month	Information about weekly installment	Comments
1			7		
2			8		
3			9		
4			10		
5			11		
6			12		
Sum of first six months			Sum of second six months		

Third 26 weeks	Fourth 26 weeks	Fifth 26 weeks	Sixth 26 weeks

Note: You must declare how much you will repay from the third 26 weeks onward.

3. I am completely aware that when I can borrow twice the amount of repayment after 26 weeks, the total outstanding amount cannot exceed the ceiling of _____ taka. In other words, when I reach this ceiling I cannot borrow more than I have repaid.
4. I am further aware that after repaying in total in principal and in interest _____ taka the rule to double the amount paid in 26 weeks will no longer be applicable. From then on I will only be able to borrow the amount repaid and I will receive loans according to the rules of the basic loan.

Signature: _____

Member's name: _____

Loanee number: _____

Group number: _____

Center number: _____

Signature of the worker (with date):   Signature of the branch manager:

_____   _____

Name (with date): _____   Name: _____

Identity Number: _____   Identity Number: _____

Rank: _____   Rank: _____

Note: (a) Amount of weekly installment must be mentioned in the column for months.

(b) This form must be filled every time the member takes a loan.

(c) This agreement must be stored in the branch office under center heading.

APPENDIX 5B: EVOLUTION OF GRAMEEN LOAN PRODUCTS

Name	Date of Commencement	Status[1]
1. General loan	August 1976	*
2. Collective enterprise loan	November 1982	*
3. Housing loan	May 1984	Continues
4. Basic housing loan	September 1987	Continues
5. Capital recovery loan	September 1990	*
6. Family loan	July 1992	*
7. Seasonal loan	July 1992	*
8. Food stock loan	March 1992	*
9. Installation of tube-well loan	November 1992	*
10. Building sanitary latrine	February 1993	*
11. Leasing	October 1993	Continues
12. Supplementary loan	October 1994	*
13. Cattle rearing	December 1994	Continues
14. Loan for homestead purchase	March 1996	Continues
15. Pre-basic housing	October 1996	Continues
16. Special general loan (scaling up)	June 1997	*
17. Seasonal loan 2	September 1997	*
18. Seasonal loan 3	September 1997	*
19. Intermediate loan	October 1997	*
20. Higher education loan for Member's children	October 1997	Continues
21. New flexible loan/flexible loan		
New flexible loan	December 29, 1999 for Jamalpur Special project	
New flexible loan	April 24, 2000, for three projects[2]	
New flexible loan	May 21, 2000, for three projects	
Flexible loan	May 22, 2000, for all zones	

Flexible loan	May 31, 2000, for all zones
Flexible loan (September 2000 edition)	September 14, 2000, for all zones and projects
Flexible loan (February 2001 edition)	February 13, 2001, for all zones and projects

22. Basic loan

Basic loan for golden members	May 24, 2000, for all zones and projects
Basic loan for regular members	May 24, 2000, for all zones and projects
Basic loan for regular members	May 31, 2000, for all zones and projects
Basic loan for golden members	May 31, 2000, for all zones and projects
Basic loan for regular members (September 2000 edition)	September 14, 2000, for all zones and projects
Basic loan for regular members (February 2001 edition)	February 13, 2001, for all zones and projects

1. Asterisk (*) denotes loans that were discontinued with the introduction of Grameen II.
2. In addition to Jamalpur, two more special zones, Nilphamari and Hobiganj, were created, encompassing poorly performing areas.

NOTES

1. Shekhar Shah, "Coping with Natural Disasters: The 1998 Floods in Bangladesh," paper prepared for the 1999 World Bank Summer Research Workshop on Poverty and Development, July 6–8, 1999, Washington DC.
2. Grameen Bank could have bought rainfall-based insurance, where the bank would be paid for damages when the rainfall exceeded a certain amount in a given period. However, it is not clear if the domestic insurance market could have paid off such insurance; the flood would have affected many other organizations insured by the insurance company, which would not have enough funds to payoff all the organizations (covariance risk). An advanced insurance market would have allowed the local insurance company to buy re-insurance in the overseas market to protect against such an occurrence.
3. David Bornstein, *The Price of a Dream* (New York: Simon & Schuster, 1996), pp. 263–264.
4. Bornstein, *Price of a Dream*, p. 264.
5. The money lenders typically charge 10% to 12% per month.
6. Carlos del Ninno, Paul Dorosh, and L. C. Smith, "Public Policy, Markets, and Household Coping Strategies in Bangladesh: Avoiding a Food Security Crisis Following the 1998 Floods," *World Development* 31(7), 2003, pp. 1221–1238.
7. Khandker was able to compare the same household before and after the flood. His sample includes Grameen borrowers. He reports that the sample household sold land, labor, and crops in advance; skipped meals; and migrated out of the village to cope with the effects of flooding. Shahidur Khandker, "Flood and Coping Ability in Bangladesh," typescript, Table 10 (World Bank, 2004).
8. Muhammad Yunus, *Grameen Bank II: Designed to Open New Possibilities* (Dhaka: Grameen Bank, 2002).
9. This was less than the $100 million Grameen requested. David Chazan, "Microcredit Dream Washed Away," *Financial Times* (London edition), October 1, 1998, p. 4. The amount borrowed from the central bank as well as the bonds were completely repaid on schedule by May 2002.
10. Susan Holcombe, *Managing to Empower: The Grameen Bank's Experience of Poverty Alleviation* (London: Zed Books, 1995).
11. The idea for the leasing loan came from the borrowers. See Asif Dowla, "Micro Leasing: The Grameen Bank Experience," *Journal of Microfinance* 6(2), 2004, pp. 137–160.

12. These loans were given for the proceeds to be used to buy a cow and fatten it for sale during the *Qurbani* festival. The duration of the loan was usually six months. The borrower could use the six months to fatten the cow, and then sell it and pay back the loan with one payment. The animals were insured with 50% co-insurance.

13. Morduch and Rutherford report the similar experience of BRAC when it introduced fortnightly repayment. BRAC switched to weekly repayment after arrears shot up. Jonathan Morduch and Stuart Rutherford, *Microfinance: Analytical Issues for India* (World Bank, Finance and Private Sector Development–South Asia Region, 2003).

14. Larance reports that the women are addressed, for the first time in their lives, by name in these center meetings. These meetings allow them to develop a shared identity with members of different clans, castes, and social status; develop friendship; share information; built networks; and exchange scare resources. Lisa Larance, "Fostering Social Capital through NGO Design: Grameen Bank Membership in Bangladesh," *International Social Work* 44(1), 2001, pp. 7–18.

15. Yunus, *Grameen Bank II,* pp. 22–23.

16. Many branches maintained attendance registries prior to 1999, but regular attendance was not a condition for the sanctioning of future loans or for enhancement of the loan ceiling.

17. James Surowiecki, *The Wisdom of Crowds: Why the Many Are Smarter than the Few and How Collective Wisdom Shapes Business, Economies, Societies, and Nations* (New York: Doubleday, 2004), p. 159.

18. For an evolution of loan products from Grameen I to Grameen II, see Appendix 5B.

The staff distributing alum at the doorstep of a borrower's house for purifying flood-contaminated water.

Borrower Bilkis Begum in her shop selling school bags and nylon ropes.

A group of women weaving baskets using funds from the bank.

A borrower in front of her betel leaf plantation.

Borrower Fatema Begum in her corner grocery cum mobile phone booth.

Borrower Anima Rani feeding her dairy cows.

Borrower Nazma Begum supervising her flat rice making factory funded by a microenterprise loan from the bank.

A beaming Khodeja with a basket of gourd (fuzzy melon) from her garden.

Amena Bagum with her husband in her poultry farm.

A borrower and her family with their leased power tiller from the bank.

Struggling member (beggar) Moron Chanda Sarkar doing brisk business with the cell phone leased out by the bank.

A small textile factory funded with a microenterprise loan.

6

Staff Incentives and Implementation of Grameen II

I n the preceding chapter, we discussed how the bank arrived at Grameen II after a long process of trial and error. A bigger challenge was the actual implementation of the changes in the field. The nuts and bolts of Grameen II had to be explained to its 13,000 staff members as well as its 2.4 million borrowers at the time. The most important challenge was to get the staff out of the "groupthink" of the core elements of Grameen I: a one-year loan with fifty-two weekly installments of equal value, and compulsory savings in the group fund with no access until ten years of membership. The staff recruited under the aegis of classical Grameen had been trained to implement the core elements of the standard model and to deal with any minor crises. As a result, they were very comfortable with the idea of disbursing loans and collecting repayments. During the transition to Grameen II, however, the former recruits, now officers and senior-level staff, had to leave that comfort zone and implement a mode of financial transaction that was unfamiliar to them. As we will see later in this chapter, this was an arduous task because the staff had been taught that there was only one correct way of doing things.

Once consensus was established regarding the basics of Grameen II, the next step was to implement the new structure in the field. New rules and regulations had to be written, a process spearheaded by co-author Dipal Barua, who was in charge of a special unit of the head office called the Coordination and Operation Department, which subsumed the tasks of the problem cell discussed in Chapter 5. The Coordination and Operation Department assigned the tasks of writing the rules to a number of working groups made up of senior managers in the bank dealing with various aspects of the implementation process. These rules included such procedures as how to change the credit ceiling and how to collect savings. In May 2000, a four-day workshop at the head office was devoted to a discussion of the rules and guidelines developed by these working groups and also to training the trainers. All senior staff from the head office (including the managing director), all zonal audit officers, administrators from the zonal offices, one area manager from each zone, and a senior staff member from the audit department of each zone attended this workshop. The officers from the area and zonal offices then held their own workshops at the zonal level to train the staff of the areas and zones. A core team consisting of staff from the zonal administration and audit offices as well as area managers and program officers was then formed to train the staff at the branch level. The zonal manager organized a workshop in a specific branch, with branch managers and staff from two to three adjacent branches in attendance. One member of the core training team from the zonal office and zonal audit department ran these workshops at the branch level during holidays.

To ensure active learning, all of the workshops were participatory and involved pedagogical tools such as role playing, quizzes, simulations, and scenario analysis. Quiz results were announced to the participants and were sent to the head office for inclusion in the personnel files of the participants.

The head office also received suggestions, amendments, and changes to the rules from staff at each level of training. This feedback raised a number of questions, suggesting to the head office that more than a simple rule book would be needed to implement Grameen II fully. As a result, implementation guidelines for the rule book were also written. The implementation guide clarified the wording in the rule books and provided examples and scenario analyses so that the staff could implement the rules correctly.

Armed with the rule book and implementation guide, staff handled the transition carefully and gradually. The head office suggested that the switch to Grameen II should start with implementing the changes at one center in a couple of branches. The idea was that by starting on a small scale, staff and mangers at the branch, area, and zonal levels would gain valuable experiences that could be used to handle larger-scale training and transformation. It was up to the respective zones and branches to decide which center under their control would be selected for transformation. Once the center was selected, staff who had excelled in the test at the end of training at the branch level were given the task of converting the center. After the staff had successfully implemented the changes in a center, the experience was shared with other workers in the branch, which allowed them to convert their own centers. The experiences of converting all the centers in a branch were then shared with other branches and the staff in the area office. This exchange of information made it possible for an area and eventually a zone to switch completely to Grameen II.

After the publication of first rule book and implementation guide, the branch staff met with the borrowers and explained the new products, rules, and regulations. They also listened to the borrowers' feedback. One field officer mentioned that he organized a "bamboo mat and stool" meeting—the traditional manner of meeting, in which people sit on bamboo mats and stools to solve the problems facing their community. The reason for organizing such meetings was to impress upon the borrowers that the bank is a community organization and that its changes had to be implemented in a communitarian way. After meeting with the borrowers, staff met with the branch manager and the area manager to share their experiences and inform them of the questions and concerns raised by the borrowers. Later the area managers met with the zonal managers, and eventually the head office staff met to incorporate this feedback into updated versions of the rules.

To keep the implementation process as interactive as possible, feedback from other sources was gathered about the experience of enacting changes in the field. The managing director and the general manager (now the deputy managing director) visited the field frequently, sometimes three times a month, with an average stay of two to three days. During these visits, the two of them would meet with scores of staff and borrowers, with meetings going on late into the night. They would also discuss the implementation process during the long car rides on their way to and from the field visits. Moreover, as in the early days of the bank, staff were encouraged to write letters directly to the managing director, Professor Yunus, expressing their opinions and reservations about the implementation process. The task forces provided additional information, noting any anomalies and problems that arose as they tried to implement the rules. Many brought up specific contradictions between what the rules suggested and what was possible in the field.

In addition to the normal channels, such as meetings with the managing director and other high officials and writing directly to the managing director, the Staff Association was used as a vehicle for providing feedback about the design and implementation of Grameen II. The Staff Association and its leaders played an important role as a source of mutual help for the staff. If an employee was unable to learn and implement the rules of Grameen II, others in the association helped him or her out. Representatives of the association visited branches, areas, and zones to learn about the implementation process and to exchange information with management about innovations in implementing Grameen II. They organized special Staff Association meetings to discuss how to overcome the problems and regularly included implementation issues in their monthly meeting with the bank's representative. The association also played an important role in the workshops about the rules of Grameen II.

This feedback from borrowers and staff at various levels was used to refine the rules and the implementation guide, and the resulting changes were disseminated in published form. Several editions of rules and implementation guidelines were produced, with each new edition highlighting the changes in bold. These highlighted sections allowed staff that were already familiar with previous editions to concentrate only on the changes. The final version of the rule book was published in July 2004 and updated in May of 2005, and has been in use ever since.

The trainers received further instructions on the final version of the rules for Grameen II at a two-day session at the bank's training institute in April 2003. The trainers were trained by senior staff of the head office, who in many cases also learned from the trainees. This additional training was conducted to finalize the transition to Grameen II. Workshops were held for the core training team at the zonal office; each area office then organized two-day workshops for branch managers, with the zonal manager and the zonal audit office in attendance. Figure 6.1 summarizes the process of developing the rules for Grameen II.

The area office training team, consisting of an area manager and a program officer not directly involved in managing the branch, organized one-day workshops at the branch level, with staff from two branches in attendance. Since the training was for a particular branch, the questions were specific; as a result, the training could be finished in one day. Further, staff from the zonal office, the zonal audit office, and the training institute attended these workshops as observers to facilitate the training and to learn about emerging issues of implementation and how to deal with them. Training at the branch level was the most crucial, as it entailed training the foot soldiers who would be directly involved in implementing Grameen II. The involved and laborious process of retraining staff suggested that along with the writing of rules and their refinement, and the publishing of various editions of the implementation guide, training the field staff was one of the most important elements of Grameen II. Table 6.1 lists the publication dates of various editions of the rule book and implementation guide.

Beginning in May, 2000, once the rules were finalized, the staff had to implement the rules to switch to Grameen II. A great deal of paperwork and meticulous changes in the accounts were required to enable the switch to Grameen II. First, staff had to convert all loans that were current into basic loans, and loans that were in arrears into flexible loans. Second, group funds had to be credited to the individual borrower, since these funds were eliminated in the new system. The staff also had to compute the interest on group funds for borrowers who were regular in their repayments; they had to credit half of the accumulated funds directly to the personal savings accounts and the rest to the special savings funds. Next, they had to enter these amounts in two separate passbooks, one for loans and one for personal savings. With the

THE PROCESS OF WRITING RULES & IMPLEMENTATION GUIDE IN GRAMEEN II

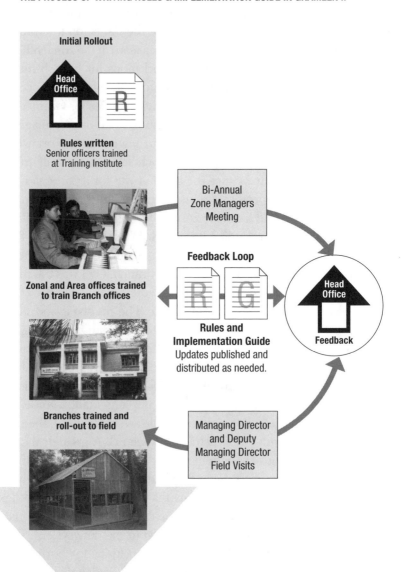

Figure 6.1   Rule writing process for Grameen II.

Table 6.1   Publication Dates of Various Editions of the Rule Book and Implementation Guide

Name of the Book	Date of Publication	Edition
Rule Book for Basic Loan	May 2000	First
Rule Book for Flexible Loan	May 2000	First
Rule Book for Basic Loan	September 2000	Second
Rule Book for Flexible Loan	September 2000	Second
Rule Book for Basic Loan	February 2001	Third
Rule Book for Flexible Loan	February 2001	Third
Rule Book for Basic Loan	October 2001	Fourth
Rule Book for Grameen Bank's Loans	March 2003	First
Rule Book for Grameen Bank's Loans	July 2004	Second
Rule Book for Grameen Bank's Loans	May 2005	Third
Flexible Loan Implementation Guide	September 2000	First
Basic Loan Implementation Guide	—	First
Flexible Loan Implementation Guide	February 2001	Second
Basic Loan Implementation Guide	February 2001	Second
Flexible Loan Implementation Guide	October 2001	Third
Basic Loan Implementation Guide	October 2001	Third
Loan Rulebook Guide	October 2003	First
Loan Rulebook Guide	June 2004	Second
Loan Rulebook Guide	June 2004	Third

introduction of the Grameen pension scheme (GPS), which at that time was voluntary, the staff had to introduce a separate passbook. These three passbooks had to be updated with each additional transaction and the passage of time. Now all types of savings—personal, special, and GPS—are recorded in one passbook.

Adjusting the group fund for borrowers who were in arrears also required a substantial amount of work for the field staff. Unlike the regular borrowers, those in arrears had to have their outstanding loan amount subtracted from their accumulations in the group fund.

The staff then had to add the accumulated interest on the remaining balance, if there was any. Finally, the remaining funds had to be distributed equally between the personal and special savings accounts.

Staff had to determine the loan amount and installment payments for the basic and flexible loan as well. In the case of the basic loan, all outstanding principal and interest from various loans first had to be merged into one amount so that they could be converted to a basic loan. Next, the staff had to figure out the installment payments as well as the loan ceiling for each borrower according to the rules. For example, suppose a borrower in good standing had a general loan of 10,000 taka with 5000 taka remaining, and a seasonal loan of 8000 taka with 2000 taka remaining. For this borrower, the loan ceiling would be 18,000 taka. For the transition to the basic loan, the borrower's old loans would be canceled and in their place a basic loan of 7000 taka (the amount outstanding from the two previous loans) with a one-year duration would be issued. After making regular payments for twenty-six weeks, the borrower could easily raise the amount by topping up this loan.

In converting defaults to flexible loans, the work was much more involved. First, the staff had to find the borrowers, which in itself was difficult and time-consuming, as many had severed all connections with the bank. Once the borrowers in arrears were found, the staff had to explain the principles of the flexible loan and, more important, get the borrowers to sign the contract. Even before meeting with the defaulter, the staff had to a lot of preparatory work. They had to study the case history of the borrower and, in particular, compute the amount of outstanding interest on the loan and the portion of the group fund owned by each borrower. After adjusting the group fund for loans outstanding, the staff had to arrive at the net amount owed to the bank. The most difficult aspect, however, was to get the borrowers to sign a contract to repay, along with specification of the installment amounts and a repayment schedule. Borrowers and their families had to be convinced that repaying the bank would be beneficial for them in the long run.[1] In addition to clerical and preparatory work, the staff had to do a lot of explaining to motivate borrowers to reestablish a connection with the bank. The staff had to explain all the changes that were made to the group funds as well as the new passbooks and the various entries in them. Some examples of defaulters who assumed flexible loans are presented in Box 6.1.

Due to the borrowers' reluctance to sign contracts, many staff members had to get very creative in finding and convincing them to take that step. In a typical case, a staff member paid a courtesy visit to get to know the borrower and to learn the names of the borrower's children and their levels of education. During the next visit, the staff member would diplomatically mention to the borrower that his or her defaulted amount was increasing, and that there is a plan to make it easy for him or her to repay loan and, in the process, open a new line of credit. The bank worker would carefully explain how much interest the borrower was paying per day on the defaulted loan and how that amount could be reduced by adjusting the outstanding amount by means of the group fund. The bank worker had to explain to the borrower why adjusting the group fund against the loan outstanding made sense, since the interest rate on the loan was 20% whereas the interest rate on the group fund was only 8.5%. Moreover, the worker had to explain the advantage of signing a contract, especially one involving access to a new line of credit (see Box 6.1). If a bank worker was successful, he or she generously shared this experience with others through formal and informal means. All of these visits took place after hours, usually in

Box 6.1   Stories about Flexible Loans

"I Have Taken the Loan, I Will Sign the Contract, and There Is No Problem"

Rehana Begum is a member of the 28/M center of the Selam Sylhet branch. She stopped paying installments after the flood of 1998 and she is in now arrears. A bank worker got in touch with her, and she rejoined the center and pledged to sign the contract. However, on the day of the signing, she announced that she would abide by all of the conditions of the contract except the one about adjusting her group fund against the amount due. She had 2169 taka saved in the group fund, and her husband forbade her from using the group fund to pay off the outstanding loan. His argument was that they had worked very hard to save this money, and he would not allow it to be used for paying off a loan, even if it meant paying 20% interest to the bank. The worker was dejected and was about to leave her house when Rehana said, "Sir, please sit down. I will sign the contract."

Box 6.1   Stories about Flexible Loans (Continued)

She said she would be willing to take 100 taka a week from her husband and use 50 taka to pay off the loan and put the other 50 taka in an individual savings account. In six to seven months she would be able to save around 1500 taka. She said she would convince her husband that this is a good compromise because through her deposits she would be able to replenish their lost savings in the group fund. The bank worker was reluctant. He said, "I will not sign a contract with you today, because if you sign the contract without the support of your husband, he will be mad at you and this will create conflict between the two of you." Rehana responded, "I have taken the loan and I will sign the contract. I will benefit by adjusting the amount due against my savings in the group fund."

"I Am the One Responsible for My Bad Luck"

Safura Begum had not attended meetings for three years and had stopped making installment payments. Many attempts had been made to regularize her loan. After publication of the rules for flexible loans, the staff contacted her again and explained to her the advantage of the flexible loan. She was noncommittal, believing that once she repaid the old loan in full, she would not be able to borrow again. She confessed that she had had problems making her payments because her husband was ill, but the main reason was the instigation of her neighbor, who advised her not to pay. When she found out the amount of her accumulated interest, she said, "I messed up by listening to others. Please let me sign up for a flexible loan." Her principal amount was 9123 taka and the accumulated interest was 6172 taka, making the total amount to be repaid a whopping 15,295 taka. She signed a contract to repay 40 taka per week. Now she is eagerly waiting for the twenty-six weeks to pass so that she can borrow twice the amount and invest in her husband's rice trading business.

"Let Me Sign the Contract and Be Relieved of My Worries"

The bank worker had been unsuccessful in tracking down Mr. Dudu Miah, a borrower in the Rangerchar branch of the Sunamganj district. The worker visited Miah's house several times but was told he was not there. His wife, however, informed the worker that he actually was home, but he was ashamed to meet with the worker because he could not pay his installments. The bank worker convinced Miah to come out and meet him. He explained to him the benefit of signing a contract, but Miah replied, "The bank can do anything they want; I cannot pay the installment" and left the house in a huff. He returned home a bit later. The bank worker had waited for him and resumed the conversation. "If you had borrowed 16,000 taka from the money lender at his interest rate you would have to pay 20,000 in interest. You only have to pay 7000 taka in interest for the bank loan. Why are you getting so frustrated? Is the bank being unfair to you? If you feel the bank is at fault, I will leave." Dudu Miah responded, "No sir, it is my fault. Okay, I will sign a contract. Let me sign the contract and relieve me of my worries. It would have been better for me if I had done this before."

Box 6.1   Stories about Flexible Loans (Continued)

The principal on his unpaid loan was 8380 taka and the accumulated interest was 6190 taka, making the gross amount due 14,570 taka. This was adjusted against the group fund amount of 3342 taka, for a net amount of 11,228 taka. He signed a contract to repay this amount with installments of 50 taka per week. When he relayed his experience of signing the contract with other borrowers in arrears, eleven of them signed contracts to repay their loans.

"You Found Me at Last"

Ms. Shabana was a member of the Fatepur-Zaintapur branch. She married a man her parents did not approve of. Her family shunned her for her defiance, so she left the area with her husband. Since 1998 she has been living elsewhere in secret and no one knew her address. She was, however, the only remaining member who had not signed the contract in that center. If she could be located and persuaded to sign the contract, the center could achieve the distinction of having 100% of its borrowers on contract.

The branch manager used all available avenues to find her. Finally, he received information that she was living in the town of Sylhet in a rental house. The branch manager accompanied the bank worker to Ms. Shabana's address. They first met her husband, who was a paramedic and was about to leave the house for work. He was quite irritated that some men he had never met were inquiring about his wife. He started asking pointed questions to determine the identities of the strangers. When Ms. Shabana heard the manager introduce himself, she came out of the house, saying, "I am the Shabana you are looking for. You have come to the right address." She introduced the bank manager to her husband. The manager explained the reason for his visit and urged her to sign the contract. It became apparent that her husband was not in favor of his wife signing a contract to repay a loan she had taken before they got married. Shabana begged her husband for permission to sign the contract. Eventually, the couple agreed to sign a contract to repay 50 taka per month. She started crying out of joy that her husband had agreed. She said, "You found me at last, sir. Even my family members do not look for me anymore." The contractual amount was 2580 taka, which she was to repay over a period of two years.

Source: Uddog, no. 88, July 2001.

the evening or on a Friday, the official holiday, when the likelihood of meeting the members and their families was high. Even former staff members who had had good relationships with especially difficult loanees were recruited to persuade the borrowers. In addition to dealing with borrowers at their own centers, these staff members would go to the centers of difficult loanees on their holidays to persuade them to sign contracts.

The first branch to completely switch over to Grameen II was the Bhason branch in the Gazipur area, in March 2001. The bank widely circulated the news that the branch had switched to *ditio onko* ("Phase II"). Converting to Phase II implied that all regular loanees in the branch had been switched to a basic loan and that all group fund proceeds, where applicable, were credited to personal savings and special savings accounts. The story of this first conversion appears in Box 6.2.

A successful switch also meant that all borrowers opened GPS accounts and that all loanees in arrears were switched to flexible loans wherever possible. In difficult cases, accounts of delinquent borrowers were cleared by offsetting the outstanding amount against savings in the group fund and personal accounts. Because these changes were done member by member, center by center, and branch by branch for the whole bank, the achievement of a full changeover to Grameen II was quite an accomplishment. All borrowers in the Bhason Gazipur branch, however, were regular in their repayments, which made switching to Grameen II relatively easy at that location. Nonetheless, once the news got out and the staff realized its full implications, other branches were inspired to try the switch to Phase II as well. As a result, a friendly competition ensued among the branches, areas, and zones. By December 30, 2001, two zones—Noakhali and Rajshahi—had completely switched to Grameen II.

While it was relatively easy to switch branches that had few problem loans, a typical branch required almost a year to complete the switch to Grameen II. The last zone to achieve this was Tangail. Table 6.2 shows the dates of switching to Phase II for the zones of Grameen Bank.

By August 7, 2002, after the successful changeover of all branches, areas, and zones, the Coordination and Operation Department began to gather information relating to the implementation process to share with staff. As before, staff members were encouraged to share their thoughts, suggestions, and concerns with the managing director. The Coordination and Operation Department would then summarize these findings and meet with the senior leadership of the bank to distill the

Box 6.2   Bhason Gazipur: The First Branch to Switch to Grameen II

I first became aware of the need to build a new type of Grameen Bank in a branch managers' meeting with the managing director of the bank held in May 2000 at the Dhaka zone. In June of the same year, the zonal manager briefed us on the rules of Grameen II, and we received a copy of the rules that month. We started informing the centers about these rules. In July there was a two-day workshop and a review meeting at the zone. In the meeting, the zonal manger asked if any of the branches has been able to separate the group fund into individual accounts. I announced that in my branch all the group funds' principal and interest had been separated and credited to the individual borrowers. In addition, the borrowers in my branch had opened 661 GPS accounts. He asked me if the borrowers were willing to switch to the basic loan. I replied that borrowers who had been members for seven to eight years were eager to switch. Older members were not that excited about switching, but they were few in number. He suggested that, initially, I should switch fifty borrowers to basic loans. On July 13 we began our journey to build a Grameen II branch by switching five members from four different centers. All my co-workers cooperated, and through our joint efforts we contacted the borrowers and their guardians. Gradually, they started switching to basic loans. We prepared a preliminary plan on how to switch my branch to Grameen II. The plan included

1. Every day we will hold two center meetings and use the venue to explain basic loan to the borrowers and their family members.
2. At least two days a week we will meet the members in their houses to brief them on the essentials of Grameen II.
3. We will get all borrowers who have been members for more than a year to open GPS accounts. By December 2000, 2069 out of 2561 members had opened GPS accounts. By February 2001, we will bring all members under the domain of GPS, and by April 2001, we will switch all members to basic loans.

We commenced the work on implementing our plan. I was worried that my staff were moving too fast and urged them to slow down the pace a bit. They responded that this was the time to do the hard work and urged me to provide them with the necessary documents and moral support. In my regular meeting with the staff, I suggested that they divide the workload among themselves. For example, half of them could work on transferring the borrowers to basic loans and the other half could concentrate on the day-to-day work of the branch. Further, I suggested that they try to switch one group from each center to basic loans every day. We started noticing progress and the successful implementation of our plan. By the end of February 2001, nineteen centers and 52% of the borrowers were completely switched to basic loans. Around that time, we were also able to sort out the accounting aspects of various loans and savings accounts. I was still worried that my staff were moving too fast. But they were inspired, and there was nothing that could stop them. At the end, on March 29, by switching 123 borrowers from nine centers to basic loans, we finished the task of switching the branch completely to Grameen II.

Box 6.2   Bhason Gazipur: The First Branch to Switch to Grameen II (Continued)

The following elements were the key to the successful switch to Grameen II:

a. Sincere efforts of the staff
b. Eagerness to be successful
c. Adoption of the proper steps
d. Intelligence
e. Enthusiasm for the work
f. Cooperation and coordination
g. Full information regarding the nature of the work

Source: Based on a narrative by Mohammad Abdus Sabir, branch manager of Bhasan Gazipur, published in *Uddog*, no. 89, November 2001.

inputs and suggestions. The department also published a number of short monitoring reports to help staff at all levels keep tabs on the implementation process. These reports summarized information about changes in repayment rates, amounts of unpaid interest in general and housing loans, the number of and balances on basic loans, the number of borrowers under flexible loans, the number of borrowers eligible to sign contracts, the number of borrowers who actually signed contracts, the rate of contract signing, and the amount of GPS and other savings. These numbers were reported in descending order across zones so that the staff could easily tell which zone was leading in the competition.

The issues related to implementation were also discussed and debated at the zonal managers' conferences. At the peak of the crisis, two meetings of zonal managers were held, as opposed to one meeting during the normal days of the bank. During implementation of Grameen II, the head office organized special zonal managers' meetings to discuss and make decisions about the process, pace, and strategy of implementation. For example, these meetings identified how to monitor the implementation process and how to measure its success. After a day of conversation and debate, a consensus was typically reached and major decisions were made at the end of the day.

The tremendous effort to change to Grameen II required much dedication and a strong work ethic on the part of Grameen staff, traits

Table 6.2   Dates of Switching to Grameen II by Various Zones

Zone	Number of Branches	Date of Entering Phase II
Rajshahi	87	December 30, 2001
Noakhali	64	December 30, 2001
Dhaka	72	February 13, 2002
Patuakhali	83	February 18, 2002
Bogra	102	February 19, 2002
Comilla	70	February 19, 2002
Khulna	75	February 20, 2002
Chittagong	74	February 20, 2002
Faridpur	73	February 27, 2002
Naraynganj	69	March 14, 2002
Sylhet	54	March 14, 2002
Dinajpur	67	March 21, 2002
Habiganj (subzone)	25	March 21, 2002
Rangpur	84	March 21, 2002
Nilphamari (subzone)	30	March 28, 2002
Jamalpur, special project	33	May 14, 2002
Mymensingh	60	June 29, 2002
Tangail	69	August 7, 2002
Total	1191	

for which these workers are well known. Although Grameen staff had learned how to work hard and negotiate complicated situations during their careers, the switch to Grameen II required far more than the ordinary effort. The staff's willingness to go above and beyond their typical duties raises an interesting question: what motivated them to take on this extra workload to implement the transition to Grameen II? As previously mentioned, many staff members were asked to meet borrowers in their homes, get trained on the new rules, and perform extra accounting work, often during holidays. The staff's tenacity and dedication in the face of such adversity speak volumes about the bank's selection and training methods. Through the rigorous selection and training process, the bank was—and still is—able to select staff with "not only an understanding of poverty, but a deep commitment to working to change that poverty."[2]

Grameen management, through transparent and participatory decision making, has created "a distinctive Grameen community." Jain (1996) points to how Grameen's "routinization of functions, induction and training, boundary maintenance, morale boosting, link-up between field offices and headquarters, zonal manager's role in organizational communication, and leadership example were critical elements in fostering appropriate organizational culture."[3] The staff take pride in working for the organization, as "they see themselves as guardians—guardians of Grameen's interests and, guardians of the interests of their *Kendra* (Center) members."[4] This pride in the bank and how it changes people's lives has been expressed by many of Susan Holcombe's respondents, one of whom commented that the "greatest happiness is finding improvement for poor people." Once staff members see firsthand how their work has changed the lives of the poor, it makes them want to work harder. Even non-officers have suggested that the bank's work is more interesting than that of the commercial bank "because they could see that their work had a direct impact on people's lives."[5]

During the early phase of the transition, staff were concerned that converting to Grameen II would mean an increased workload. The management believed, however, that once the transition was complete, the workload would actually decrease dramatically. An internal study based on time spent by staff showed that the transition to Grameen II and the increased computerization has reduced staff workload by 40%. The in-house journal, *Uddog*, published several articles in which staff mentioned reduced workload as one of the most beneficial aspects of Grameen II.

This reduction in workload came from several factors. The first is the reduction of loan types. Second, accounts were made more transparent and simple, with very clearly marked passbooks. Because of the enhanced transparency and simplicity of the rules, workers had to spend less time resolving misunderstandings and, consequently, less time in center meetings. Branch staff members are provided with pre-printed repayment figures for each weekly meeting. If every bor-rower pays according to the repayment schedule, the staff have nothing to write on the document except for their signatures. Only deviations are recorded. The only paperwork that remains to be done at the meeting is to enter figures in the borrowers' passbooks.

These schedules and passbooks are sent to the area offices for entry into the computer. Prior to the implementation of Grameen II, the bank experimented with putting computers in the branches, but found that many of the units were underutilized as the data of a branch was insuf-ficient to take advantage of the large capacity of a personal computer. Besides, any software or hardware problems would disrupt the data entry work until the problem could be fixed. Moreover, a single machine could not be used to back up its own data. Grameen Commu-nication, a sister organization, now runs an Information Management Center (IMC) in every area office. On average, four computer opera-tors employed by Grameen Communications work in the IMC; their salaries are paid through a contract with Grameen Communications. These operators run and maintain the computers that are kept in area offices. Each computer keeps records for three branches. The presence of several computers makes it possible to back up the data, and in case of software or hardware problems with one computer, another machine can be used for data entry. Computers in the area offices are now used to manage accounts and print reports on all monthly closings of the branches, MIS reports, and even vouchers for petty expenses. Previ-ously, the branch staff had to produce these reports manually. Comput-ers are now used for data management for 1548 out of 1861 branches. For all new branches, the record keeping is computerized from day 1.

Even more evidence of the reduced workload lies in the simplified process of year-end closing, where the branch is required to balance its books to find out if it is showing a profit or a loss. In the past, staff needed weeks of continuous work to finish the closing, for which they were handsomely rewarded in the form of a special bonus. While workers still receive a bonus for their help, computerization and streamlining of loan products have made the closing process far less time-consuming. Grameen was in negotiations with a company to provide PDAs (personal digital assistants). However, such devices are still too expensive to be cost-effective. There is also a plan to use smart cards in future. The cost of maintaining detailed financial records for accounting and management purposes is anticipated to come down even further when the bank is able to introduce these innovations.

In addition to reducing the workload of the staff, the bank also took initiatives to reduce costs. One obvious means was to take advantage of the time saved by computerization and the streamlined loan processing and savings collection tasks and use these surplus hours to increase the number of borrowers that each worker in the branch has to manage. The bank now requires each worker to manage at least ten groups, or 500 borrowers, instead of the previous standard of 400 borrowers. The increased efficiency of computerization and the complete transfer to Grameen II in the near future will make it possible for one staff member to manage 600 borrowers.

Initially, there was only Flexible Loan 1 (*chukti rin* 1); this applied to a loan that was in arrears but had not yet been declared as bad debt and written off. Each area was given a target of signing 1000 contractual loans within six months from the day of the loan's introduction. Out of the 100 staff in each area, the one responsible for signing the largest number of contracts was to receive a cash reward of 1000 taka and a certificate. Since the implementation of bankwide competition, similar contests based on various criteria have commenced within the bank. Initially, bank workers were given a financial incentive to get a borrower with a delinquent loan that had been written off to sign a contract for a Flexible Loan 2 (*chukti rin* 2); staff members who were able to collect bad debts would get 5% of the collected debt. One staff member collected 1,500,000 taka in bad debts and in the process earned additional income. However, this cash incentive applied only to loans that had been declared bad prior to 2000. This cutoff date was introduced to make sure staff wouldn't deliberately try to turn a loan into a bad debt in order to collect the cash. In addition, the criteria for writing off bad debts have been made more stringent since 2000 as part of Grameen II.

The bank has recently halted the offering of monetary incentives for collecting bad debt (*ku rin*) prior to the cutoff of 2000. It is revisiting the whole issue because it wants to redirect the incentives to borrowers by encouraging them to repay the written-off debts. An aggressive campaign to rid the bank off all bad debts through a competition between the zones has now begun under the leadership of the deputy managing director of the bank. He personally calls every zonal manager weekly to monitor the progress of collection of such loans, and his staff produce a daily report monitoring the collection of bad debts. Like other information, the daily monitoring report is widely shared with the staff to enhance competition. The amount of bad loans collected is now one of the criteria used to determine the best worker, best branch, best area, and best zone.

The successful switch to Grameen II has changed the tasks performed by a bank worker. In addition to the usual tasks, such as collecting loans and saving deposits, maintaining the saving passbook, and sharing information, staff are now encouraged to explain the difference between Grameen Bank and other credit-granting institutions. The current model of financial intermediation of Grameen Bank differs significantly from the models used by NGOs in Bangladesh. For one thing, the interest rate charged by the bank is lower: a maximum 100 taka interest per 1000 taka borrowed from Grameen, compared with 150 taka interest per 1000 taka borrowed from other institutions. Grameen borrowers can also borrow at 8% interest to build a house or pay for homestead land. Other institutions do not offer a housing loan, and the only alternative is to borrow from the House Building Finance Corporation at a 15% interest rate. In addition, there is no prepayment penalty on loans from Grameen Bank. If a borrower repays the full amount after a few months, he or she only has to pay interest for the duration of the loan use; in other organizations, borrowers have to pay interest for the full duration of the loan. Grameen borrowers can also borrow again after paying installments diligently for the first twenty-six weeks of loan duration. Borrowers of other organizations have to wait until they have fully repaid a loan before they can borrow again. Finally, unlike the case with other organizations, Grameen borrowers can vary the installment amount and the duration of the loan.

Grameen borrowers' children can also receive scholarships and loans for higher education. No such opportunity exists at other organizations. If a borrower of the bank dies, his or her dependents receive 1000–2000 taka from the Central Disaster Fund. If a borrower or her husband dies, their outstanding loan is forgiven by virtue of the loan insurance program. A borrower at other organizations does not receive death benefits, nor are loans forgiven at the death of the borrower or her husband. Grameen Bank is also legally authorized to collect deposits from nonmembers, and the bank pays 8.5% on savings deposits and 12% on time deposits. Other organizations are not allowed to collect savings from nonmembers, and they pay at most 6% interest on savings deposits. Unlike borrowers at other organizations, Grameen borrowers do not have to pay a non-refundable admission fee or a yearly renewal fee of 20 taka or more.

As the previous discussion shows, the bank worker's task is a difficult one. It is a testament to Grameen's strong institutional culture that staff members are willing to do such hard work. The obvious question is what motivates them to do such tedious tasks, not to mention the unpleasant duty, at times, of looking into the eyes of the poorest of the poor and asking them to repay the bank on time.

In addition to direct and indirect monetary compensation, celebration, competition, and public recognition are the tools used to reward staff under Grameen II. Recognition comes in various forms: publication, in the official calendar of the bank, of the pictures of staff of the first branch that moved into Phase II; public recognition of staff, branch, area, and zone staff in the annual zonal manager's conference; and congratulatory letters for successful performance, with copies sent to all staff.

Staff and branches under Grameen II are rewarded for achieving their targets by means of a star system (see Figure 6.2). There are five stars, each with a different color representing a particular target. Stars are given for being free of loans outstanding, losses, or any out-

BADGE OF HONOR

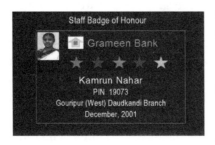

Ten Indicators to Assess Poverty Level

1. The members and their family are living in a tin-roofed house or in a house worth at least 25,000 taka, and the family members sleep on cots or a bed instead of the floor.
2. The members drink pure water of tubewells, boiled water, or arsenic-free water purified by the use of alum, purifying tablets or pitcher filters.
3. All of the children of the members who are physically and mentally fit and are above the age of six either attend or have finished primary school.
4. The member's minimum weekly installment is 200 taka.
5. All the family members use a hygienic and sanitary latrine.
6. The family members have sufficient clothing for daily use. Further, the family has winter clothes such as kanthas (light wraps made out of used clothing), wrappers, sweaters, quilts, blankets etc. to protect them from cold, and they also have nets to protect them from mosquito bites.
7. The family has additional sources of income, such as a vegetable garden, fruit-bearing tree, etc., to fall back on these sources when they need additional income.
8. The borrower maintains an average annual balance of 5000 taka in her savings accounts.
9. The borrower has the ability to feed her family members three square meals a day throughout the year; essentially, the family does not face any food insecurity.
10. All family members are conscious about their health. They have the ability to take immediate actions for proper treatment and can pay for medical expenses in the event of illness of any member of the family.

Red Star
If all borrowers cross poverty threshold according to the "Ten Indicators"

Brown Star
If all borrowers children in center attend school

Purple Star
Individual staff who brings more deposits than outstanding loans to his/her borrowers

Blue Star
Individual staff who contribute to branch profit

Green Star
No overdue loans in centers under their management

Figure 6.2   Star system to rate staff performance.

standing balance with the head office; perfect school enrollment of borrowers' children; and having all the borrowers under a staff cross the poverty threshold according to the ten indicators in Chapter 2.

Staff can earn a green star for having no loans outstanding in the centers under their management. Blue stars are rewarded to individual workers who earn a profit, which the bank monitors by determining income and expenditures accruable to each worker. The worker's cost is measured by adding salary, bonuses, allowances for food and conveyance, and the projected interest costs of deposits that they manage. The fixed cost of managing a branch is allocated proportionately to the number of workers, and this is added to the cost figure. The worker's income is measured by the projected interest income of the loans that he or she manages. Profit by each worker is the difference between the cost and income measured according to these variables. A worker will earn a purple star if at the end of the two periods (June and December) the amount of deposits under the worker exceeds the amount of loans outstanding. He or she will earn a brown star if all the children of the borrowers in the worker's center attend school. Finally, a worker will earn the highly coveted red star if all of his or her borrowers have crossed the poverty threshold according to the "ten indicators" developed by the bank. Table 6.3 shows the numbers of stars earned by the staff in various years.

Similar indicators of staff performance are used in rewarding branches with stars. The first three stars—green, blue, and purple—are assigned based on internal reporting, while the last two stars—brown and red—were to be assigned by an independent research institute that would certify achievement of the two targets (i.e., all children in school and all borrowers crossing the poverty threshold).[6] When a branch receives all five stars, it is deemed to have completed the bank's mission. Staff earning stars display them proudly, prompting others to work hard to earn their own stars (see the badge in Figure 6.2). The head office sends letters to all of the branches highlighting staff achievements at the individual and branch levels, leading to a friendly competition between the staff and between the branches. This benefits the bank by inducing staff to work hard to achieve the ultimate goal of the bank—poverty alleviation. Table 6.4 shows the branch-wise distribution of stars for various years.

The latest addition to the methods of public recognition for staff accomplishments is the Grameen Bank Gold Cup competition. The

Table 6.3 Numbers of Stars Earned by Workers Each Year

Year	Total Number of Workers	Numbers of Workers Receiving One Star	Numbers of Workers Receiving Two Stars	Numbers of Workers Receiving Three Stars	Numbers of Workers Receiving Four Stars	Numbers of Workers Receiving Five Stars	Numbers of Workers Receiving at Least One Star	Percentage of Workers Receiving at Least One Star
2002 (mid-year)	9,075	1,228	1,146	536	120	44	3,074	34
2002 (year end)	8,620	2,306	1,356	828	162	63	4,715	55
2003 (mid-year)	9,060	2,129	1,720	1,064	250	139	5,302	59
2003 (year end)	9,290	1,631	2,164	1,713	465	259	6,232	67
2004 (mid-year)	9,201	1,762	2,125	2,033	1,099	568	7,587	82
2004 (year end)	9,724	1,506	1,706	2,703	1,493	717	8,125	83
2005 (mid-year)	10,226	2,097	2,273	2,844	3,796	888	8,815	86

Table 6.4 Number of Stars Awarded by Branch and by Year

Year	Total Number of Branches	Branches with One Star	Branches with Two Stars	Branches with Three Stars	Total Number of Stars	Percentage of Branches Receiving at Least One Star
2000 (year end)	1160	202	95	6	303	26
2001 (mid-year)	1160	226	114	6	346	30
2002 (mid-year)	1175	244	160	103	507	43
2002 (year end)	1178	367	236	169	772	66
2003 (mid-year)	1200	378	334	218	926	77
2003 (year end)	1230	355	370	304	1029	84
2004 (mid-year)	1287	309	431	395	1135	88
2004 (year end)	1363	273	366	371	1158	85
2005 (mid-year)*	1561	314	378	431	1312	84

*160 and 29 branches had received four and five stars, respectively, by the middle of 2005.

Gold Cup is awarded to the best-performing zone. In addition, two other zones are rewarded first and second runner-up status. The selection process occurs in two steps. First, zones are evaluated on the basis of the performance of the staff and the branches. To evaluate the performance of the zone based on staff criteria, the respective percentages of staff receiving a star, earning a profit, and managing more than 500 borrowers are used to calculate an average score. The average score for the branch is calculated based on the percentages of branches that achieved a star, earned a profit, did not have to use funds from the head office, and collected more than 25% of its deposits from nonmembers. The zones that score the top three scores based on these combined criteria make the cut for the final round of competition.[7] In the final round, zones selected from the preliminary round are evaluated based on nine positive criteria and two negative criteria. The positive criteria include number of stars per worker, profit, total deposits, deposits from nonmembers, balance on special investment loans, number of education loans per branch, outstanding loans and balance on deposits per borrower, and number of actual scholarships as a percentage of potential scholarships in each zone. The negative criteria include the amount of embezzlement and number of dropouts per branch in each zone. Each zone receives 10 points for securing the top position according to the positive and negative criteria; second- and third-place finishers are given 6 and 3 points, respectively. The points for negative criteria are then deducted to arrive at a net score, with first place going to the zone scoring the highest. The Dhaka zone received the first Grameen Gold Cup in 2003; second and third places went to the Chittagong and Noakhali zones, respectively.

Using the same methods, the bank publishes a mid-year prediction as to which zone is likely to win the competition at the end of the year. These predictions are inducements for zones that are lagging to improve their performance in the next six months.

Soon after the first Grameen Gold Cup competition, the bank realized that some of the zones would never have a chance of winning because of their particular geography and socioeconomic conditions. To remedy this bias, a separate award was declared for these weaker zones: Jamalpur, Tangail, Habiganj, Rangpur, Sylhet, Niphamari, Mymensingh, and Dinajpur. Borrowing the vocabulary of the English Football League, the overall competition essentially consisted of a premier league the football league for the next level of teams.[8] The problem zones received awards for making the most progress according to their own set of positive and negative criteria. Progress was computed by comparing year-end figures for successive years. Only zones showing an increase in positive items and a decrease in negative items received scores. The weaker zones now have made such a dramatic turnaround in their performance, however, that the bank has cancelled this competition. The erstwhile weaker zones now compete with the other zones for the prestigious Grameen Gold Cup.

The bank has also started to reward individual workers, branch managers, branches, areas, and zones for achieving records in year-end performance in certain areas. Table 6.5 summarizes the salient features of this award.

Table 6.5   Selection Criteria for Record-Setting Performance by Staff, Branch, Area, and Zone

Record Statistic	Award Recipient	Selection Criteria	Award
Management of largest number of active borrowers	Bank worker	Sum of monthly numbers over twelve months	Certificate and 2000 taka in prize bonds
Highest profit per borrower	Branch, area, and zone	Year-end net profit divided by total number of borrowers	One crest and 1000 taka in prize bonds
Highest profit among branches more than a year old	Branch	Total year-end profit	One crest and 1000 taka in prize bonds
Highest reduction in loss	Branch, area, and zone	The difference between last year's loss and the current year's loss	One crest and 1000 taka in prize bonds

Table 6.5   Selection Criteria for Record-Setting Performance by Staff, Branch, Area, and Zone (Continued)

Record Statistic	Award Recipient	Selection Criteria	Award
Lowest cost to earn 1 taka	Branch	Year-end cost divided by year-end income	One crest and 1000 taka in prize bonds
Largest disbursement of loans including special investment loans	Branch, area, and zone	Total loans disbursed divided by total number of borrowers	One crest and 1000 taka in prize bonds
Largest disbursement of special investment loans	Worker and branch manager	Total special investment loans divided by the total number of borrowers	One certificate and 2000 taka in prize bonds
Largest disbursement of bridge loans	Worker and branch manager	Total number of loans disbursed in a year	One certificate and 2000 taka in prize bonds
Largest collection (amount) of bad debts or debts that have been written off	Worker and branch manager	Total amount collected with and without contract in a year	One certificate and 2000 taka in prize bonds
Largest collection of housing loans	Worker and branch manager	Total amount collected in a year	One certificate and 2000 take in prize bonds

In addition to this variety of incentives, staff of Grameen Bank are also eligible for voluntary retirement after ten years or more of active service with the bank. Upon retirement, staff members receive a lump-sum gratuity that is very generous by Bangladesh standards.[9] Since this benefit was introduced in 1994, 5118 staff members have retired and received a total of 2.48 million taka, or $47.23 million, as of September 2004. This makes the average pension 0.48 million taka, or $9228, per staff retiree.[10] During the process of implementing Grameen II, in the year 2000 a significant number of staff took the option of early retirement. Event though the bank lost some experienced workers, it was able to replace them with new workers who were not indoctrinated in classical Grameen and hence could be trained in Grameen II with less resistance or opposition. Many of the retirees are now gainfully employed in other credit-granting institutions that are still using the classical Grameen type of credit delivery mechanism.

As Table 6.6 reveals, the bulk of the retirements occurred during the development and implementation of Grameen II (1999–2002). The table gives the number of optional retirements taken by the staff each year.

The transition to Grameen II now is complete, and the bank recently reached a couple of milestones: it disbursed $5 billion worth of loans cumulatively, and it has more than 5 million members. Centers that were moribund are now full of life; those that were losing money and had miserable repayment rates are now

Table 6.6   Optional Staff Retirements at Grameen Bank by Year

Year	Number of Officers*	Number of Non-Officers	Total
1994	3	0	3
1995	14	66	80
1996	39	90	129
1997	12	38	50
1998	132	201	333
1999	277	433	710
2000	537	940	1477
2001	364	497	861
2002	397	264	661
2003	481	77	558
2004	266	77	343
2005	328	139	467

*Officers include deputy managing director, general manager, deputy general manager, assistant general manager, senior principal officer, principal officer, senior officer–selection grade, senior officer, and officer.

making huge profits, and their repayment rate is near perfect. Precisely because the hardship of rebuilding now seems like a distant memory, however, we must be careful not to forget the pain and hard work that it demanded. The staff—the foot soldiers of the bank—bore the brunt of these hardships. It is they who had to rebuild the bank center by center and branch by branch. During the height of the crisis, 80% of the borrowers repaid on time and per schedule. It was the other 20% who needed all the extra incentives to pay back. Here is where the role of the staff was supremely important. It was they who had to convince the borrowers that repaying the bank would be to their advantage. It was they who listened to the borrowers' reasons for not paying on time and who found a way for them to repay small amounts and rejoin the bank. It was they who worked out the rehabilitation plan with the borrowers and got them to repay on time. It was they who worked on holidays to institute the broad and meticulous changes in accounting required for the seamless transition to Grameen II. It was the hard work of the staff and the willingness of the borrowers to repay that made it possible to cross the amazing thresholds of 5: 5 million members and disbursement of $5 billion in cumulative disbursed loans.

NOTES

1. It should be clear that all these changes in accounting were made possible with the computerization of record keeping. The task would have been more difficult if the staff had had to make all of these changes manually.
2. Susan Holcombe, *Managing to Empower: The Grameen Bank's Experience of Poverty Alleviation* (London: Zed Books, 1995), p. 111.
3. Pankaj Jain, "Managing Credit for the Rural Poor: Lessons from the Grameen Bank," *World Development* 24(1), 1996, p. 88.
4. Stuart Rutherford, "Grameen II at the End of 2003: A 'Grounded View' of How Grameen's New Initiative Is Progressing in the Villages," typescript (Dhaka: MicroSave, 2004).
5. Holcombe, *Managing to Empower,* p. 117.
6. The research institution could not complete its task, and the bank is now using internal means—for example, using the audit office—to verify the claims.
7. The preliminary selection criteria have been updated recently. Instead of percentage of workers and branches earning one star, the criteria now are the percentages of workers and branches earning the first three stars: green, blue, and purple.
8. Readers in North America can substitute the baseball analogy of the major and minor leagues.
9. For example, if a staff member retires after ten years of service, his gratuity will be based on 50% of his last salary. Half of this stated amount will be multiplied by 130 to arrive at a one-time gratuity, and the other half will be multiplied by 130 to determine the health benefit on retirement. If a staff member retires after the full term (twenty years of service) the gratuity will be based on 80% of basic salary. Half of that amount is multiplied by 200 to determine the one-time gratuity, and the other half will be multiplied by 144 to determine the health benefit on retirement.
10. Muhammad Yunus, *Grameen Bank at a Glance* (Dhaka: Grameen Bank, 2004), p. 16.

7

The Education Loan and a Program for the Poorest

For the last several years, Syman had been earning her living by begging door to door in the village. She had worked as a house-maid for many years, and washing dishes had taken a toll on her hands. Because her hands were infected, she could no longer work as a maid and had to beg instead. She was fifty years old. Even though she had a tough life, she still had her pride. Married off at the age of twelve, she returned to her parents after only one year because her husband abused her. A year later she was married again, this time as a second wife. In this marriage she was mistreated by the first wife, and the ill treatment increased when her husband started to pay more attention to Syman with the birth of her son. Five years later she was blessed with a daughter. Her husband, how-ever, died the same year, and the first wife forced her out of the house. When she returned to her natal home for the second time, she could feed her children only by working as a housemaid. Through hard work and sheer tenacity, she raised the children and was even fortunate enough to get them married. However, her son left her to live with his in-laws within six months of his marriage, and her daughter and son-in-law came to live with her. She thus had to depend for support on the son-in-law, who was a landless laborer.

Destitute women such as Syman, in all likelihood, would not be accepted as members of any microfinance institution. Because of an innovative program for beggars, however, Syman is now a member of Grameen Bank. She owns a small business selling miscellaneous items in the village; the business is funded by an interest-free loan from the bank. Her customers are the same households that she used to visit for handouts.[1]

Microfinance providers in Bangladesh, including Grameen Bank, have been criticized for their failure to include the hardcore poor, such as Syman.[2] The low representation of the very poor in the client base of MFIs has been called "mission drift." After all, the original mission of microfinance institutions was to help the poor irrespective of the intensity of their poverty. Some commentators have suggested that microfinance may not be an appropriate tool to alleviate the poverty of this group. Instead of credit, they believe that the hardcore poor need grants and guaranteed employment to break free. In addition, they need funds not only for investment but also for food and shelter, and they need help in using these funds appropriately so that they can earn income from their investments. The poorest, some argue, may also need such "survival measures" or "protection measures" as voluntary savings facilities and emergency consumption credit facilities, instead of "promotional" measures such as credit for self-employment.[3]

There is no consensus as to who constitutes the hardcore poor. Clearly, the most logical choice is to use some level of income as a cutoff point. Hashemi (1997) defines the hardcore poor as people who live on an income that provides them a daily per-capita intake of 1740 calories, compared with the poverty line figure of 2112 calories, or on a per-capita income of less than 60% of the poverty line.[4] H. Z. Rahman (1998), on the other hand, defines the hardcore poor as people with an average income of 3757 taka per person per year for 1994 and with an average landholding of 15 decimals only. The hardcore poor as defined by Rahman (1998) had an income level 48% below the poverty-level income and consumption of 1800 calories or less.[5] As mentioned in Chapter 2, the World Bank's study defined extreme poverty as income below 80% of the poverty line.

Some researchers recognize the difficulty of separating the hardcore poor from the moderate poor based on income alone. As a result, other indicators, such as possession of minimum clothing and access to safe drinking water and sanitation, have been used to identify the poorest more precisely. Sen and Begum (1998) settled on three indicators: occupation, housing structure, and land ownership. After examining the data based on these characteristics, the two authors concluded that "the prospective poorest clientele would be agricultural laborers residing at *jhupri* or single structure thatch with land owned up to 0.5 acres."[6] The use of this "housing structure" indicator for identifying the hardcore poor was confirmed by Rahman and Razzaque (2000).[7]

The definition used in the World Bank's Voice of the Poor project[8] is a bit more involved. According to this study, the extreme poor are those who (1) do not possess land or a house of their own; (2) are in families that have no income-earning male member; (3) are in families mostly headed by women; (4) meet their food needs by begging; (6) have no access to institutional or noninstitutional credit; (7) have no access to health care facilities and are less informed about illness and treatment; and (8) are excluded by the society as revealed by a lack of invitations to social celebrations.[9] Datta (2004) adds that small children of this group are a burden, whereas adult children are a source of income.

Researchers have tried to identify reasons for the exclusion of the poorest from the programs of MFIs. R. I. Rahman (1998b) explains their exclusion by invoking demand- and supply-side factors.[10] Demand-side factors, she points out, entail self-exclusion by the poorest themselves. The poorest do not have supporting inputs such as land, capital, additional working family members, human capital in the form of education, and knowledge of running a business. As a result, these individuals will receive a low return from using credit in non-farm activities, which, in turn, discourages them from participating in a risky, low-return credit program. Low returns may also discourage the MFIs from providing loans to the poorest, thus acting as a supply-side deterrent as well. This factor, in addition to a lack of specific targeting of the hardcore poor by the NGOs, is a supply-side deterrent that has excluded this group from membership in MFIs.[11] Another supply-side factor that Rahman (1998b) noted is geographical targeting. Because MFIs choose areas with access to better infrastructure, the programs left out the poorest individuals, who tend to live in large numbers in areas that are geographically inaccessible and ecologically vulnerable.[12] Datta (2004) mentions that membership selection criteria such as permanent settlement, residency, and the requirement to save compulsorily also tend to exclude the poorest.

Evans, Adams, and Mohammed (1999), on the other hand, suggest that inherent barriers attributable to microfinance programs, as well as the nature of clients, compel these programs to exclude the hardcore poor. Among program-related barriers, insufficient funds of MFIs preclude programs from including the poorest individuals. Membership requirements, such as regular attendance in group meetings, payment of fees, mandatory savings, and participation in educational and planning activities can also prevent the poorest from receiving credit. Groups themselves might also exclude the poorest as a way to prevent liability. Evans and co-authors (1999) found that groups tend to exclude the poorest women whose husbands are known to have wasted money in gambling (also see Datta 2004) or whose husbands work as migratory laborers. If, as in the latter case, a woman's husband has to leave his resident village during harvest season to look for work, his absence makes it extremely difficult for her to continue the installment payments. In addition, the need to keep the repayment rates high might encourage bank workers to exclude the poorest from membership.

The potential clients or borrowers themselves may also be responsible for their exclusion from membership. Participation in a credit program requires that households possess sufficient time to attend meetings and enough cash reserves for savings. Clients who suffer from perpetual ill health and are vulnerable to repeated crises, both natural and personal—an important identifier of the hardcore poor— might be discouraged from participating in a credit program on the basis that it just might not work for them. In addition, another important subgroup of the poorest, female-headed households, are subject to economic and social discrimination as they may not be able to meet the resource requirements for participation in credit programs. Low levels of education among potential clients might keep them from understanding the benefits of credit and participating effectively within a group setting. Finally, clients may prefer not to borrow because they feel that credit is not in their best interest.[13]

From its inception, Grameen used specific targeting of the poor and gave priority to the poorest of the poor, whom it recognized as needing special attention. Professor Yunus recalls the story of a beggar named Sufia Khaton from the early days of Grameen Bank (this is not the Sufia mentioned in Chapter 2). Because of her low status, no one wanted to include her in their group. Professor Yunus arranged for her to join a group on his personal guarantee, but the experiment ran into a snag: to the annoyance of her fellow group members, she wanted to borrow only 10 taka as a loan, compared with the average loan size of 500–1000 taka at that time.[14] The other members thought she was joking and urged her to borrow at least 100 taka, but she could not imagine borrowing more than 10 taka. After much persuasion, Professor Yunus finally convinced her to borrow 30 taka, which she repaid promptly.[15]

The main objective of Grameen Bank is to alleviate poverty by providing credit and savings facilities for all kinds of poor people. This goal relies, however, on the poor using these resources to earn income through self-employment. Under the classical Grameen model, the first two persons to receive credit had to be the neediest of the group. Grameen's latest training manual for new staff provides an algorithm on how to choose such members. The guidelines clearly suggest that the poorest of the poor should get top priority in receiving bank membership. A recently published guideline suggests that the following be given membership priority:

- Widowed, deserted, and divorced women; beggars; those who receive *jakat* or *fitra*;[16] milk-nurses, messengers and sweepers; and those who live either separately or in the paternal home but whose living conditions (and those of any children) are miserable—for example, living in a home with a leaky roof and not enough protection against rain and wind.
- Those who earn their livelihood by supplying physical labor in other people's houses (e.g., earth diggers, road builders, brick breakers, and similar workers); those whose home has only one room, or a roof made of polythene, or a single or

double tin roof; those who own less than half an acre of land and have very few income-earning members in the household; and those who are unable to meet their basic expenses and are unable to send their children to school, or send their children to work in other people's houses.

- Those whose household has many members, of whom very few are income earners; those from households where the prospective member, his or her spouse, or their children earn their living by working in other people's houses; those unable to send their school-aged children to school for lack of income or lack of resources such as land; and those whose household contains members able to work but unable to earn because of a lack of capital.

- Those whose household includes no males able to work; and those who sleep on the floor or on a bamboo mat or have no furniture other than a bamboo cot, mosquito net, mattress, and quilt.

- Landless women who are involved in productive income-earning work but own no capital and carry on their businesses by borrowing small amounts of money from others.

- Those who must buy their rice all year round to eat; and farmers who must borrow from money lenders to finance their crops and must repay after harvesting.

- Those whose daily income is less than 100 taka or whose monthly income is less than 3000 taka.

- Those who, lacking farmland of their own, farm land that is mortgaged, leased, or sharecropped.

- Those in households whose men are day laborers or van or rickshaw pullers, or whose women maintain their families through petty crafts such as bamboo or cane work, sewing, or needlework, with capital of less than 3000 taka.

One should note that these criteria for groups that should get top priority mirror the defining characteristics of the hardcore poor suggested in the World Bank's Voices of the Poor study.

The hardcore poor, however, are not a monolithic group. They include the ecologically vulnerable, people who have lost everything because of river bank erosion or who live in "char" and inaccessible areas; and the life-cycle vulnerable, the old and the incapacitated, and women who have lost their husbands and are forced to live in destitution.

Despite its good intentions, Grameen missed a portion of the hard-core poor. Hashemi (1997) conducted a survey of four villages to determine the reasons for target group households not joining the credit programs of Grameen Bank and BRAC (Bangladesh Rural Advancement Committee). He reported that the majority of the target group self-selected themselves out of the credit programs. Amin, Rai, and Topa (2003), Fujita (2000), and Ito (1999) also reported that Grameen Bank missed the poorest of the poor in their respective study villages.

These troubling findings prompted many researchers to investigate the reasons for the exclusion. Ito (1999) suggests that the poorest are excluded from the Grameen program because of a perception that they would be unable to service installment payments with their limited earning capabilities. She argues that because of the escalation in loan size, the threshold income necessary to service the loan has gone up; as a result, the poorest with limited income are not included in the program. Moreover, the need to start repayment within a few weeks of the loan requires that the household have an alternative and predictable source of income so that repayment can be financed. This requirement tends to favor the better off among the poor.

Hashemi notes that a majority of his respondents (49%) reported that they did not join the programs "because people felt that they would be unable to pay back the loan money and would therefore be stuck with debt for which they would have to eventually be forced to sell off what little possessions they still had. They refused to be burdened with still another debt."[17] About a quarter of the women in Hashemi's survey did not join because they were afraid that they would be shunned for leaving their homes to meet with males (i.e., the bank workers) who are not related to them in violation of social and religious norms. Thirteen percent of women reported that they were excluded by other members of the group because they were perceived as "high risk" in the sense that they would not be able to repay the loan on time. This result was confirmed by a later survey of the target group (Hashemi and Schuler, 1997): people who were qualified to join the bank but chose not to, and former members who had dropped out of the bank. Hashemi and Schuler (1997) found that their sample consisted of two distinct groups. One group did not have a reliable source of income from which to pay weekly installments. The other consisted of women who were "married to men who were irresponsible and likely to appropriate, or had appropriated, the woman's entire loan without providing the money for weekly installments."[18]

Dipal Barua, the co-author of this book, spearheaded one of the earliest attempts to include the poorest while he was the zonal manager in Patukhali during the early 1980s. At his directive, the branches were required first to include members with landholdings between 0 and 10 decimals. Once the branch had included everyone in that group, staff were allowed to recruit members from the next landholding class (i.e., 10 to 20 decimals). The recruitment was to be stopped when they reached the final threshold of 50 decimals of landholding. The objective ensured that the poorest, measured by land ownership, got top priority in receiving membership in the bank. Another approach that Grameen used to include the poorest of the poor consisted of "share raising" a goat with a vulnerable member, through which the bank would buy a goat for a member to raise. Instead of paying the bank in cash, however, the borrower would repay the bank with two goat litters. In the process, the member would eventually come to own the goat. The idea was to give in-kind credit and ask for repayment in kind from the poor who would not be able to make regular repayments on a standard loan. The goat loan program was based on a system known as *pushon*, which had been widely practiced in rural Bangladesh for centuries.[19]

The bank also developed built-in responses to reduce the tendency of potential members to exclude themselves out of fear that they would not be able to repay the bank during hard times. One plan Grameen has implemented to combat this problem is the provision of in-kind loans as mentioned above. Other options include giving consumption loans during the lean season; leasing out agricultural equipment, such as thrashing machines and treadle pumps; and providing interest-free loans to be repaid over two harvest periods. To meet their subsistence needs, the desperate poor are forced to borrow against their land at a high interest rate, which makes it impossible for them to reclaim the land from the wealthy—a common means of dispossession and pauperization in Bangladesh.[20] Grameen developed a special loan for the poor so that they could release mortgaged-out land from the wealthy. These options were available to local-level staff, enabling the bank to close the "implementation gap"—the difference between public pronouncements about targeting the poorest and the reality in the field. All these measures were designed to help the poorest stay with the bank and take advantage of this narrow window of opportunity to change their economic conditions.

Prior to the introduction of Grameen II, the bank ran two pilot projects for the destitute—one in Arihazar, near the capital city of Dhaka, and another in Melandah, in the Jamalpur district, in the northeast part of the country. Dipal Barua was responsible for running the project in Melandaha. The district of Jamalpur was a prosperous area during the heyday of jute trading. Its weather and topography were most suitable for jute production—water for six months of the year so that the jute could grow, rot, and turn into fiber. But after the collapse of the jute market in the face of competition from cheaper synthetic alternatives, the area fell into economic depression. Jamalpur is also subject to river bank erosion and recurring floods; moreover, its poor soil makes it unsuitable for profitable agriculture. As a result of bad geographical conditions and the fact that it took farmers a long time to switch to alternative crops like rice, the area has a poor economic base.

The objective of the project was twofold: first, to bring the destitute and the vulnerable in the area under the project umbrella and try to improve their quality of life, and second, to see if Grameen Bank or a variation of this model could be developed to meet the needs of the hardcore poor.

The pilot project in Melindah in Jamalpur entailed first preparing a list of the destitute in the area. The list included the following categories of individuals:

- Those who had lost their capital and all sources of income
- Those who had lost their home because of river bank erosion and had no source of income

- Those who did not have a house of their own and lived in someone else's home and earned their livelihood from begging
- Those who were abandoned/widowed/divorced
- Those who were indebted to another bank or institution but did not have the capacity to repay the loan
- Those who could do physical work but did not have anyone to support them (for example, older widows)
- Those who could not manage even two square meals a day and were hungry most of the time
- Those women whose husbands were handicapped and could not earn a livelihood, forcing the women to beg for a living
- Those who had lost everything due to natural disasters such as a storm, tidal wave, or flood and presently had no capital to earn a livelihood
- Those who were orphaned
- Those who were old, could not work, and had no one to help them
- Thieves and petty criminals who lived as social outcasts

Based on these criteria, the project staff prepared a preliminary list of destitutes in the area who were not members of the bank at that point. The staff then determined the true status of the people through further investigation and field visits, eliminating those who did not belong in the list. After a final list was prepared, the project staff compiled a detailed life history of each person, including an economic history of the family, current health conditions, past and present marital status, and the chief factors responsible for the person's current destitution. The history also included information about the nature of houses and the assets owned, such as the amount of land, number of livestock and poultry, types and quantity of furniture, and types of clothing.

After studying the detailed life history of each person on the list, the project officer identified the skills that individual possessed. Further, he asked them how they would use the funds that the bank was willing to provide. Based on this information, the project officer prepared proposals for rehabilitating the destitutes that would utilize their prior work experience in an income-earning project. For example, the officer proposed sanctioning loans to fund a project to make bamboo stools by a destitute who had prior experience in this craft. Further, the proposal included ideas about how to market the products as well as potential problems in implementing the plan. The project initially identified 300 members who qualified and disbursed its first loan in June 1996.

To develop a system targeting only the poorest of the poor, the project staff created diaries on the loanees detailing the changes they experienced after each round of loans. These changes included increased ownership of livestock and poultry; acquisition of utensils, furniture, and bed frames; and an increase in the number of meals.

These diaries and the surveys on the status of the borrowers provided a rich trove of information on the extent and depth of poverty. Asif Dowla, a co-author of this book, created a database documenting the change in the asset base of each borrower after a loan cycle to help provide an understanding of how successive loans lead to asset build-up. During this process, he wanted to lump together the numbers of ducks and chickens owned prior to and after receipt of the loans in one category labeled poultry. The project staff pointedly suggested that such lumping would fail to capture the chronic and systemic nature of the poverty faced by the destitute. The staff person suggested that to capture the depth of poverty a much sharper distinction among the poor is necessary. He pointed out a hardcore poor person will not raise ducks during the dry season because she does not have access to ponds and other water bodies where the duck can scavenge for food such as duckweeds and snails. If her ducks go into a privately owned pond, the owner of the pond will seize them. The hardcore poor, therefore, can raise ducks only during the monsoon season, when low-lying areas are flooded and the ducks can swim at will. Similarly, the hardcore poor would not want to raise pigeons because they cannot afford a coop placed high above the ground to prevent the jackals from eating them. These observations point out clear differences even among the poorest of the poor.

A cursory look at the database reveals characteristics shared by all the hardcore poor identified for the project. The target individual has a large family with few income earners and a meager daily income of 10 to 40 taka, or one-half to one kilogram of rice earned mostly through begging. Many of these poor lease goats to earn some extra income.

On a good day, they are able to eat two meals consisting mostly of rice and lentils supplemented occasionally with roasted red peppers, and they have only one set of clothing such as a *sari* and *lungi* (sewn sarong worn by men). The group includes a high percentage of divorced, widowed, or abandoned women or women whose husbands are handicapped or mentally retarded and are unable to earn a livelihood. All of them borrow from money lenders at 10 to 15 taka interest per month, and all owe a sizable sum to the money lenders. Most of these people are functionally landless. The major reason for their current status is the loss of land to river bank erosion, and rich and powerful people in the village grabbing their land by falsifying land records. In many cases, they have been forced to sell whatever land they had to pay for legal fees or to buy medicine for a family member.

The project staff made a concerted effort to build a separate structure, free from the influence of the Grameen model, because of the recognition that such a structure may be necessary to cater to the special needs of the poorest. For example, under the new program, the loans for the destitute were individual rather than group loans. Also, there was no group tax on the loan, and the borrower could repay the loan early if he or she wished without incurring penalties. The initial loan size was a mere 500 taka, and borrowers were required to save 2 taka per week.[21] All these departures were adopted out of the realization that the very poor need more generous credit terms in order to succeed. Further, the hardcore poor tend to lack self-confidence and are afraid to borrow money. A majority of the first-time loans were used to finance petty trading, paddy husking, poultry raising, and the selling of puffed rice. These activities were safe and would yield a quick return, enabling the borrowers to make repayments on time and in the process boosting their confidence. Moreover, the borrowers were already familiar with these activities and could easily manage their investment, which improved their chances of being successful.

At the end of December 2003 the project had 919 members, most of whom had built a sizable asset base by using several rounds of loans. The rapid build-up of assets and the borrowers' improved living conditions convinced the bank that the destitute had graduated from their lowly status and were ready to join mainstream rural life. Due to the project's overwhelming success, the bank has recently converted it to a regular branch of Grameen Bank.

In the current restructuring of Grameen, the bank revisited these earlier experiences in helping the hardcore poor. As an alternative to the somewhat involved process of identifying and helping every type of destitute, the bank has narrowed its focus to beggars only. Under all feasible criteria, the beggars are really the poorest of the poor, and under Grameen II the bank has developed a special program for them. The objective of the program is to ensure that there will be no beggars in Grameen II's area of operation. This is the first program of its kind, targeting the disabled, the old, and the infirm— the poorest even among the hardcore poor. Hulme and Mosley (1996) suggest that MFIs have stayed away from this group since the success of their ventures depends on the use of self-employment in low-demand, high-competition markets for goods and services.[22]

In the program for beggars, the branch is required to make a list of the beggars in its area and develop ideas to help them to quit begging. Each staff member initially takes responsibility for one beggar, and gradually the number of beggars under his or her management is increased. The beggar member is exempt from Grameen rules: he or she does not have to belong to a group, save, attend meetings, or make regular repayments, and the members can make up their own rules. Also, the average loan size is between 500 and 1000 taka, compared with the current average loan size of 5490 taka for regular bank members. Hardcore poor members do not have to pay any installments, and there is no time limit on repayment. More important, the loans are interest-free; in addition, the borrowers can choose the installments and duration of the loan. These members can also borrow the amount repaid in the first thirteen weeks of the loan, instead of the twenty-six weeks used for regular members.

Most of the hardcore poor members are quite old and do not want to assume debt at this stage of their lives. To allay their fear of dying in debt, the bank covers their loans for free under the loan insurance program and their family members will receive a one-time allotment of 500 taka in death benefits. Interest-free loans are also given to these members to buy quilts, mosquito nets, and umbrellas, and the members are required to pay only 2 taka per week as installments to pay off these loans. As mentioned earlier, the objective of all these departures from the classical Grameen model, as well as the inclusion of such popular initiatives under Grameen II as loan insurance and death benefits, is to ease the beggars' burden and build their confidence. This will be the first time in their lives that many of them have the chance to use an umbrella, a mosquito net, or a quilt. The powerful experience of sleeping under a mosquito net for the first time is captured by an unusual request by a struggling member, Afilatunnessa: her wish was that she be given her last bath under the net.[23]

The most popular activity for beggar members is to carry a collection of popular consumer items with them wherever they go. These items, such as snacks, sweets, and cosmetics, are bought with loans from the bank, and members can sell these items at their convenience. Others have used the money to make and sell cane furniture; to buy goats, sheep, or poultry; and to start a business selling dried fish. Each member receives an identity badge with her picture, name, and the Grameen Bank logo. She displays the badge as she goes about her daily life, publicizing that she is a member of the bank and that this powerful national institution stands besides her. While the beggar member is not required to give up begging, she is encouraged to take up an income-generating activity so that she can quit begging when her daily income increases. The members are strictly forbidden, however, from repaying the bank with income from begging. Presently, most of the loans have a maximum of 2000 taka with an average installment of 20 to 30 taka per week. In some cases, however, the member can get goods worth 2000 taka on credit from the local grocery shop with a guarantee from the bank. This is especially useful for members who cannot count and find it difficult to keep track of their purchases and amounts due.

To ensure that the program is working to its potential, Grameen staff members are encouraged to come up with innovative means of incorporating the beggars into the bank's structures. Regular bank group members are encouraged to help the bank identify the destitutes in their village and to become mentors to these individuals. The group chair acts as a liaison between hardcore poor members and the bank, maintaining regular contact with them. A bank worker is assigned to each beggar member and meets with her regularly to help her find additional sources of income. The group and the center are also responsible for helping these members find alternative sources of income. This reliance on one another within the banking system creates a sense of ownership for the program among the regular members of the bank. The involvement of members, in addition to bank workers, in implementing the project builds the confidence of the beggar member and helps ease the transition from begging to petty trading. The most important role, however, is played by the bank workers in charge of the beggar. Their job is to assure the beggars that they can run the business and to help them do so.

There are other means used to rehabilitate beggars besides disbursing loans and helping them become petty traders. For instance, the bank has started leasing mobile phones to the beggars. This enables the beggars to sell roving phone services for cash—a good fit with the mobility of the beggar. The bank may also buy raw materials that the beggar can use to produce something the bank could then sell on her behalf—a put-out system. Another possibility is to start a piece-rate project with the beggar as the partner. In such a project, the bank acts as a venture capitalist as well as a business development and marketing agency for the goods produced. The bank could buy a milch cow that the beggar could raise. The beggar would then share part of the income from selling milk, and the bank would help him or her find buyer for the milk. Table 7.1 reports the current status of the beggar member program.

The biggest hurdle currently facing the program is self-doubt on the part of the beggars. It is hard to convince them that they can change their lives by using credit from the bank. This is the problem of self-exclusion mentioned in the literature on the hardcore poor. Anthropologist Arjun Appadurai argues that aspirations about the good life exist in all societies. However, the capacity to aspire is unevenly distributed; the rich are more aware of the various manifestations of the good life, which they use to improve their material conditions:

Table 7.1   Current Status of the Beggar Program (Cumulative to December 2005)

Zones	Number of Branches Implementing the Program	Number of Members	Full Membership in the Bank	Current Number of Members	Amount of Loans Disbursed (Hundred Thousand Taka)
Rangpur	95	4,367	80	4,126	24.68
Narayngang	81	7,106	26	6,984	49.39
Bogra	73	1,915	8	1,874	20.12
Khulna	85	2,553	17	2,511	13.36
Patuakhali	71	2,464	7	2,419	17.61
Chittagong	86	2,131	57	2,001	22.78
Mymensingh	70	3,735	6	3,662	29.55
Dhaka	80	6,907	106	5,173	31.33
Noakhali	89	6,709	33	6,646	38.27
Comilla	85	5,635	52	5,483	34.48
Rajshahi	101	2,063	2	2,018	15.73
Tangail	72	2,338	2	2,018	15.73
Dinajpur	71	2,429	0	2,402	17.22
Nilfamari	54	3,937	57	3,799	27.55
Faridpur	85	2,809	12	2,730	14.85
Sylhet	65	1,621	29	1,551	10.32
Jamalpur	54	1,875	9	1,840	10.61
Habiganj	44	1,280	14	1,251	8.49
Pabna	56	1,670	8	1,640	10.41
Barisal	76	1,313	12	1,280	9.04
Jinaidah	71	1,350	4	1,324	10.24
Total	1,564	66,207	548	62,988	435.18

If the map of aspirations . . . is seen to consist of a dense combination of nodes and pathways, relative poverty means a smaller number of aspirational nodes and a thinner, weaker sense of the pathways from concrete wants to intermediate contexts to general norms and back again. Where these pathways do exist for the poor, they are likely to be more rigid, less supple, and less strategically valuable, not because of any cognitive deficit on the part of the poor but because the capacity to aspire, like any complex cultural capacity, thrives and survives on practice, repetition, exploration, conjecture, and refutation.[24]

Appadurai adds that "empowerment has an obvious translation: increase the capacity to aspire, especially for the poor."[25] Staff and members of regular groups are recruited to build the beggars' confidence, and members who have done well in the regular program act as examples of the good life and prosperity that can be achieved by being a member of the bank—as an "aspirational node" (see Box 7.1).

In a similar vain, Nobel Laureate Rabindranath Tagore explored how a lack of confidence perpetuates poverty:

The poor are greater in number than the rich in all countries. If this is so, then which country should be especially categorized as . . . poor? The answer to this question is that the country in which the poor have no opportunities to become rich through earnings is poor. In a country where the poor too have enough confidence in themselves, this is reckoned to be a great resource. It is not enough to say that we do not have enough money. The real thing is that we do not have enough confidence in ourselves. What is needed most, is, therefore, instilling confidence in people's mind and not providing them with begging bowls. . . . When we were very young, we used to be fearful of ghosts. In reality the fear of ghost[s] is nothing but weakness in oneself. . . . The fear of poverty is [like] the fear of ghost[s]. We can get rid of this fear if we can come together.[26]

Thus far our discussion has focused on a specific program targeted to include those living in truly wretched circumstances within the bank's program. The flexible conditions for loan products as well as the generous terms for savings withdrawals under Grameen II have the potential

Box 7.1 Self-Reliant Sabur Ali

Sabur Ali was one of eight children. His parents had very little land, and the family used to depend on the income from his mother's trading business. His sisters got married and went on to live with their husbands. Since his mother was always away on business and his father could not cook, the family needed someone to cook for them. Sabur Ali married while only 16 so that his wife could cook for the family. Soon they had a baby daughter, and in the meantime, he started his own trading business. When his daughter was only three years old, his wife contracted tuberculosis. He used up his capital from the business to pay for his wife's health care. She died anyway, and his daughter contracted typhoid after his wife's death. To save her, he used up what capital he had left to pay doctor fees. He lost his only daughter and then his parents to other diseases.

With no family for support, he was alone, and a powerful neighbor took advantage of his vulnerability and took over his land. He did not have any money to hire a lawyer, and even if he did, he probably would have lost it in paying for one. After losing his land, the only asset he had, Sabur left his village heartbroken and joined his sister's family in a neighboring village. His sister found him a wife, but the marriage lasted for only two weeks. In the meantime, he accumulated a huge debt in his business and was forced to abandon it. After all of these successive personal tragedies, he gave up on life and began visiting the mausoleums of Sufi saints in the country and in India. In between his trips to the mausoleums, he lived in his sister's grandson's porch on a makeshift bed and earned his livelihood by begging. He bought the bed and a mosquito net from the proceeds of his begging. He could earn 20–30 taka daily by begging, and he used the money to buy food, which was prepared by his granddaughter.

One day a motorbike hit him from behind and he lost several teeth. Because of old age and the many tragedies he faced, he became bitter and quite despondent. His luck changed when he met the bank workers, who urged him to become a struggling (beggar) member of the bank. He received an interest-free loan of 1000 taka, which he has since used to buy goods for his trading business. Now he roams the village and sells condiments and female accessories. He makes 30–40 taka a day from his trading business and begging, and pays only a 20-taka installment per week. At the twilight of his life, now at age 70, Sabur Ali has finally become self-reliant and finds that life has a lot to offer him.

to attract the hardcore poor to join and stay with the bank. As mentioned earlier, a common refrain of the hardcore poor who opt out of the program is that they will not be able to pay the installments regularly. Under classical Grameen, their only recourse in such situations was to drop out of the bank. Group responsibility was also a hindrance to the inclusion of the poorest, because regular borrowers did not want to include such persons in their group. Under Grameen II, a regular borrower having trouble paying installments regularly can take the temporary option of switching to a flexible loan and choosing an installment schedule consistent with her ability to repay. Unrestricted access to personal savings also helps to ameliorate repayment problems.

The inability of the hardcore poor to make regular installment payments is a reflection of their vulnerable position. They simply do not have the income necessary to maintain fixed repayment schedules. In many cases, a repayment problem is caused by illness in the family, especially the husband, and the need to pay for treatment instead of repaying a loan. Disdain from the group is also mentioned as a cause of dropout by the poorer members.[27] Grameen II attempted to minimize these problems by allowing the poorest of the poor to have individual loans and to choose their own repayment schedules along with the possibility of variable installments. Moreover, as mentioned earlier, in extreme cases of repayment problems, borrowers have the option to switch to a flexible loan instead of dropping out. This allows them extra time to get their finances in order.[28]

A large number of members drop out because they feel that they do not need the money from the bank anymore for a number of reasons, mostly related to improvement in their economic condition. Rutherford (2004) has labeled these borrowers "retirees." These members dropping out also gives the bank a chance to replace them with new members who are poor, which is the official policy of the bank. Strict adherence to the official policy of giving priority to the most vulnerable members, like widows and landless laborers, while excluding the better off, should allow the bank to replace retirees with the truly destitute.

From its inception, Grameen Bank has always encouraged its members to send their children to school. Grameen's original focus on female membership was due to the staff's realization that to make a fundamental change in the lives of the poor, credit must be channeled to the women.[29] A fact borne out empirically in Bangladesh, as well as many other parts of the world, is that when women have financial resources, they use them primarily for the welfare of their family. Within the family, significant additional financial resources are used for the children, especially to pay for school fees and educational supplies.

This emphasis on the importance of children's education was later codified by the borrowers into the Sixteen Decisions—the social charter adopted by the members in 1984. Decision 7 states, "We shall educate our children and ensure that they can earn to pay for their education." Bank workers remind borrowers of these pledges in the regular center meetings and encourage borrowers to send their children to school.

During its earlier days, the bank promoted children's education by helping to establish schools in the centers. A borrower who had taken more than one loan from the bank was required to contribute 1 taka per week to the Children's Welfare Fund, which was used to build a schoolroom in the center house, to pay a teacher, or to buy textbooks at cost from the bank. The teachers were members' children and local youths. Instruction in reading, writing, arithmetic, and forms of physical and creative expression were provided in center houses in the mornings and evenings. The bank worker helped the members set up these schools and hire the teachers. The bank also distributed free textbooks received from UNICEF. In 1990, around 4000 such schools were managed by the centers.[30] However, with the rapid expansion of government schools in the rural areas and with parents opting to send their children to these schools, the center schools eventually became unnecessary.

Anecdotal evidence suggests that increased income from the use of credit is used for children's education, and that access to credit has increased the demand for children's education. Theoretical analysis suggests, however, that increased credit may have an ambiguous effect on children's schooling. This ambiguity occurs because children are both consumption and production goods: the family derives satisfaction from having children and benefits from their use in family enterprises. An increase in income due to credit, then, will lead to higher demand for education of the children, or what theoreticians call "income effects." Credit that facilitates owning and using more capital, however, could increase the productivity of children's work, thereby making it too costly to send them to school instead of using them in a family enterprise. This is known as the "substitution effect." However, the higher income made possible by the increased productivity of children will increase the income of the household in the long run. This chance at long-term wealth induces borrowers to raise more and better-educated children.

Because credit directly increases the income and wealth of the recipient, it can also increase the demand for children. In addition, many MFIs, including Grameen Bank, provide non-credit services or social intermediation, such as vocational training, organizational help, and social development instruction aimed at improving health, literacy, leadership skills, and social empowerment.[31] Chase (1997) suggests that these non-credit services could also lead to higher demand for children's education by increasing its perceived benefit.

Wydick (1999) identifies two effects of microcredit on children's education. He labels the first one the "family-labor substitution effect." Wydick suggests that credit, through the increased use of capital, could increase the productivity of family labor and, as a result, increase the cost of sending the children to school. This echoes the "substitution effect" mentioned previously. He calls the other effect the "household-enterprise-capitalization effect." In this case, an increase in credit may lead the family to substitute hired labor for child labor if the credit relaxes the constraint on working capital needs. Using data from Guatemala, Wydick found that the relationship between access to credit and schooling is not unequivocally positive.

Maldanado, González-Vega, and Romero (2003) identify several more routes through which credit might affect schooling.[32] Research shows that when households face interruptions to their income due to crisis, they tend to take their children out of school as part of a coping mechanism.[33] By providing access to regular and emergency loans and promoting the build-up of income-earning assets, Maldanado and co-authors believe that the use of credit from the MFIs makes it less likely that children will be withdrawn from school in response to adverse shocks. They call this the "risk-management effect." These researchers point out that additional activities made possible through credit may also increase the demand for child labor. This is similar to Wydick's "family-labor substitution effect."[34] The empirical exercise of Maldanado and co-authors, however, shows that credit from MFIs increases children's schooling, mainly through income and risk management channels.

This research team also points out that, compared with men, women show a greater desire to educate their children. MFIs' specific targeting of women for delivery of credit will help increase their power to influence household schooling decisions. The improved bargaining position and empowerment of women, these researchers believe, will increase the schooling of children, an outcome they term "gender effect." In the context of Bangladesh, a different gender-associated effect is also pertinent. An increase in credit-related activities causes the female to reduce the time spent on household chores—slack which must be picked up by the children, most likely the female child, thereby reducing her schooling.[35]

This brief survey of theoretical results suggests that credit can have an ambiguous effect on the education of children. To find the truth among the various theories regarding the credit-education relationship, researchers have tried to verify empirically if credit from Grameen Bank increases the likelihood of borrowers' children enrolling in school. Although her results were based on a very limited sample, Todd (1996) found that 100% of the female children of Grameen borrowers had some schooling, compared with only 60% of girls in the control group—households that would qualify for a loan from the bank but chose not to participate. In the case of boys, Todd found that the participation rate was 80% for borrowers compared with 62% for non-borrowers. She then used a more accurate measure of schooling: the number of years of schooling annually completed by each child as a percentage of the number of years he or she should have completed, given the child's age. This measure is an attempt to capture the true effect of credit on schooling. Once again, the Grameen borrowers came out ahead: 62% of possible school years completed, compared with 44% for the control group children. Todd suggests that girls are receiving more schooling than boys because "boys can earn cash income for their families as young as eight years old." Such a simple comparison between the borrowers and the control group and the use of a small sample make the results, however, subject to the many biases mentioned earlier.

The World Bank study corrected for these biases by using a better methodology: a larger sample size chosen scientifically to control for various biases mentioned in Chapter 2. It found that a 1% increase in credit to women by Grameen Bank increased the probability of a girl's school enrollment by 1.86%. However, similar increases in credit to men did not affect a girl's enrollment. The response for boy's schooling, however, was much higher: a 1% increase in credit provided to women and men increased the probability of boy's schooling by 2.4% and 2.8%, respectively. This suggests that there is a strong preference for boy's schooling among Grameen Bank members, despite attempts to increase member awareness of the benefits of female children. Pitt and Khandker (1998) suggest that the reason for this may be that a girl's activities form a close substitute for a woman's activities. It is the female child who assumes the mother's household responsibilities when the mother becomes involved in a self-employment project.[36]

Using the same data set with a slightly different estimation technique and a different measure for educational attainment, however, Jessica Chase (1997) was able to replicate Pitt and Khandker's results for boys' school enrollment.[37] She found that boys in Grameen families have a higher probability of school enrollment as well as greater levels of educational attainment. Unlike Pitt and Khandker (1998), she did not examine how credit to men and women affect the schooling of boys and girls. Nor did she find any evidence of an effect of Grameen membership on girls' schooling. Rather, Chase (1997) found that credit had a neutral effect on the schooling of girls: neither the demand for more education nor the demand for more household labor had an effect on Grameen girls' school attendance. She suggests that the different impacts on male and female children of Grameen's credit may involve circumstances beyond the bank's control. If given an opportunity to educate one child and keep one at home, Chase believes, the family may choose educating the boy over the girl because the family is more likely to reap the benefits of investment in a boy's education. The family may perceive that the return on educating a male child is higher than that for a female child. One of Todd's respondents noted that "daughters need some education, but not too much. If we spend a lot of taka on the daughter's education there is no return to us, she will take it all to another household."[38] The same sentiments were captured by a survey conducted by Chase to identify the reasons for a lack of current enrollment in school: 8% of boys in the sample mentioned that "parents did not want" them to have an education, compared with 27% of girls citing this reason.

We should point out that these studies were based on a survey conducted in the early 1990s. In the last decade and a half, the country as a whole has made a remarkable turnaround in female school enrollment. In 1991 only 20% of Bangladeshi females could read and write, making them among the least educated females in the world. Today more than 50% of females in the country are enrolled in school, which matches the 50% of males enrolled. Bangladesh is one of the few countries in the developing world that has achieved this degree of parity across gender lines. By the end of the twentieth century, the gross enrollment rate in primary education was over 100%, and the gender gap in education at the primary level had been eliminated.[39] Similar improvements occurred in secondary schools. Since 1994 the enrollment of girls in secondary school has increased at a rate of 13% per year, while boys' enrollment has increased by 2.5% per year.[40] This success is largely attributable to several incentive programs implemented by the Bangladesh government to redress gender inequity in enrollment.

An earlier project was the food for education (FFE) program, introduced in 1993. This program was meant to replace the *palli* (rural) food rationing system, of which 70% of the beneficiaries were not poor even though the program was meant for the poor. To remedy this misuse of resources, the government replaced the ration system with the FFE program, in which landless and very poor families were rewarded with allocations of rice or wheat for sending their children to school. This program involved a two-step targeting mechanism. First, two or three unions from an economically backward, low-literacy area were targeted for each of the 460 rural *thanas*. Within each union, households that met at least one the following conditions were selected to receive FFE benefits:

- A landless or near-landless household that owns less than half an acre of land
- The household head's principal occupation is day laborer

- The head of the household is a female (widowed, separated from husband, divorced, or with a disabled husband)
- The household earns its living from low-income professions (e.g., fishing, pottery, weaving, blacksmithing, cobbling)

Once a household was selected to participate in the FFE program, it was entitled to a free ration of up to 20 kilograms of wheat or 16 kilograms of rice per month in exchange for sending its children to a primary school. If a household had only one primary school–age child (six to ten years old) who attended school, that household was entitled to receive 15 kilograms of wheat or 12 kilograms of rice per month. To be eligible for 20 kilograms of wheat or 16 kilograms of rice, a household was required to send more than one child and all of its primary school–age children to school. To maintain the family's eligibility, children had to attend 85% of total classes in a month. To maximize this educational encouragement, the program was implemented in 1255 unions covering 27% of the country.

Evaluation by the International Food Policy Research Institute (IFPRI) suggests that the program was indeed successful in increasing primary school enrollment, especially for girls, and in promoting school attendance and reducing dropout rates. However, the study also found that the quality of education in FFE schools suffered because of the increased enrollment.[41] Research at the World Bank reports that the program was not cost-effective and suffered from high levels of leakage: it cost 1.59 taka to transfer 1 taka in benefits, and the benefits accrued to the non-poor.[42] As a result, the government replaced the transfer in kind with a cash stipend program known as the Primary School Stipend Program. Students in the FFE program were enrolled in this program automatically. The program now includes an additional 40% of poorest students and it gives a stipend of 100 taka per month to qualified students.

Another program aimed at increasing the education of children, and especially at promoting gender equality in enrollment, is the Secondary School Scholarship Program. This program is different from FFE and it is geared toward female students at the secondary level. Female students participating in this program receive a stipend and tuition subsidy to defray the cost of their education. To receive the transfer, the student has to maintain a 75% attendance rate, receive a score of at least 45% on school tests, and remain unmarried. Various reports suggest that the program has been successful in attaining its objective of increased enrollment for girls (Khandker, Pitt, and Fuwa, 2003; Arends-Kuenning and Amin, 2000).

Again, the bank has always encouraged borrowers to send their children to school. In 2000, to identify the enrollment status of the borrowers' children, the bank conducted a survey of the members' households. Table 7.2 reports the results of the survey. The table shows that a total of 2.23 million children, about 46% of them female, attended school at that time. A large number of them (82,429) were studying at a higher secondary level and another 23,220 were pursuing post-secondary education. However, compared with the boys, female children were lagging in school enrollment.

To directly encourage the borrowers' children to get an education, Grameen Bank started a monthly scholarship program in 1999. Children of borrowers who have been members for more than a year, own a share of the bank, and have made all of their installment payments in the preceding year qualify for such awards. As shown in the following table, there are five types of scholarship based on varying criteria: a primary scholarship for performance on a fifth-grade test, a lower-middle scholarship based on an eighth-grade test score, a middle scholarship based on a regional-level secondary school certificate test score, an

Category of Scholarship	Branch-Level Award (Tk)	Area-Level Award (Tk)	Zonal Award (Tk)	Head Office Award (Tk)
Primary	50	75	100	500
Lower middle	75	100	125	500
Middle	100	150	200	500
Upper middle	125	200	250	500
Cultural	125	200	250	500

Table 7.2   Results of Survey on the Status of Borrowers' Children's Education, 2000*

Level	Male	Female	Total	Percentage Female
Grades 1–5	611,834	535,623	1,147,457	47
Grades 6–8	260,004	232,830	492,834	47
Grades 9–10	140,076	121,777	261853	47
Higher secondary (grades 11–12)	48,136	34,293	82,429	42
Bachelor's	12,271	5,649	17,920	32
Bachelor's with honors	2,702	989	3,691	27
Bachelor's in Engineering	162	15	177	8
Medicine	126	24	150	16
Postgraduate	910	371	1,281	29

*Ignores students who were waiting to be admitted in higher secondary and post–higher secondary programs.

upper-middle scholarship based on a regional-level higher secondary school certificate test score, and a cultural scholarship for excellence in extracurricular activities such as sports, community service, music, acting, poetry recitation, dancing, and essay writing. More than one scholarship is granted for each of these categories at the various levels of the bank: branch, area, zone, and the head office.

Half of these scholarships are reserved for female students; the rest are awarded based on an open competition between male and female students. This preferential treatment of female children is consistent with the targeting of women as members and the goal of promoting education for girls. It is also consistent with government policies, such as the exclusive targeting of female students for scholarships in secondary schools and the quota of one-third of the seats in local government going to females, in addition to allowing them to compete for open seats.

Numerous studies, based on data from countries at different levels of development, suggest the benefits of educating girls. The consensus as to the "win-win" nature of these benefits is so overwhelming that the authors of a background paper for the World Bank's World

Development Report titled it "Girls' Education Is *It*–Nothing Else Matters (Much)."[43] In addition to private benefits such as higher wages and greater return on investments, society as a whole benefits from educating girls. Research at the influential Council on Foreign Relations suggests that educating girls reduces fertility and family size, improves the health of the children and reduces child mortality, increases the likelihood of children attending schools, and empowers women in the family and in society.[44]

Ideally, both girls and boys should be encouraged to attend school. However, when resources are limited, using these resources to educate girls is more efficient due to the higher social return on educating females. Moreover, such a program allows society to redress long-standing biases against women. In the context of Bangladesh, subsidizing girl's education will also redress the issue of unequal access to education. Nath (1997) shows that school enrollment of children increases with an increase in land ownership. He reports that an increase in enrollment related to land ownership is more pronounced for boys than for girls, as boys of households with more than 200 decimals of land are 130% more likely to enroll in school, compared with only 56% of girls.[45] Nath further found that girls in all social groups, except for that of educated mothers, are less likely to enroll in school.

Unlike the government's Secondary School Scholarship Program, however, the bank's scholarship program also rewards male students. Many people feel that the government program's exclusion of male children is unfair, especially to poor households who have to bear the expenses to send their children to school. Research suggests that the secondary scholarship program has exacerbated the problem of child labor among boys. With the use of annual data and a more sophisticated methodology, Khandker, Pitt, and Fuwa (2003) found that the secondary scholarship program for girls actually reduces the enrollment of boys in coeducational schools.[46] These same researchers found that the Food for Education program, which was directed at both boys and girls, reduced the incidence of child labor.[47] These results suggest that Grameen's objective of including both male and female children in the scholarship program is well founded.

Table 7.3   Scores of Borrowers' Children Taking the SSC and HSC Examinations*

GPA	SSC-2004	HSC-2004	SSC-2005	HSC-2005
5.00	111 (4)	47 (0)	481	158
4.00–4.99	1,001 (524)	610 (129)	2,199	1,509
3.50–3.99	992 (1,035)	777 (329)	3,045	2,280
3.00–3.49	1,238 (1,122)	958 (577)	3,589	2,649
2.00–2.99	1,619 (1,532)	1,258 (753)	3,264	2,272
1.00–1.99	665 (413)	284 (167)	1,198	847
Total	5,626 (4,630)	3,934 (1,955)	13,776	9,715

*Numbers in parentheses are the results from 2003.

The performance of borrowers' children in nationwide tests suggests that the scholarship program is making a difference. Table 7.3 reports the performance of borrower's children in the Secondary School Certificate and Higher Secondary School Certificate examinations in 2003–2005.

In the absence of rigorous scientific evidence—for example, controlling for other factors such as student and teacher attendance, study habits, and family environment—it is difficult to associate the scholarship program with the success of students on these tests. However, we might be able to extrapolate the effect of the program by using the evaluation of a similar program in Kenya. A Dutch NGO chose schools randomly and gave scholarships to girls excelling in the sixth-grade exams. Economists Michael Kremer, Ed Miguel, and Rebecca Thornton evaluated the effectiveness of the program and found that having girls compete for the scholarships led to major improvement in test scores.[48] They found that the program also improved the test scores of students who did not qualify for the scholarships: boys who were ineligible for awards and girls with low test scores who were unlikely to win them. This result suggests that the incentive to learn had a spillover effect; that is, it improved the efforts even of students who did not qualify for the scholarship.

Grameen Bank is now more than twenty-five years old. The first generations of borrowers are close to retirement age, and many of their children are entering university. From the very beginning, the bank has been committed to making qualitative changes in the lives of its borrowers—a commitment it continues to fulfill by encouraging borrowers to educate their children and helping them to do so. In addition to the scholarship, another avenue through which the bank is helping to improve children's education is by providing additional sources for paying for their schooling, especially at the undergraduate and graduate levels.

The bank's internal survey shows that significant numbers of the borrowers' children are, in fact, attending school. Despite the significant progress in enrollment, however, the survey also reveals that there was a dramatic drop in enrollment in post–higher secondary education programs in the year 2000. There was also a much greater drop in the enrollment of female students after higher secondary education, due mainly to the cultural prerogative that females should be married and raising a family by a certain age (see Box 7.2). Despite the bank's efforts and the value attached to higher education in the society as a whole, cost is an impediment to children's continued education. When borrowers are queried about their dreams for their children, a common

Box 7.2   Nurjahan's Dream

Nurjahan, like most Grameen borrowers' children, was born into poverty. Her father is a teacher in the religious school, and the family's only asset is 0.4 decimal of homestead land. Her mother is a member of the bank and earns her living working as a tailor, a livelihood made possible by a loan from the bank. Nurjahan and all of her siblings are going to school; economic hardship could not undermine their desire to learn.

Nurjahan has been an excellent student all along. She received merit scholarships from the government for excelling in regional-level examinations at the primary and junior levels. Despite her academic feats, however, her parents could not afford to pay for her continued education; when she was in the ninth grade, they married her off. She was divorced within four months of the marriage because her father could not pay the agreed-upon dowry. Nurjahan earned the cost of her own education by working as a tutor, and in 1995 and 1997 she passed the Secondary School and Higher Secondary School Certificate examinations, respectively, with flying colors. Every month while she was studying medicine she paid the 2000 taka for her educational expenses with a contribution from her parents and a higher education loan from the bank.

Nurjahan is now a practicing physician. She is repaying her loan at the rate of 2000 taka per month. She wants to repay the loan quickly so that the money can be used by others less fortunate than her.

response is that they hope their children will not be members of Grameen Bank. Even though such a response seems paradoxical, there is a valid rationale for it. Grameen Bank is a bank for poor people, and like all good parents, borrowers do not want their children to be poor as adults.[49] The majority of borrowers hope that their children will become educated and join government service, become successful businessmen, or get involved in another respectable occupation (Rahman et al., 2002).[50] These rising aspirations for children's education and future is fairly widespread among all classes in the country (Hossain and Kabeer, 2004). It is the hope of the bank's leaders that when they retire, borrowers' children will take the helm of the bank.[51] However, to achieve this dream, the bank and the borrowers will have to find a way to cover the cost of a proper education for the children.

The high cost of education beyond the post-secondary level is cited in the 2000 internal survey as one of the top reasons for the drop in school enrollment of borrowers' children.[52] Even though primary education is free, families end up paying hidden fees or bribes to teachers for these so-called free services (Tietjen, 2003). Moreover, the schools face serious problems with absentee teachers and poor-quality instruction.[53] As a result, families that can afford the costs end up using private tutoring, which adds to the overall price of education. According to Education Watch 2001, the average annual expenditure per primary pupil by household (i.e., private cost) is 82 taka per month or about 1000 taka per year.[54] The private cost of education increases at a growing rate with the level of education. The cost of post-secondary education increases rapidly because of the student's need to leave home, stay in a dormitory, and pay for room and board.

To ease the burden of the cost of university-level education, in 1997 the bank introduced an education loan for the children of borrowers. Even though the education loan was not part of Grameen II, it was instrumental in getting many of the borrowers back to the centers after the repayment problem in original Grameen. Unlike the situation in wealthier countries, where the government provides such loans, Grameen Bank— a member-owned institution—decided to provide these loans to finance higher education for the children of its members. All children of borrowers who are on a basic or flexible loan and have been members of the bank for at least a year are eligible to receive such loans.[55]

The loan finances all costs of higher education, from admission to a course to the successful completion of that course: admission fees, education supplies, tuition, room and board, and so on. The loan is given to students pursuing graduate or postgraduate degrees and for professional education in medicine, engineering, agriculture, and teaching, in both public and private institutions. Students who qualify through admission tests to enter university and professional programs such as medicine, engineering, agriculture, and teacher training are eligible for higher education loans. The amount of the loan depends on the nature of the course and its duration. Table 7.4 shows the loan amounts for various courses. Table 7.5 provides the breakdown of annual costs for some representative courses.

This cost schedule applies only in the case of a public institution. Although private universities are much more expensive, the bank is still willing to pay for such an education if the private university agrees to exempt 25–50% of the expenses. Once a student provides such assurance from a private university, the bank will finance the rest of the expenses. The specified cost schedule assumes that the course will run and finish on schedule. In the case of a schedule delay of six months, the zonal manager can increase the amount of the loan to pay for the added expenses of room, board, and educational supplies. Increases in the loan necessitated by a schedule delay of more than six months must be approved by the Coordination and Operation Department at the head office.[56]

Table 7.4   Loan Amounts for Various Types of Courses

Type of Course	Duration, in Years	Loan Amount
MBBS (medicine)	5	105,000 taka
BDS (dentistry)	4	84,000 taka
Engineering	4	75,000 taka
BA (honors), B.Ag., and BBA	4	77,000 taka
Postgraduate (M.Ag. and MBA)	2	38,000 taka

Table 7.5   Breakdown of Annual Costs for Some Representative Courses

Year	Admission, Tuition, Supplies, and Other Costs	Room and Board	Total (Budget)
	MBBS (Medicine)		
1	15,000	16,000	31,000
2	–	16,000	16,000
3	10,000	16,000	26,000
4	–	16,000	16,000
5	–	16,000	16,000
Total	25,000	80,000	105,000
	BA (Honors), B.Ag., and BBA		
1	4,000	16,000	20,000
2	3,000	16,000	19,000
3	3,000	16,000	19,000
4	3,000	16,000	19,000
Total	13,000	64,000	77,000
	Master's, Including M.Ag. and MBA		
1	3,000	16,000	19,000
2	3,000	16,000	19,000
Total	6,000	32,000	38,000

Once the loan is approved, the amount is transferred to a current account owned jointly by the borrower and the student. The student can withdraw the amount allocated for tuition and other fees at the beginning of each year, and the yearly funding for room and board will be transferred on a quarterly basis. The area manager examines the progress report of the student and, upon satisfaction, approves the transfer of funds for the next year's education. During the course of study, no interest is charged on the loan. After a month of the student's receipt of the final approved installment amount of the loan, a

5% service charge is added to the outstanding amount from that day onward. A year after the successful completion of the course, the student begins repaying the loan through monthly installments that include a principal amount plus the service charge. The monthly installment amount is determined in consultation with the student.

The student must pay back the loan over the number of years for which the loan was approved; a student must, for instance, pay off a five-year loan plus the service charge for a medical degree in five years. The student can, however, repay the loan earlier than the scheduled time by paying higher installments. They do not have to pay a service charge if they can repay the entire loan amount before the start of installment payments. Table 7.6 reports the status (as of December 2005) of the education loan.

A 5% interest rate is less than the commercial rate and the rate charged on a typical loan from Grameen Bank. This low interest rate thus amounts to a subsidy from the bank to the borrowers, because the alternative cost is a lot higher. The bank is willing to subsidize the higher education of the borrowers' children because it will fulfill their lifelong dreams to see their children become educated so that they will not have to become members of the bank (see Box 7.3). In return, the borrowers will be loyal to the bank and feel that they are being rewarded for their ownership of the bank. In addition to loans for higher education, the bank extends "coaching loans" for preparatory courses so that students can score high on the admission test and thus get admitted into an undergraduate program in a university. Borrowers' children who have attained a minimum GPA of 4.0 in both Secondary School and Higher Secondary School Certificate examinations qualify for such a loan. The loan can be used only toward the fees for such courses; students have to arrange their own funding for room and board. A service charge of 5% is applied to the loan amount from the day it is sanctioned. If a student is successful in achieving admission into an undergraduate program and wants a higher education loan, the coaching loan will be added to the higher education loan. Although the student will have to pay a service charge on the coaching loan, he or she will receive the

Table 7.6 Status of the Education Loan Program (Cumulative to December 2005)

Course of Study	Number of Students			Total Amount (Hundred Thousand Taka)	Total Disbursement to December 2005*	Total Repayment to December 2005
	Male	Female	Total			
Bachelor's (honors): general subjects	6509	1701	8210	5449.85	1774.78	16
Master's: general subjects	516	125	641	168.81	118.29	7
BBA	142	8	150	94.65	42.07	1
MBA	19	1	20	8.04	5.73	1
Bachelor's: agriculture/ veterinary/ fisheries	147	17	164	104.59	44.80	2
Master's: agriculture/ veterinary/ fisheries	36	1	37	16.82	11.40	0
Bachelor's: engineering/ textile/computer and marine engineering	224	8	232	142.76	59.22	1
Medicine and dentistry	85	18	103	81.48	47.25	3
Total	7678	1879	9557	6067	2103.54	31

*Approved loans are disbursed quarterly during the course of study.

higher education loan interest-free until the end of the program. Students who fail to enter a university and do not want a higher education loan will have to repay the bank for the prep courses through installments within a year of the loan's sanction.

Box 7.3   Looking for My Mother's Face in the Crowd

My name is Monishanker Dewan. My mother has been an honorable member of Center number 47 of the Jhawdanga branch under the Khulna zone of Grameen Bank since 1993. My father was a primary school teacher and retired from his job in 1992. Other than homestead land, we do not own any land, and my father accumulated a huge debt to pay for the educational expenses of his three children. He paid off part of these debts from his pension. In 1996–1997, I was admitted to a four-year BBA course at Rajshahi University. During that time my elder brother was studying in the same university, and to pay for our educational expenses my parents borrowed more money. My mother used to send me some money out of her meager income acquired by using the loan from Grameen Bank.

My parents ran into debt to pay for the BBA degree that I received in 1992 with a 3.15 GPA. In the meantime our family finances were in a dire state, and I almost gave up the dream of studying for an MBA. During this time of desperation, my mother's branch manager became a beacon of hope for me and my family. He suggested that I take an education loan from the bank, and with the help of this loan, in 2004 I received an MBA with a 3.46 GPA. Now I am an officer trainee in the Srinagar branch under the Naraynganj zone of Grameen Bank. As part of my training, I talk to the borrowers in the centers, and I can see the reflection of my mother's face among them.

Source: Grameen Bank Quarterly Education Newsletter, issue 1, December 2004.

By providing education loans, the bank is trying to correct an imperfection in the capital market. Like its predecessor giving collateral-free credit to the poor, the bank is now venturing to meet the needs of the borrowers' children. If the capital market were perfect, as stipulated in the literature and in textbooks, anyone wishing to pursue higher education should be able to borrow from an institution to finance it. The borrowers would pay off the bank in the future by means of higher, predictable income streams made possible by an education financed through credit. Unfortunately, financial institutions are unable to provide such loans for human capital formation. One reason is that, unlike land and other nonmovable assets, expected future income cannot be used as collateral against a loan. Financial institutions cannot take ownership of the human capital acquired through loans and sell it to pay off the debt in the case of default. Moreover, they do not know if the student will be able to complete the program or will be able to get a job to pay off the debt. Milton Friedman (1962) suggested that imperfection in the credit market will lead people to underinvest in education to acquire human capital. Such underinvestment will be more pronounced in the case of the poor. Critics argue that microcredit cannot solve the problem of poverty by remedying the imperfection in only one market—the market for financial and physical capital that conditions the lives of the poor.[57] By providing an education loan for the children of the borrowers, the bank is attempting to remedy the imperfection in another market: the market for human capital.

In advanced countries such as the United States, as well as in many developing countries and countries in transition, the government provides education loans to remedy such imperfections in the capital market. In the United States, the current interest rate on a student loan is 3.5%. This is lower than the rate for other forms of commercial credit such as mortgages, credit cards, and consumer loans because of the explicit guarantee to the lending institution by the federal government against default. In Bangladesh it is Grameen Bank, a for-profit company, that is providing the loan. There are, however, some interesting similarities between Grameen's program and the government programs in advanced countries. In both cases, for example, repayment is secured from the future income of the students. This is known as "deferred payment" or "income-contingent repayment."[58] However, Grameen's loan program differs from many student loan programs in a fundamental way. Lending to students can be disaggregated into several distinct functions: (1) originating the loan, (2) providing the capital, (3) guaranteeing or bearing the risk of default, (4) subsidizing some of the cost of borrowing, and (5) servicing and collecting.[59] In the loan programs of other countries, these functions can be performed by separate entities. For example, the private banks or the universities themselves can originate the loan, and the parents bear the risk. Also, all loan programs entail subsidies, explicit or implicit, from the government. In the case of Grameen's education loan program, functions 1–5 are all performed by the bank. Even borrowers who are on a flexible loan (which is akin to a rescheduled loan) can qualify for an educational loan. By giving such a loan, the bank signals to its borrowers that it genuinely cares about their welfare without regard to their credit history.

These loans will redress the long-standing inequality in access to higher education for the benefit of children of the poor. A recent paper reports that only 9% of young people from poor households are enrolled in college, compared with 24% for the entire population.[60] Clearly, funding for education is a compelling need among the poor.

In this chapter, we examined several new initiatives of Grameen Bank. Even though these were not among the core elements of Grameen II, the initiatives send a clear signal to the borrowers that the bank genuinely cares about the welfare of the poor and the destitute. To help achieve its overall goal of lessening the incidence of poverty, the bank is providing interest-free loans to the destitute, and giving scholarships and below-market loans to the borrowers' children. We have shown how these have benefited the beggars as well as the borrowers and their families.

NOTES

1. Syman's story was profiled on *BBC News.*
2. David Hulme and Paul Mosley, *Finance Against Poverty, Vol. 1* (London: Routledge, 1996); Dipanker Datta, "Microcredit in Rural Bangladesh: Is It Reaching the Poorest?" *Journal of Microfinance* 6(1), 2004, pp. 55–81.
3. Hulme and Mosley, *Finance Against Poverty*; David Hulme and Paul Mosley, "Finance for the Poor or the Poorest? Financial Innovation, Poverty, and Vulnerability," in *Who Needs Credit? Poverty and Finance in Bangladesh,* edited by G. D. Wood and I. A. Sharif (Dhaka: University Press, 1997); Iffath Sharif and Geof Wood, "Towards New Frontiers of Finance: Summary and Findings," paper prepared for the final session of the 2nd International Workshop on Poverty and Finance: Emerging Institutional Issues in Microfinance, 1998.
4. Syed M. Hashemi, "Those Left Behind: A Note on Targeting the Hardcore Poor," in *Who Needs Credit?,* eds. Sharif and Wood, p. 253.
5. H. Z. Rahman, "Bangladesh: Dynamics of Rural Poverty," paper presented at the International Conference on Poverty: Emerging Challenges, organized by the Bangladesh Institute of Development Studies (BIDS) in association with Grameen Trust and Local Government Engineering Department (LGED), Dhaka, February 9–11, 1998.
6. Binayak Sen and Sharifa Begum, *Methodology for Identifying the Poorest at the Local Level,* Technical Paper no. 27, "Macroeconomics, Health and Development" series (World Health Organization, 1998).
7. A. Rahman and A. Razzaque, "On Reaching the Hard Core Poor: Some Evidence on Social Exclusion in NGO Programmes," *Bangladesh Development Studies* 26(1), 2000, pp. 1–35.
8. As part of the World Development Report on Poverty, the World Bank commissioned a study that involved a conversation with the poor to delineate their own perspective and experience of poverty. The study involved talking to 20,000 poor men and women from twenty-three countries, and Bangladesh was one of the countries included in the sample.
9. R. Nabi, D. Datta, S. Chakrabarty, et al., "Consultation with the Poor: Participatory Poverty Assessment in Bangladesh," paper prepared for the NGO Working Group of the World Bank (Dhaka, 1999).
10. Rushidan I. Rahman, *The Hard Core Poor and NGO Intervention* (Dhaka: Bangladesh Institute of Development Studies, 1998).
11. Atiur Rahman, M. A. Razzaque, M. M. Rahman, et al., "On Reaching the Hardcore Poor: Redefining NGO Strategy," paper prepared for NOVA consultancy, (Dhaka: Bangladesh Institute of Development Studies, 1998).

12. Sharma and Zeller conclude that branches of these programs tend to be located more in "poor pockets of relatively well-developed areas than in remote, less developed regions." Monohar Sharma and Manfred Zeller, "Placement Outreach of Group-Based Credit Organizations: The Cases of ASA, BRAG, and PROSHIKA in Bangladesh," *World Development* 27(12), 1999, p. 2123. In contrast, Ravallion and Wodon report that while the traditional banks are attracted to areas that favor the non-poor, Grameen Bank places its branches in areas that favor the poor. Martin Ravallion and Quentin Wodon, "Banking on the Poor? Branch Location and Nonfarm Rural Development in Bangladesh," *Review of Development Economics* 4(2), 2000, pp. 121–139.

13. T. Evans, A. Adams, R. Mohammed, et al., "Demystifying Nonparticipation in Microcredit: A Population Based Analysis," *World Development* 27(2), 1999, pp. 420–421.

14. The current average size of the loan is 5500 taka.

15. Preface to guideline for beggar members (original in Bengali), Grameen Bank, January 2004.

16. Forms of alms in Moslem society.

17. Hashemi, "Those Left Behind," p. 253.

18. Syed M. Hashemi and Sidney Schuler, *Sustainable Banking with the Poor: A Case Study of Grameen Bank,* JSI Working Paper no. 10 (Washington, DC: John Snow International Research and Training Institute, 1997), p. 8.

19. David Bornstein, *The Price of a Dream* (New York: Simon & Schuster, 1996), p. 266.

20. Hashemi and Schuler, *Sustainable Banking*, pp. 49–50.

21. One may question why Grameen is giving credit, as many commentators believe that the "hardcore poor are not 'bankable' in their own or their neighbour's eyes," and that instead of credit they need employment and direct assistance. Research by Sen shows that lack of initial capital prevented the chronic poor from escaping poverty by taking advantage of high-return non-agricultural opportunities. Binayak Sen, "Drivers of Escape and Descent: Changing Household Fortunes in Rural Bangladesh," *World Development* 31(3), 2003, pp. 522–523.

22. Hulme and Mosely, *Finance Against Poverty, Vol. I,* p. 131.

23. According to Islamic ritual, all dead bodies have to be washed before burial.

24. Arjun Appadurai, "The Capacity to Aspire: Culture and the Terms of Recognition," in *Culture and Public Action,* edited by V. Rao and M. Walton (Stanford, CA: Stanford University Press, 2004), p. 69.

25. Appadurai, "Capacity to Aspire," p. 70.

26. R. Tagore, "Sambaya Niti," in *Collected Works of Tagore*, Vol. 14, p. 313 (translated from Bengali and quoted by eds. Binayak Sen and Atiur Rahman in *South Asia Poverty Monitor: The Bangladesh Chapter,* June 1998).

27. M. R. Karim and Mitsue Osada, "Dropping Out: An Emerging Factor in the Success of Microcredit-Based Poverty Alleviation Programs," *Developing Economies* 36(3), 1998, pp. 257–288.

28. Rutherford reports that flexibility of loan repayment and open access to savings are being implemented rather slowly at the field level. Stuart Rutherford, "Grameen II at the End of 2003: A 'Grounded View' of How Grameen's New Initiative Is Progressing in Villages," typescript (Dhaka: MicroSave, 2004).

29. Some studies show that money given to a woman is usually handed over to a male member of the family. Some have erroneously concluded that this is evidence that women are not empowered by microfinance. As Naila Kabeer shows, such a binary definition of female empowerment fails to capture the much more complex and nuanced nature of empowerment and bargaining that goes on in the household with the infusion of credit from MFIs. She correctly points out that what matters most for empowerment is whether the female actively participates in the use of the credit. Naila Kabeer, *Money Can't Buy Me Love? Re-Evaluating Gender, Credit, and Empowerment in Rural Bangladesh,* Discussion Paper no. 363 (IDS, 1998).

30. Pankaj Jain, "Managing Credit for the Rural Poor: Lessons from the Grameen Bank," *World Development* 24(1), 1996, pp. 79–89.

31. Signe-Mary McKernan, "The Impact of Micro-Credit Programs on Self-Employment Profits: Do Non-Credit Program Aspects Matter?" *Review of Economics and Statistics* 84(1), 2002, pp. 93–115.

32. Jorge H. Maldonado, Claudio González-Vega, and Vivianne Romero, "The Influence on the Education Decisions of Rural Households: Evidence from Bolivia," paper prepared for the Annual Meeting of the American Agricultural Economics Association, Montreal, July 27–30, 2003.

33. Hanan G. Jacoby and Emmanuel Skoufias, "Risk, Financial Markets, and Human Capital in a Developing Country," *Review of Economic Studies* 64(3), 1997, pp. 311–335; R. Kanbur and L. Squire, "The Evolution of Thinking about Poverty," in *Frontiers of Development Economics: The Future in Perspective,* edited by G. Meier and J. Stiglitz (Washington, DC: World Bank, 2001).

34. Maldonado and his co-authors label the increase in demand for children's schooling due to non-credit services provided by MFIs "education effect."

35. Mark Pitt and Shahidur Khandker, "The Impact of Group-Based Credit Programs on Poor Households in Bangladesh: Does the Gender of the Participants Matter?" *Journal of Political Economy* 106(5), 1998, p. 986.

36. Pitt and Khandker, "Impact of Group-Based Credit Programs," p. 986.

37. Jessica Chase, "The Effect of Microfinance Credit on Children's Education: Evidence from the Grameen Bank," unpublished undergraduate honors thesis in economics, Harvard University, 1997.

38. Helen Todd, *Women at the Center: Grameen Bank Borrowers after One Decade* (Boulder, CO: Westview Press, 1996), pp. 200–201.

39. Naomi Hossain and Naila Kabeer, "Achieving Universal Primary Education and Eliminating Gender Disparity," *Economic and Political Weekly* 39(36), 2004, pp. 4093–4100.

40. S. Khandker, M. Pitt, and N. Fuwa, *Subsidy to Promote Girls' Secondary Education: The Female Stipend Program in Bangladesh* (Washington, DC: World Bank, 2003).

41. Akhter Ahmed, *Feeding Minds While Fighting Poverty: Food for Schooling in Bangladesh,* International Food Policy Research Institute (available at http://www.ifpri.org/pubs/ib/ib4/ib4_resultsBang.pdf).

42. Karen Tietjen, *The Bangladesh Primary Education Stipend Project: A Descriptive Analysis* (Partnership for Sustainable Strategies on Girls' Education, 2003).

43. Surjit S. Bhalla, Suraj Saigal, and Nabhojit Basu, "Girls' Education Is It–Nothing Else Matters (Much)," back ground paper for World Development Report, 2003.

44. Barbara Herz and Gene Sperling, *What Works in Girls' Education: Evidence and Policies from the Developing World* (New York: Council on Foreign Relations, 2004).

45. S. R. Nath, "Social Factors Underlying Gender Variation of School Enrollment: Case of Rural Bangladesh," *Journal of Rural Development* 27(1), 1997, p. 129.

46. Also see Mary Arends-Kuenning and Sajeda Amin, *The Effects of Schooling Incentive Programs on Household Resource Allocation in Bangladesh,* Policy Research Division, Working Paper no. 133 (New York: Population Council, 2000).

47. Martin Ravallion and Quentin Wodon, "Does Child Labor Displace Schooling? Evidence on Behavioral Responses to an Enrollment Subsidy," *Economic Journal* 110, 1999, pp. 158–175.

48. Michael Kremer, Edward Miguel, and Rebecca Thornton, *Incentives to Learn*, Harvard University, 2004 (available at http://www.educationnext. org/unabridged/20052/57.pdf).

49. This notion of greater class mobility is widely accepted as a fact in rich countries. However, in poor countries class mobility is rather limited; a poor person's children are more likely to be poor, and the most important means of improving class mobility is higher education.

50. A. Rahman, R. Rahman, M. Hossain, et al., *Early Impact of Grameen: A Multi-Dimensional Analysis* (Dhaka: Grameen Trust, 2002).

51. In some of the oldest operational areas of the bank, such as Tangail, borrowers' children now constitute 40% of the staff.

52. The monthly scholarship amount provided by the government secondary school program is equal to what a child can earn from two to four and a half days of work.

53. A recent World Bank study reports that on average 15.5% and 17.6% of teachers are absent in primary and secondary schools, respectively. Nazmul Chaudhury, Jeffrey Hammer, Michael Kremer, Karthik Muralidharan, and Halsey Rogers, *Roll Call: Teacher Absences in Bangladesh* (Washington, DC: World Bank, 2005).

54. Tietjen, *Bangladesh Primary Education Stipend Project*, p. 19.

55. Adopted children and other dependents of the borrowers do not qualify to receive such loans.

56. Political unrest such as strikes and extended work stoppages can affect the smooth running of an academic session, especially for public institutions. Private institutions are relatively better at making up for lost time, as they include allowances for such disturbances in their academic calendars.

57. Rehman Sobhan, *A Macro Policy for Poverty Eradication through Structural Change,* Discussion Paper no. 2005/03 (World Institute for Development Economics Research, 2005).

58. D. Albrecht and A. Ziderman, *Deferred Cost-Recovery for Higher Education: Student Loan Programs in Developing Countries,* Discussion Paper no. 137 (Washington, DC: World Bank, 1991).

59. Bruce D. Johnstone, *Student Loans in International Perspective: Promises and Failures, Myths and Partial Truths,* International Comparative Higher Education Finance and Accessibility Project, Center for Comparative and Global Studies in Education, Graduate School of Education (Buffalo, NY: SUNY, 2001), p. 14.

60. Alia Ahmad, "Inequality in the Access to Education and Poverty in Bangladesh," part of the ongoing project Access to Secondary Education and Poverty Reduction in Bangladesh, 2003.

8

Conclusion

F arida Begum, a member of Grameen Bank since 1993, now owns fifty-five rickshaws. Until a few years ago she wore used clothes and did not own any plates or glasses. Now she has a well-stocked crockery and glassware cupboard. Previously, nobody would lend her even 25 cents; now people gladly hand over 25,000 taka, no questions asked. Even though she lacks electricity, she owns a TV and a cassette player powered by batteries. These newfound riches are all due to her membership in Grameen Bank. Hidden behind the assets and luxury goods, however, lies a tale of struggle and misfortune.

When Farida was very young her village home was wiped out by the mighty river Padma. Her family moved to the town of Faridpur and her father took a job managing the property and other business of a rich landlord. In return, he received a salary and a place to live. Eventually he saved enough money to buy a small plot in the town and they were able to move into their own home, but there was not enough money to send Farida and her siblings to school. At the tender age of fourteen she was married off to a folk singer whose extended family of ten depended on his seasonal income. The first challenge Farida faced was to persuade her husband to give up folk singing for a profession with a higher and more predictable income. Her husband found a job cleaning date trees and collecting sap from them. She sold some of the date juice to other households in the village and reduced the rest into molasses to sell in the market. Unfortunately, tending the trees was seasonal work. During the off season Farida's husband worked as a day laborer and occasionally drove a rickshaw. Her in-laws did not appreciate her hard work, and after the birth of their first daughter the young family was forced to set up their own household. They build a house with a roof made of hay from the remnants of wheat plants. Farida did not even have a cot to sleep on: everybody slept on a bamboo mat on the mud floor. The roof leaked during the rainy season, and during the periods of torrential rain she was forced to take shelter on the neighbor's porch. She did not even have a plate; all she owned was one bowl. She would serve her husband food first in the bowl, and she would eat afterward. A used milk can served as a drinking glass. The juice from the date trees was her breakfast, and her lunch consisted of plain rice with green papaya added to increase the volume so that the three of them would have enough to eat.

She learned about Grameen Bank from her husband's aunt and joined without telling her husband, though she got permission from her mother-in-law. Initially her husband objected, but when Farida told him about her plan to buy him a rickshaw with the loan money, he relented. She indeed used the first loan of 3000 taka to buy a rickshaw for her husband, which allowed him to keep all the income for the family. Farida paid the weekly installments with the income from the rickshaw, and even managed to save 5 to 10 taka a month. Her next loan was for 5000 taka. She used 3000 taka to buy two used rickshaws and used the rest to fix them. She rented out two of the three rickshaws that she now owned and used the income to build a temporary garage. She used 1400 taka out of the 6000 taka of her third loan to buy a heifer from her father-in-law. With her savings and the remaining loan amount she bought three more used rickshaws and one rickshaw van. She used her daily income to repair these rickshaws, and she ended up owning six regular rickshaws and one rickshaw van. With so many rickshaws to manage, her husband quit driving and leased out the rickshaws, and started repairing them in their garage.

Her fourth loan was for 8000 taka, which she topped up with the proceeds from the sale of the heifer for 8000 taka. She bought ten additional used rickshaws, at a price of 19,000 taka, from another owner and paid him 16,000 taka from her total funds. She drew on her savings to fix the new batch of rickshaws and eventually paid off the loan from the bank as well as the credit balance of 3000 taka with the previous owner with the rents from the rickshaws.

By repeatedly and successfully buying used rickshaws at a discount,[1] fixing them, and renting them out, and also buying heifers, which she fattens and sells for a profit, Farida has built up a sizable base of assets that are generating the income to enable her to move out of poverty. She has used the income to build a brick house with a corrugated tin roof, and she has set up a shop selling rickshaw spare parts. She has repaid all loans from the bank on time; her only remaining loan is for a village pay phone. Table 8.1 shows the current value of the assets built with proceeds from her bank loans.

But Farida Begum is not finished. She plans to take a large special enterprise loan to expand her shop and wants to send her daughter to the university for advanced studies.

Granted, Farida Begum is an exceptional success story; not every borrower of the bank can be as successful as she. She is the manager of

Table 8.1 Farida's Assets

Asset Number	Description	Market Value (Taka)
1	Rickshaws (55)	165,000
2	House	150,000
3	Furniture	50,000
4	Rickshaw garage	10,000
5	Cow	5,000
6	Rickshaw spare parts shop	8,000
7	Balance on three GPS accounts	19,000
8	Balance on personal savings account	725
9	Balance on special investment account	4,273
10	Balance on *palli* phone savings account	15,000
11	Balance on savings account in Rupali Bank	5,000
	Total value	432,441 ($6653)

her enterprises and her husband is a willing partner. In most cases, the female borrower needs help from the male member of the family to be truly successful, sometimes having to hand over to him the actual management of the loans. Still, her story suggests that it is possible for a nearly destitute person to become a rickshaw queen over time; all that she needed was a helping hand. There is a famous quote attributed to Julius Nyerere, the founder of modern Tanzania. When US President Ronald Reagan suggested that poor countries needed to lift themselves by the bootstraps, Nyerere responded that the president should wait until they get the boots before offering such advice. Grameen Bank gave Farida an opportunity to buy the boots so that she could lift herself by the bootstraps. The boots were not free; Farida used the income from investments funded by loans that had to be repaid on time to buy these proverbial boots.

Farida started her membership in the bank in the early 1990s under Grameen I. Now she is enjoying her good fortune under Grameen II. The flexibility inherent in Grameen II will allow her and her family to improve their economic condition even more in the years ahead. Table 8.2 summarizes the differences between Grameen I and Grameen II along with the reasons for the changes.

The task of Grameen I was to prove to a skeptical world that the poor are creditworthy and bankable. The relative success of microfinance-related schemes in Bangladesh and in many other countries has firmly established the creditworthiness of the poor. The repayment crisis faced by Grameen Bank in late 1990s called into question this virtually universal fact. Unlike the case with Grameen I, the doubt this time was whether the poor with large unpaid loans would feel a need to rejoin the bank and repay the debt. The turnaround in repayment rates and the huge success in getting borrowers to come back to the bank and even to repay loans that had been written off have put all such doubts to rest.

The fact that the poor always pay back has been proven conclusively. The obvious question is why this is so. Economists have grappled with this question; the answer obviously depends on the nature of the model proposed by the theorists. Economic theory suggests a number of factors: the poor pay back because the group as a whole is made liable for

Table 8.2   Comparison between Grameen I and Grameen II

Grameen I	Grameen II	Reasons for Change
No provision to save for pension	Borrower deposits a fixed monthly amount in Grameen pension scheme (GPS)	To help borrowers build a nest egg for retirement To provide borrowers with an ownership stake in the bank
Obligatory savings accumulated in the group fund refundable after ten years of membership	Savings accumulated in obligatory special investment account refundable after three years of membership	To allow borrowers to save a lump-sum amount and then transfer the ownership to them as soon as feasible and convenient
Amount of weekly personal savings same for all borrowers	Amount of weekly personal savings varies with loan amount from 5 to 50 taka per week	To encourage borrowers with large loans to save more, as larger loan size reflects greater saving capabilities
No encouragement to save in contractual accounts	Borrowers encouraged to save in any of several contractual savings schemes that fits their needs	To allow borrowers to save for specific reasons, such as to pay for the marriage and education of the children, to create a large asset base, and to meet other long-term needs
No initiative to collect savings from nonmembers	Active campaigns underway to collect savings from nonmembers	To enable the bank to fund credit operation from its own sources
Borrowers unable to borrow against their savings	Borrowers free to borrow against their savings	To encourage borrowers to save To enable borrowers to use "bridge loans" to meet short-term discrepancy between income and expenditure rather than using up savings meant for long-term needs

(*continues*)

Table 8.2   Comparison between Grameen I and Grameen II (Continued)

Grameen I	Grameen II	Reasons for Change
Multiple loan products	One prime loan product–the basic loan	To streamline accounting To make the total amount owed transparent to borrowers To prevent borrower and staff from using one loan product to pay off another
Mostly one-year loans, with some exceptions	Loan duration can vary from three months to three years	To synchronize the supply of credit to borrower with his or her investment needs
Installment size fixed	Installment size variable during the loan period and can be tailored to needs of the borrower	To allow borrower to match the repayment schedule with the business environment and income flow, which is bound to change over time
Lump-sum and one-time repayment not allowed	Repayment subject to negotiation between staff and borrower at any time, although the minimum payment due depends on the duration of the loan	To allow borrowers to repay at their own convenience
Staggered loan distribution with two members receiving the loan first, then another two, and finally (in most cases) the group chair	Member can receive loan at any time irrespective of what others are doing	Borrowers' ability to repay now well established, obviating the need to stagger loans to see if anyone has repayment problems; even if a borrower runs into trouble repaying the loan, he or she can always switch to a flexible loan
No new borrowing until the previous loan is repaid in full	A borrower, under certain conditions, can borrow the amount repaid in the first six months without repaying the loan in full	To allow the borrows to take advantage of a new business opportunity through the infusion of fresh credit

Table 8.2   Comparison between Grameen I and Grameen II (Continued)

Grameen I	Grameen II	Reasons for Change
Loans disbursed in one go	Loan disbursement can be varied and borrowers can receive credit in tranches	To match the need for credit over the investment cycle of the borrower
A common loan ceiling imposed for the whole branch	Borrowers each have their own loan ceiling based on savings and the performance of their group, center, and branch; it can be increased	To reward borrowers for good performance To take account of borrowers' loan use and investment capacity To reward borrowers for the performance of others and thus use group and center membership positively
No hard and fast rules for a decrease in loan ceiling	Loan ceiling can be decreased based on performance of borrower (e.g., missing center meetings or installment payments)	To discourage borrowers from missing center meetings and installment payments
Part of loan (5%) sanctioned to borrowers deposited in a compulsory savings account (group fund) managed by the group	Borrowers required to deposit part of the loan amount in two individually owned savings account: a personal savings account with open access (2.5%) and an obligatory savings account with restricted access (2.5%)	To allow borrowers to manage their own savings without the hassle of dealing with the group
Family responsible for loan of deceased borrower, and female borrower responsible for loan outstanding even if her husband dies	Contributing to a special savings account allows borrowers to ensure that outstanding loan will be paid off after their death, and extra contribution enables female borrower to cover loan outstanding against death of husband	To alleviate borrower's fear about leaving debt behind for their families To protect female borrowers from poverty after the death of main income earner of the family

(continues)

Table 8.2   Comparison between Grameen I and Grameen II (Continued)

Grameen I	Grameen II	Reasons for Change
Borrower becomes defaulter if she cannot repay the full amount in fifty-two weeks	Borrower becomes defaulter if she cannot pay the amount due according to repayment schedule within six months for basic loan	Six-month cutoff period acts as an early warning device in that if irregularities arise in the first six months of the loan, repayment in full at the end of maturity term is unlikely
Borrower could not become a defaulter from failure to make timely deposits in savings accounts	Borrower who fails to make four consecutive monthly GPS deposits will be treated as defaulter	Deposit in contractual saving accounts considered a sign of good behavior; serial failure to make deposit considered a sign of impending problem with loan payments
Defaulter could borrow from the group fund	Defaulter cannot borrow from her savings account until all arrears are paid off	To ensure accumulated savings are used to pay off loan before they can be used for other purposes
No special program for the hardcore poor	Special program with easier loan terms, savings requirements, and repayment conditions for beggars	To emphasize that the need of the poorest of the poor for credit and savings is different from that of the regular poor
Funds for disbursement for new bank branches borrowed from head office at 12% interest	New branches can be self-financed from day 1 by mobilizing savings from members and nonmembers prior to disbursement of credit	To ensure that branches reach profitability quickly and be self-reliant

the individual loans (joint liability contract), loan repayment is rewarded with larger loans (dynamic incentives), default is penalized by social sanctions (social collateral), and installment payments are small and frequent ("a little at a time").[2] Some even suggest that the main reason for the high repayment rate is the management structure of the lending institutions. Interestingly, practitioners know that the poor always pay back; they see it every day and do not need the insights of the theorists to convince them that it is true. One can use the analogy of a trapeze performer. If you ask her why she does not fall off during the high-wire act, she will likely answer that her long experience of repeated performances has convinced her that she will not fall. She will, in other words, cite her own experience instead of invoking a theory from physics.

But the question remains as to why the poor repay. The most obvious answer is self-interest. MFIs such as Grameen Bank are the most economic and secure source of credit for the poor, who do not want to risk cutting off this option. Practitioners, however, also know that some do not repay even though they can, as became amply evident during the repayment crisis Grameen faced in 1999. They also know that most repayment problems have a human dimension. If one insists on repayment at any cost, the borrower may have to sell assets, withdraw children from school, or face the public shame of being branded a defaulter. This might lead her back to the path of poverty, thus defeating the original mission of the program.

The challenge for the financial institution is to discover the real reasons for the repayment problem and give the borrower another chance by issuing a fresh loan and allowing her to repay the total amount in small installments until she can get back on her feet. Grameen always did this informally, and in many case local staff did it on their own initiative. Grameen II formalized this option. In addition to formalizing the option of rescheduling loans, Grameen II introduced many other innovations:

- Ramping up voluntary savings mobilization, including open access and contractual savings accounts
- Taking advantage of unmet savings needs of the poor by providing avenues to save for retirement and other long-term needs
- Making it easy for the members and nonmembers to save by providing secure and diversified savings products
- Taking advantage of the bank's legal standing to provide savings services to nonmembers and using this medium to achieve self-sufficiency and secure funding for loans
- Getting new branches to be self-reliant as soon as possible and turning them into profit-making centers by using savings deposits from nonmembers to disburse credit

- Establishing loan insurance program for the borrowers and their husbands
- Encouraging individual loans and individual savings
- Recognizing the vulnerability of the poor and allowing them a temporary reprieve to reschedule loan in arrears by using flexible loans
- Making incentives to repay transparent by tying individual loan ceilings with repayment records and savings behavior
- Turning the group into a vehicle for positive feedback by rewarding the borrowers with larger loans based on the performance of the group, center, and branch
- Making regular attendance a condition for increased loan size and penalizing members for missing meetings beyond a certain number by reducing their loan ceiling
- Providing large loans to borrowers with higher investment capacity to hasten the process of moving out of poverty
- Using internal resources to increase membership
- Aggressively monitoring the system by collecting detailed information and sharing it within the organization
- Creating an early warning system by examining the quality of loans after six months
- Topping up loans after a clean record of repayment for the first six months of a loan
- Using material and moral incentives to get staff on board for large-scale change in the organization
- Using public recognition through the "star system" to reward good performance by the staff
- Using system-wide competition to improve performance at all levels of the bank: branches, areas, and zones
- Accepting beggars as members in a special program to reach out to the destitute
- Establishing loans to fund the higher education of the borrowers' children
- Establishing scholarships at different levels to encourage education of the borrowers' children
- Outsourcing data management from the branches to a sister organization by creating Area Information Management Centers (AIMCs)

- Computerizing the audit system by enabling the auditors to use pen drives (i.e., flash memory devices) to collect data from AIMCs for pooling and analysis

We have described how these innovations helped the bank survive the repayment crisis the late 1990s. As the history of Grameen II suggests, however, even a well-run institution can be subject to large-scale problems. Being a pro-poor organization with more than 5 million poor people as owners, Grameen has a special responsibility to avoid crises that could jeopardize its very existence. Grameen has successfully dealt with the repayment crisis, but that does not mean it will not face crises in the future. Now the bank has the added responsibility of guaranteeing the safety and sure return of the savings of its members and the general public.

Grameen Bank faces challenges that could create problems in the future. Some of these challenges lie outside the bank's control, and there is little it can do about them. Some areas served by the bank are affected by poor geographical conditions: river bank erosion, poor access, and a generally low level of economic activity. Even though the bank does not issue loans to finance agricultural activities, its performance and, in particular, its repayment rates are closely tied to the agricultural cycle.[3] The bank's performance is also affected by macroeconomic conditions. So far, the macroeconomic environment has been quite beneficial. Inflation has been kept under control and the rate of growth in GDP has been significant. The most important external challenge has been the recurrent floods. The bank has a good disaster plan, which was instrumental in overcoming the effects of the flood of 2004. This plan involves disaster preparedness and steps for post-disaster rehabilitation. The bank urges members to save more, to stock non-perishable food items, and to immunize livestock at the onset of flood season, in the month of June. After the flood, the bank uses the Center Disaster Fund and Rehabilitation Fund from headquarters to provide short-term credit for post-flood rehabilitation. Ideally, the bank should be able to reduce the risk of financial problems caused by flooding by buying flood insurance from a local provider, who could in turn pass on the risk to companies outside the country by buying re-insurance.

Grameen now holds a large stock of savings by its borrowers and the general public. The current strategy is to loan out the proceeds and park part of the cash in time deposits with commercial banks. Ideally, the bank should be able to invest these funds in the local stock market to generate a sizable return so that it can easily honor the savings contracts when they mature. So far, the bank has been able to invest a small fraction of the savings in the stock market by issuing the Grameen Mutual Fund One. The small size of the initial public offering reveals the limited absorbing capacity of the capital market. Since the stock market crash in November 1996, the government has failed to restore confidence in the sanctity of market transactions. Moreover, it has not adopted policies to increase activity in the market. As a result, the capital market is underdeveloped, with a capitalization of only 6.7% of GDP. The high interest rate offered on long-term savings instruments by the government has deterred the development of the equities market and distorted the market for issuing private debt securities. Since the local capital market is not likely to pick up in the near future, the government could allow Grameen Bank to invest its large deposits in mature financial markets outside the country. Given the high probability of devaluation of the Bangladeshi taka in the future, even low-rate, high-quality US Treasury bonds would be a worthwhile investment on behalf of Grameen borrowers. Such an option would allow the poor of Bangladesh to benefit from global financial intermediation. Frustration over the inability to use the financial market as an aid to the poor is aptly captured in a recent working paper for the World Institute for Development Economics Research of United Nations University written by the former chairman of Grameen Bank, Professor Rehman Sobhan:

> Regrettably, few finance ministers in the developing world have registered the crucial lessons from the micro-credit revolution that the poor are bankable and creditworthy. The logic of this discovery would be to enable micro-credit organizations to graduate into corporate banks, owned by the poor. This, indeed, is the path followed by the Grameen Bank, which is a corporate body with over two million shareholders, composed mostly of poor women, who are also the clientele of the Bank. Bangladesh and indeed a number of other

developing countries are ready to sustain many more such banks, owned by the poor and serving the poor. Given the high level of non-performing loans in the regular banking system of Bangladesh, the fact that Grameen Bank, with a credit volume comparable to the largest commercial banks, can limit its portfolio of nonperforming loans in the range of 5 per cent, demonstrates that it has the capacity to operate as a competitive bank whilst serving the needs of the poor. There is, today, no reason why such organizations, of the maturity of Grameen Bank, should not graduate into the macrofinance system by accessing the deposits of the public and even marketing its assets at the global level, through such financial instruments as securitization, which are in widespread use in more advanced financial systems.[4]

Another challenge the bank has to face is increasing competition from credit-granting NGOs. Large numbers of institutions provide microfinance in the rural areas of Bangladesh, and it is quite common to have more than one microfinance provider operating in any given area. In certain parts of the country, 40 to 125 institutions provide microfinance services within a subdistrict.[5] The leadership of the bank, however, does not believe that increased competition is a factor that must be reckoned with. They point out that several zones of the bank are extremely profitable despite intense competition; moreover, the redesign of the bank was motivated by the need to address internal weaknesses of the system rather than in response to increased competition. The bank managers believe that the potential for expansion is underutilized, and that the problem is one of unmet demand, as revealed by the phenomenon of "overlapping," where an individual borrows from several institutions. Field research suggests that MFIs are able to supply credit to only 45–50% of the target group. The loans provided by MFIs constitute around 5% of total private credit in the economy.[6]

Grameen is aware of its competitive environment. Being a firm in a competitive industry, the bank differentiates its product and has created products that meet the specific needs of the members. Currently, the bank is providing products that take care of the borrowers' children's education, health, retirement, and debt burden upon death. The rapid increase in membership and the accumulation of savings since the launch of Grameen II suggest that the product differentiation strategy is working. Currently, Grameen is in an advantageous position compared with its rivals in the NGO sector. Being a formal institution and having a legal mandate, the bank is able to collect savings from nonmembers. The government has capped the interest rate of its microfinance operations at 11% flat, or 22% on a declining-balance basis. Effective July 2004, Apex Institution PKSF has instructed its partner organizations (POs) to reduce their interest rate to 12.5% flat or 25% declining balance The POs of PKSF are in direct competition with Grameen Bank in many geographical areas. Grameen's current interest rate of 10% flat puts it at a competitive advantage over its rivals. However, many of the competitors charge higher interest rates and pay lower deposit rates, and their labor costs are also lower than Grameen's. These factors would seem to decrease Grameen's advantage over its rivals.[7]

The microfinance industry in Bangladesh is highly competitive, and it will not be difficult for others to change their loan products to meet the challenge from Grameen. Because of increased competition, it is far easier to switch from one MFI to another, and "waiting times" for credit delivery are far shorter than they were a decade ago.[8] Once the terms of loan products are made similar, the MFIs will have to compete on the basis of services provided. In the face of competition, Grameen Bank must be efficient and customer friendly, and the best way to implement this is by listening to the members and to continuously search for improvements in its delivery of products and services. Of course, this is what the bank did as part of its redesign. Introducing flexibility came about as a result of the bank listening to the borrowers. Borrowers report approval of the open-access savings account and the ability to save for retirement at an attractive rate. They also like the fact that they can borrow more if necessary after six months and that they can borrow at any time. In the old system they had to wait a whole year before they could borrow, which made it impossible to synchronize the credit demand with supply.

Grameen II has implications for the global microfinance industry as well. The Grameen model has been replicated in more than 110 countries. Grameen's credit methodology is being replicated in two ways. One approach is the Build-Operate-Transfer (BOT) model, in which Grameen experts provide on-site technical assistance and help to set up a Grameen replication. The first BOT model was initiated in Myanmar. At present, there are BOTs replicating Grameen II in Kosovo, Turkey, Zambia, and India. Another approach is financial and technical assistance provided to organizations wishing to replicate the Grameen model. Interested organizations visit Grameen Bank to participate in training, exposure, and workshop programs, and individualized financial and technical assistance packages are developed for potential replicators based on their needs. It is not clear what the sequence for replications should be, or whether and how quickly the old replicators should switch to Grameen II.

The Grameen Generalized System has been designed with the inherent flexibility to deal with catastrophes Bangladesh may face at the micro or macro level such as floods, famines, and lack of financial opportunities. Grameen Bank has initiated many strategies to take advantage of its environment. For example, it has diversified its loan products with a focus on the needs and potential of future generations of Grameen members. Education loans provided by Grameen are helping to develop a future generation of Grameen members with the education and skills to help their parents to run micro-enterprises. Currently, micro-enterprises loans make up 22% of the Grameen portfolio. This is expected to rise to a minimum of 30% by the end of 2006, as more and more members graduate to micro-enterprise loans and develop small and medium-size enterprises. This is one way in which Grameen plans to face the challenges of making optimal use of its huge savings and guaranteeing the high interest rates of such savings. This strategy is beneficial to both Grameen and its members, because on the one hand it helps to build social capital, and on the other hand it provides investment opportunities for both parties. Another example of Grameen Bank's innovative approach to giving the best income-generating opportunities to its rural members is the creation of a link between them and larger businesses or enterprises with up-to-date technology or sizable capital. The "phone ladies" program is a good example of this type of linkage.

Grameen Bank is an expanding organization, and its success depends on the innovativeness and creativity of its staff, who work hard at the grassroots level. Innovations of Grameen II are attracting large number of clients, and more staff are being added as Grameen expands its operations. At present the challenge is to maintain the skills of the staff with the use of motivation and incentives in different ways. The most important asset working for the bank is the members' willingness to repay and remain loyal to the bank despite their difficult economic conditions. The bank's unadulterated trust in the creditworthiness of the poor and their ability and willingness to repay, along with the dedication of its staff and the skills of its management, will allow it to overcome any future obstacles.

The success of Grameen II has emboldened the bank to plan for the future. It hopes that by the year 2010 (see Figure 8.1):

- Membership will reach 15 million. The goal is that no poor woman will be left out. Membership in the bank will be exhaustive, including all of the poor and poorest in the villages of Bangladesh.
- The bank will open two branches a day, a rate that will enable it to reach the target of 15 million members by the year 2010.
- All beggars in the villages will become members of Grameen Bank.
- Half of the borrowers will be on microenterprise or special investment loans.
- There will be 1 million phone ladies.
- A minimum of 100,000 medical, engineering, and master's degrees will be funded by education loans.
- The bank will distribute 50,000 scholarships per year.
- Branch staff will no longer do office work such as accounting and report writing as a result of the increased use of computers.

We began this book with the story of Gazi Malek, who died free of debt. We also met many other people: Sufia Khatoon, the stool maker, to be distinguished from Sufia Khaton, who was afraid to borrow even 100 taka; Shahnur, who chased the mirage of the good life

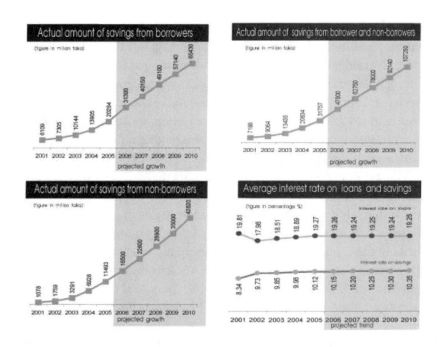

Figure 8.1 **Actual growth of Grameen Bank and projected growth for the next decade.**[9]

all the way to Libya, only to be heartbroken; Sharmila, who was surprised that the bank found her when her own family did not bother to seek her out; Farida, who became a rickshaw queen; and Laily Begum, the first phone lady, who, by calling the prime minister, also a female, challenged the conventional wisdom that illiterate women cannot be trusted with the most important tool of information technology: the mobile phone. There is a common theme in the lives of all these people: they are all members of Grameen Bank in good standing. They repaid the loans from the bank on time. Some took extra time to repay and thus became what accounting jargon refers to as "portfolio at risk." But they did not stay "at risk" for long. As soon as their economic conditions improved, they repaid the bank. These poor people repaid the bank despite other immediate and more pressing needs for the funds. They could have bought new books for their children, fixed the roof of their house, or bought new bullocks for their farms. But they resisted all these temptations and repaid the bank. Others had to be nudged back to the bank and persuaded to sign a contract. Through the creation of Grameen II, a new and improved financial service delivery mechanism, the bank was able to convince these borrowers in trouble of the importance of rejoining the bank. Even the beggars, under no obligation to repay, are paying off their loans to the bank and giving up begging for a living.

The experience of Grameen II suggests that not only do the poor pay back, but they also save a great deal. Although practitioners and researchers have vouched for the saving capability of the poor despite their low income, Grameen II offers one of the first sound proofs of the saving capability of the poor on a large scale. It has shown that all the poor need is a safe, reliable, and supportive financial institution that is willing to come to them and collect their savings in a public meeting. Grameen II has also shown that the poor employ a rich and complicated saving strategy. They save for the long term to meet specific needs such as retirement and children's marriages. They also save for the short term to overcome temporary shortfalls between income and expenses. At times of crisis, however, if their short-term savings are insufficient to meet their needs, they choose to borrow rather than deplete their long-term savings. What's more, what they borrow, they always pay back. This reaffirmation of honor and pride among the poor may well be Grameen's greatest gift to the world.

NOTES

1. She used her sixth loan and her own savings to buy forty rickshaws from the police at an auction in the capital city of Dhaka.
2. For a recent survey of these theories, see Chapters 4 and 5 in Beatriz Armedariz de Aghion and Jonathan Morduch, *The Economics of Microfinance* (Cambridge, MA: MIT Press, 2005).
3. Forty-four percent of the bank's loans are invested in agriculture, livestock, and fisheries. Grameen Bank, *Annual Report–2003* (Dhaka: Grameen Bank), p. 24.
4. Rehman Sobhan, *A Macro Policy for Poverty Eradication through Structural Change,* Discussion Paper no. 2005/03 (World Institute for Development Economics Research, 2005), p. 7.
5. Map no. 7, *Maps on Microcredit Coverage in Upazilas of Bangladesh,* (Palli Karma-Sahayak Foundation, 2004).
6. Hassan Zaman et al., *The Economics and Governance of Non Governmental Organizations (NGOs) in Bangladesh,* Poverty Reduction and Economic Management Sector Unit, South Asia Region (World Bank, 2005).
7. Even though Grameen Bank is not formally unionized (there is informal but effective workers' representation through the staff association), it follows a national salary scale set in the nationalized commercial banks by the Collective Bargaining Agency. In addition, Grameen has a generous retirement package that also increases the cost of labor.
8. Zaman et al., *Economics of Governance.*
9. Most of the growth in membership and branches occurred in 2005–2006. The growth projection is made on the assumption that the rapid growth in membership and branches will subside once the branches achieve their full capacity of 600 borrowers per bank worker. The interest rate on loans is a weighted average of the interest rate on basic loans (20%), housing loans (8%), higher education loans (5%), and loans for struggling members (0%). The average interest rate dropped in 2002 because of the introduction of education loans and loans to struggling members. Similarly, the interest rate on savings is an average of the interest rate on simple savings (8.5%), GPS accounts of various maturities, and other contractual savings discussed in Chapter 4. The average interest rate increased in 2002 because of the introduction of GPS and other contractual savings accounts.

Bibliography

Ackerly, B. 1995. "Testing Tools of Development: Credit Programmes, Loan Involvement, and Women's Empowerment." *IDS Bulletin: Getting Institutions Right for Women in Development* 26, no.3: 56–68.

Agarwal, B. 1997. *"Bargaining" and Gender Relations: Within and beyond the Households.* FCND Discussion Paper no. 27. Washington, DC: International Food Policy Research Institute.

Ahmad, Alia. 2003. "Inequality in the Access to Education and Poverty in Bangladesh." Part of the ongoing project Access to Secondary Education and Poverty Reduction in Bangladesh.

Ahmed, Akhter. 2001. *Feeding Minds While Fighting Poverty: Food for Schooling in Bangladesh.* International Food Policy Research Institute. Available at http://www.ifpri.org/pubs/ib/ib4/ib4_resultsBang.pdf.

Alauddin, Rezwan. 2005. *Connecting People in Rural Communities through ICT: Grameen Telecom Experience.* Asian Development Bank Institute. Available at http://www.adbi.org/files/2004.12.08.cpp.connecting. rural.ict.pdf (accessed January 9, 2006).

Albrecht, D., and A. Ziderman. 1991. *Deferred Cost-Recovery for Higher Education: Student Loan Programs in Developing Countries.* Discussion Paper no. 137. Washington, DC: World Bank.

Ambec, Stefan, and Nicholas Triech. 2003. *Roscas as Agreements to Cope with Social Pressure.* Working Paper no. 103. Center for Studies in Economics and Finance, University of Grenoble.

Amin, Ruhul, Ashrad U. Ahmed, J. Chowdhury, et al. 1994. "Poor Women's Participation in Income-Generating Projects and Their

Fertility Regulation in Rural Bangladesh." *World Development* 22, no.4: 555–565.

Amin, Ruhul., Robert B. Hill, and Yiping Li. 1995. "Poor Women's Participation in Credit-Based Self-Employment: The Impact of Their Empowerment, Fertility, Contraceptive Use, and Fertility Desire in Rural Bangladesh." *Pakistan Development Review* 34, no. 2: 93–119.

Amin, Ruhul, Yiping Li, and Ashrad U. Ahmed. 1996. "Women's Credit Programs and Family Planning in Rural Bangladesh." *International Family Planning Perspectives* 22: 158–162.

Amin, Sajeda, Ashok Rai, and Giorgio Topa. 2003. "Does Microcredit Reach the Poor and Vulnerable? Evidence in Northern Bangladesh." *Journal of Development Economics* 70: 59–82.

Aminuzzaman, Salahuddin, Harald Baldersheim, and Ishtiaq Jamil. 2003. "Talking Back! Empowerment and Mobile Phones in rural Bangladesh: A Study of the Village Phone Scheme of Grameen Bank." *Contemporary South Asia* 12, no. 3: 327–348.

Anderson, Siwan, and Mukesh Eswaran. 2005. *What Determines Female Autonomy? Evidence from Bangladesh.* Working Paper no. 101. Bureau for Research in Economic Analysis of Development.

Appadurai, Arjun. 2004. "The Capacity to Aspire: Culture and the Terms of Recognition." In *Culture and Public Action,* eds. V. Rao and M. Walton. Stanford, CA: Stanford University Press.

Arends-Kuenning, Mary, and Sajeda Amin. 2000. *The Effects of Schooling Incentive Programs on Household Resource Allocation in Bangladesh.* Policy Research Division, Working Paper no. 133. New York: Population Council.

Armendariz de Aghion, Beatriz, and Jonathan Morduch. 2005. *The Economics of Microfinance.* Cambridge, MA: MIT Press.

Ashraf, Nava, Dean Karlan, and Wesley Yin. 2004. *Tying Odysseus to the Mast: Evidence from a Commitment Savings Product in the Philippines.* Working paper, Princeton University.

Aubert, Cecile, Alain de Janvry, and Elisabeth Sadoulet. 2004. *Creating Incentives for Micro-Credit Agents to Lend to the Poor.* Working Paper Series 988, Department of Agricultural and Resource Economics, University of California at Berkley.

"Banks Turn to 'Unfair Means' to Dodge Rules." 2004. *Daily Star Web Edition* 5(103), September 5. Available at http://www. thedailystar.net/2004/09/05/d40905050252.htm.

Barua, Dipal Chandra, and Diane Diacon. 2003. *The Impact of the Grameen Bank Mobile Phone Programme on the Lives and Housing of Rural Women in Bangladesh.* Grameen Shakti and Building and Social Housing Foundation.

Bayes, A. 2001. "Infrastructure and Rural Development: Insights from a Grameen Bank Village Phone Initiative in Bangladesh." *Agricultural Economics* 25: 261–272.

Begum, S. 2003. "Pension and Social Security in Bangladesh." Mimeo. Dhaka: Bangladesh Institute of Development Studies.

Bhalla, Surjit S., Suraj Saigal, and Nabhojit Basu. 2003. "Girls' Education is *It*—Nothing Else Matters (Much)." *World Development Report.*

Bornstein, David. 1996. *The Price of a Dream.* New York: Simon & Schuster.

Byron, Rejaul Karim. 2004. "Cabinet Nods to Bank Law Changes." *Daily Star Web Edition* 5(26), June 22. Available at http://www. thedailystar.net/2004/06/22/d4062201077.htm.

Cain, M., S. R. Khanam, and S. Nahar. 1979. "Class, Patriarchy, and the Structure of Women's Work in Rural Bangladesh." *Population and Development Review* 5, no.3: 405–438.

Chase, Jessica. 1997. "The Effect of Microfinance Credit on Children's Education: Evidence from the Grameen Bank." Unpublished undergraduate honors thesis in economics, Harvard University.

Chaudhury, Nazmul, and Jeffrey S. Hammer. 2003. *Ghost Doctors: Doctor Absenteeism in Bangladeshi Health Centers.* Policy Research Working Paper no. 3065, World Bank.

Chaudhury, Nazmul, Jeffrey Hammer, Michael Kremer, et al. 2005. *Roll Call: Teacher Absence in Bangladesh.* Washington, DC: World Bank.

Chazan, David. 1998. "Microcredit Dream Washed Away." *Financial Times,* London Edition, October 1: 4.

Counts, Alex. 1996. *Give Us Credit.* New York: Times Books/Random House.

d'Ansembourg, B., and Ichiro Tambo. 2004. "GrameenPhone Revisited: Investors Reaching Out to the Poor." *DAC Journal* 5(4): 15–55.

Datta, Dipanker. 2004. "Microcredit in Rural Bangladesh: Is It Reaching the Poorest?" *Journal of Microfinance* 6, no.1: 55–81.

del Ninno, Carlos, Paul Dorosh, and L. C. Smith. 2003. "Public Policy, Markets, and Household Coping Strategies in Bangladesh: Avoiding a Food Security Crisis Following the 1998 Floods." *World Development* 31, no. 7: 1221–1238.

Dowla, Asif. 2004. "Micro Leasing: The Grameen Bank Experience." *Journal of Microfinance* 6, no. 2: 137–160.

———. 2006. "In Credit We Trust: Building Social Capital by Grameen Bank in Bangladesh." *Journal of Socio-Economics* 35, no.1: 102–122.

Duflo, Esther, William G. Gale, Jeffrey Liebman, et al. 2005. *Saving Incentives for Low- and Middle-Incomce Families: Evidence from a Field Experiment with H&R Block*. Retirement Security Project, Working Paper no. 2005-05. Washington, DC: Brookings Institution.

Evans, T., A. Adams, R. Mohammed, et al. 1999. "Demystifying Nonparticipation in Microcredit: A Population-Based Analysis." *World Development* 27, no. 2: 419–430.

Fafchamps, Marcel, and Susan Lund. 2003. "Risk-Sharing Networks in Rural Philippines." *Journal of Development Economics* 71: 261–287.

Faridi, Rashid. 2003. "Microcredit Programs in Bangladesh: Assessing the Performance of Participating Women." Mimeo. Department of Economics, Virginia Polytechnic Institute and State University.

Friedman, Milton. 1962. *Capitalism and Freedom*. Chicago: University of Chicago Press.

Fujita, Koichi. 2000. "Credit Flowing from the Poor to the Rich: The Financial Market and the Role of Grameen Bank in Rural Bangladesh." *Developing Economies* 38(3): 343–373.

Gale, William G., J. Mark Iwry, and Peter R. Orszag. 2005. "The Automatic 401(k): A Simple Way to Strengthen Retirement Savings." *Tax Notes* 106, no. 10: 1207–1214.

Gerstner, Louis V. 2002. *Who Says Elephants Can't Dance? Inside IBM's Historic Turnaround*. New York: HarperCollins.

Goetz, Anne Marie, and Rina Sen Gupta. 1996. "Who Takes the Credit? Gender, Power, and Control over Loan Use in Rural Credit Programs in Bangladesh." *World Development* 24, no. 1: 45–63

Government of the People's Republic of Bangladesh. 1983. *The Grameen Bank Ordinance.* Ordinance no. XLVI.

Grameen Bank. *Annual Report—2003.* Dhaka: Grameen Bank.

"Grameen Grief." 1998. *Financial Times*, London Edition, October 1: 23.

Gugerty, Mary Kay. 2003. "You Can't Save Alone: Testing Theories of Rotating Savings and Credit Associations in Kenya." Mimeo. University of Washington.

Hallman, Kelly K. 2000. *Mother-Father Resource Control, Marriage Payments, and Girl-Boy Health in Rural Bangladesh.* Food Consumption and Nutrition Division, Discussion Paper no. 93. International Food Policy Research Institute.

Hashemi, Syed M. 1997. "Those Left Behind: A Note on Targeting the Hardcore Poor." Chapter 11 in *Who Needs Credit? Poverty and Finance in Bangladesh,* eds. Geoffrey Wood and Iffath Sharif (Dhaka: University Press).

Hashemi, Syed M., and Sidney Schuler. 1997. *Sustainable Banking with the Poor: A Case Study of the Grameen Bank.* JSI Working Paper no. 10. Washington DC: John Snow International Research and Training Institute.

Hashemi, Sidney M., Sidney Schuler, and Ann P. Riley. 1996. "Rural Credit Programs and Women's Empowerment in Bangladesh." *World Development* 24, no. 4: 635–653.

Herz, Barbara, and Gene Sperling. 2004. *What Works in Girls' Education: Evidence and Policies from the Developing World.* New York: Council on Foreign Relations.

Himmelstein, David U., Elizabeth Warren, Deborah Thomas, et al. 2005. *Market Watch: Illness and Injury as Contributors to Bankruptcy.* Health Affairs web exclusive, Feb. 2. Available at http://content.healthaffairs.org/cgi/reprint/hlthaff.w5.63v1.

Holcombe, Susan. 1995. *Managing to Empower: The Grameen Bank's Experience of Poverty Alleviation.* London: Zed Books.

Hossain, Mahabub. 1988. *Credit for Alleviation of Rural Poverty: The Grameen Bank in Bangladesh.* Research Report no. 65. Washington, DC: International Food Policy Research Institute.

Hossain, Naomi, and Naila Kabeer. 2004. "Achieving Universal Primary Education and Eliminating Gender Disparity." *Economic and Political Weekly* 39, no. 36: 4093–4100.

Hulme, David. 1999. *Impact Assessment Methodologies for Microfinance: A Review.* IDPM, University of Manchester.

Hulme, David, and Paul Mosley. 1996. *Finance against Poverty, Vol. 1.* London: Routledge.

————. 1997. "Finance for the Poor or the Poorest? Financial Innovation, Poverty, and Vulnerability." In *Who Needs Credit? Poverty and Finance in Bangladesh,* eds. G. D. Wood and I. A. Sharif. Dhaka: University Press.

Ito, Sanae. 1999. "The Grameen Bank: Rhetoric and Reality." Unpublished Ph.D. dissertation, University of Sussex, Brighton.

Jacoby, Hanan G., and Emmanuel Skoufias. 1997. "Risk, Financial Markets, and Human Capital in a Developing Country." *Review of Economic Studies* 64, no. 3: 311–335.

Jain, Pankaj. 1996. "Managing Credit for the Rural Poor: Lessons from the Grameen Bank." *World Development* 24, no. 1: 79–89.

Jain, P., and M. Moore. 2003. *What Makes Microcredit Programmes Effective? Fashionable Fallacies and Workable Realities.* Working Paper no. 177. Sussex, Institute of Development Studies.

Johnstone, D. Bruce. 2000. *Student Loans in International Perspective: Promises and Failures, Myths and Partial Truths.* International Comparative Higher Education Finance and Accessibility Project, Center for Comparative and Global Studies in Education, Graduate School of Education. Buffalo: SUNY.

Kabeer, Naila. 1998. *Money Can't Buy Me Love? Re-evaluating Gender, Credit and Empowerment in Rural Bangladesh.* Discussion Paper no. 363, IDS.

————. 2004. *Snakes, Ladders and Traps: Changing Lives and Livelihoods in Rural Bangladesh (1994–2001).* Joint CPRC-IDS Working Paper, Brighton and Manchester.

Kanbur, R., and L. Squire. 2001. "The Evolution of Thinking about Poverty." In *Frontiers of Development Economics: The Future in Perspective,* eds. G. Meier and J. Stiglitz. Washington, DC: World Bank.

Karim, M. R., and Mitsue Osada. 1998. "Dropping Out: An Emerging Factor in the Success of Microcredit-Based Poverty Alleviation Programs." *Developing Economies* 36(3): 257–288.

Khaled, Khondkar Ibrahim. 2004. "Need for Trade Union Reform." *Daily Star Web Edition* 4(244), January 31. Available at http://www.thedailystar.net/2004/01/31/d401311501104.htm.

Khalily, M. A., and Richard L. Meyer. 1993. "The Political Economy of Rural Loan Recovery: Evidence from Bangladesh." *Savings and Development* 17, no. 1: 23–38.

Khandker, Shahidur. 1996. "Grameen Bank: Impact, Costs, and Program Sustainability." *Asian Development Review* 14, no. 1: 97–130.

———. 1998. *Fighting Poverty with Microcredit: Experience in Bangladesh.* New York: Oxford University Press for the World Bank.

———. 2003. *Micro-Finance and Poverty: Evidence Using Panel Data from Bangladesh.* Policy Research Working Paper 2945. Washington, DC: World Bank.

———. 2004. "Flood and Coping Ability in Bangladesh." Table 10. Typescript, World Bank.

Khandker, S., M. Pitt, and N. Fuwa. 2003. *Subsidy to Promote Girls' Secondary Education: The Female Stipend Program in Bangladesh.* Washington, DC: World Bank.

Kremer, Michael, Edward Miguel, and Rebecca Thornton. 2004. *Incentives to Learn.* Harvard University. Available at http://www.educationnext.org/unabridged/20052/57.pdf.

Kurmanalieva, Elvira, Heather Montgomery, and John Weiss. 2003. "Microfinance and Poverty Reduction in Asia: What's the Evidence?" Paper presented at the Annual Conference on Microcredit and Poverty Reduction, organized by the Asian Development Bank Institute in Tokyo, December 5.

Larance, Lisa. 2001. "Fostering Social Capital through NGO Design: Grameen Bank Membership in Bangladesh." *International Social Work* 44, no. 1: 7–18.

Ligon, Ethan. 2001. *Dynamic Bargaining in Households (with an Application to Bangladesh).* Working Paper, University of California at Berkeley.

Maldonado, Jorge H., Claudio González-Vega, and Vivianne Romero. 2003. "The Influence on the Education Decisions of Rural Households: Evidence from Bolivia." Paper prepared for the Annual Meeting of the American Agricultural Economics Association, Montreal, Canada. July 27–30.

Maloney, C., and A. B. S. Ahmed. 1988. *Rural Savings and Credit in Bangladesh.* Dhaka: University Press.

Maps on Microcredit Coverage in Upazilas of Bangladesh. Map no. 7. Palli Karma-Sahayak Foundation (PKSF), 2004.

McKernan, Signe-Mary. 2002. "The Impact of Micro-Credit Programs on Self-Employment Profits: Do Non-Credit Program Aspects Matter?" *Review of Economics and Statistics* 84, no. 1: 93–115.

McKernan, Signe-Mary, Mark Pitt, and David Moskowitz. 2005. *Use of the Formal and Informal Financial Sectors: Does Gender Matter? Empirical Evidence from Rural Bangladesh.* Policy Research Working Paper no. 3491, January, World Bank.

Menon, Nidhiya. 2003. "Consumption Smoothing in Micro-Credit Programs." Typescript. Department of Economics, Brandeis University.

Meyer, Richard L. 2002. *Track Record of Financial Institutions in Assisting the Poor in Asia.* Research Paper no. 49, Asian Development Bank Institute.

Morduch, Jonathan. 1999. "Between the State and the Market: Can Informal Insurance Patch the Safety Net?" *World Bank Research Observer* 14, no. 2: 187–207.

———. 2005. "Smart Subsidy for Sustainable Microfinance." *Finance for the Poor* 4, no. 4, Asian Development Bank.

Morduch, Jonathan, and Stuart Rutherford. 2003. *Microfinance: Analytical Issues for India.* Finance and Private Sector Development, South Asia Region, World Bank.

Mullainathan, S., and R. Thaler. 2000. "Behavioral Economics." Mimeo no. 00-27, Department of Economics, MIT.

Nabi, R., D. Datta, S. Chakrabarty, et al. 1999. "Consultation with the Poor: Participatory Poverty Assessment in Bangladesh." Paper prepared for the NGO Working Group of the World Bank, Bangladesh.

Nanda, Priya. 1999. "Women's Participation in Rural Credit Programmes in Bangladesh and Their Demand for Formal Health Care: Is There a Positive Impact?" *Health Economics* 8: 415–428.

Nath, S. R. 1997. "Social Factors Underlying Gender Variation of School Enrollment: Case of Rural Bangladesh." *Journal of Rural Development* 27, no. 1: 123–138.

Naved, R. 2000. *Intrahousehold Impact of the Transfer of Modern Agricultural Technology: A Gender Perspective.* FNCD Discussion Paper no. 85. Washington, DC: International Food Policy Research Institute.

Noponen, Helzi, and Paula Kantor. 2004. "Crisis, Setbacks and Chronic Problems: The Determinants of Economic Stress Events among Poor Households in India." *Journal of International Development* 16: 529–545.

Osmani, Lutfun N. Kahn. 1998. "The Grameen Bank Experiment: Empowerment of Women through Credit." In *Women and Empowerment: Illustrations for the Third World,* ed. Haleh Afshar. London: Macmillan.

Pitt, Mark. 1999. "Reply to Jonathan Morduch's 'Does Microfinance Really Help the Poor? New Evidence from Flagship Programs in Bangladesh.'" Typescript. Department of Economics, Brown University.

Pitt, Mark, and Shahidur Khandker. 1998. "The Impact of Group-Based Credit Programs on Poor Households in Bangladesh: Does the Gender of the Participants Matter?" *Journal of Political Economy* 106, no. 5: 958–996.

Pitt, Mark M., Shahidur Khandker, and Jennifer Cartwright. 2003. *Does Micro-Credit Empower Women? Evidence from Bangladesh.* Policy Research Paper no. 2998, World Bank.

Pitt, Mark M., Shahidur Khandker, Omar Haider Chowdhury, et al. 2003. "Credit Programs for the Poor and the Health Status of Children in Rural Bangladesh." *International Economic Review* 44, no. 1: 87–118.

Pitt, Mark, Shahidur Khandker, Signe-Mary McKernan, *et al.* 1999. "Credit Programs for the Poor and Reproductive Behavior in Low Income Countries: Are the Reported Causal Relationships the Result of Heterogeneity Bias?" *Demography* 36, no. 1: 1–21.

Public Thumbs Up for Grameen One. 2005. Financial Express, July 24. Available at http://www.aims-bangladesh.com/press/2005.07.24_fe.html.

Quisumbing, Agnes R., and Benedicte de la Briere. 2000. *Women's Assets and Intrahousehold Allocation in Rural Bangladesh: Testing*

Measures of Bargaining Power. Food Consumption and Nutrition Division Discussion Paper no. 86. Washington, DC: International Food Policy Research Institute.

Rahman, Aminur. 1999. *Women and Microcredit in Rural Bangladesh: Anthropological Study of the Rhetoric and Realities of Grameen Bank Lending.* Boulder, CO: Westview Press.

Rahman, A., R. Rahman, M. Hossain, and S. Hossain. 2002. *Early Impact of Grameen: A Multi-Dimensional Analysis.* Dhaka: Grameen Trust.

Rahman, A., and A. Razzaque. 2000. "On Reaching the Hard Core Poor: Some Evidence on Social Exclusion in NGO Programmes." *Bangladesh Development Studies* 26, no. 1: 1–35.

Rahman, Atiur, M. A. Razzaque, M. M. Rahman, et al. 1998. "On Reaching the Hardcore Poor: Redefining NGO Strategy." Paper prepared for NOVA consultancy. Dhaka: Bangladesh Institute of Development Studies.

Rahman, H. Z. 1998. "Bangladesh: Dynamics of Rural Poverty." Paper presented at the International Conference on Poverty: Emerging Challenges, organized by Bangladesh Institute of Development Studies (BIDS) in association with Grameen Trust and LGED, Dhaka, February 9–11.

Rahman, H. Z., Mahbub Hossain, and Binayak Sen. 1996. *1987–1994: Dynamics of Rural Poverty in Bangladesh.* Dhaka: Bangladesh Institute of Development Studies.

Rahman, Omar. 1997. "The Effect of Spouses on the Mortality of Older People in Rural Bangladesh." *Health Transition Review* 7: 1–12.

———. 2000. "Living Arrangements and the Health of Older Persons in Less Developed Countries: Evidence from Rural Bangladesh." Paper presented at the technical meeting "Population Ageing and Living Arrangements of Older Persons: Critical Issues and Policy Responses," Population Division, Department of Economic and Social Affairs, United Nations Secretariat, New York, February 8–10.

Rahman, Rushidan Islam. 1998a. *Rural Households' Attitude towards Savings and Demand for Saving Services"* Save the Children USA.

———. 1998b. *The Hard Core Poor and NGO Intervention.* Dhaka: Bangladesh Institute of Development Studies.

Rao, Vijayendra. 1997. "Wife-Beating in Rural South India: A Qualitative and Econometric Analysis." *Social Science and Medicine* 44: 1169–1180.

Rashid, Mansoora, and Robert M. Townsend. 1994. *Targeting Credit and Insurance: Efficiency, Mechanism Design, and Program Evaluation.* Discussion Paper no. 47, Education and Social Policy Department, World Bank.

Ravallion, Martin, and Quentin Wodon. 1999. "Does Child Labor Displace Schooling? Evidence on Behavioral Responses to an Enrollment Subsidy." *Economic Journal* 110: 158–175.

———. 2000. "Banking on the Poor? Branch Location and Non-farm Rural Development in Bangladesh." *Review of Development Economics* 4, no. 2: 121–139.

Reuters. *BD may ban trade unions in banks.* Available at http://www.paksearch.com/br98/Feb/28/BDMAYBAN.htm.

Richardson, Don, R. Ramirez, and M. Haq. 2000. *Grameen Telecom's Village Phone Programme in Rural Bangladesh: A Multi-Media Case Study.* Guelph, Ontario: TeleCommons Development Group.

Rutherford, Stuart. 2002. *Money Talks: Conversations with Poor Households in Bangladesh about Managing Money.* Finance and Development Research Programme Working Paper no. 45. Institute for Development Policy and Management, University of Manchester.

———. 2004. "Grameen II at the End of 2003: A 'Grounded View' of How Grameen's New Initiative Is Progressing in Villages." Typescript. Dhaka: MicroSave.

———. 2005. E-mail communication with author, January 7.

"SB Gets Kind to Tk 170cr Loan Defaulter." 2002. *Daily Star Web Edition* 3(928), April 19. Available at http://www.thedailystar.net/dailystarnews/200204/19/n2041901.htm#BODY4.

Schriener, Mark. 2003. "A Cost-Effectiveness Analysis of the Grameen Bank of Bangladesh." *Development Policy Review* 21, no. 3: 357–382.

Schuler, Sidney Ruth, and Syed M. Hashemi. 1994. "Credit Programs, Women's Empowerment, and Contraceptive Use in Rural Bangladesh." *Studies in Family Planning* 25, no. 2: 65–76.

Schuler, Sidney, Syed Hashemi, and Shamsul Huda Badal. 1998. "Men's Violence against Women in Rural Bangladesh: Undermined or Exacerbated by Microcredit Programmes?" *Development in Practice* 8, no. 2.

Schuler, Sidney Ruth, Syed M. Hashemi, and Ann P. Riley. 1997. "The Influence of Women's Changing Roles and Status in Bangladesh's Fertility and Contraceptive Use." *World Development* 25, no. 4: 563–575.

Schuler, Sidney, Syed Hashemi, Ann Riley, et al. 1996. "Credit Programs, Patriarchy and Men's Violence against Women in Rural Bangladesh." *Social Science and Medicine* 43, no. 12: 1729–1742.

Sebstad, Jennifer, and Monique Cohen. 2001. *Microfinance, Risk, and Poverty.* Washington, DC: World Bank.

Sen, A. K. "Gender and Cooperative Conflicts." In *Persistent Inequalities: Women and World Development,* ed. I. Tinker. Oxford: Oxford University Press, 1990.

Sen, Binayak. 2003. "Drivers of Escape and Descent: Changing Household Fortunes in Rural Bangladesh." *World Development* 31, no. 3: 513–534.

Sen, Binayak, and Sharifa Begum. 1998. *Methodology for Identifying the Poorest at the Local Level.* Technical Paper no. 27, "Macroeconomics, Health and Development" series. Geneva: World Health Organization.

Shah, Shekhar. 1999. "Coping with Natural Disasters: The 1998 Floods in Bangladesh." Paper prepared for the World Bank Summer Research Workshop on Poverty and Development, July 6–8. Washington, DC.

Sharif, Iffath, and Geof Wood. 1998. "Towards New Frontiers of Finance: Summary and Findings." Paper prepared for the final session of the 2nd International Workshop on Poverty and Finance: Emerging Institutional Issues in Microfinance.

Sharma, Monohar, and Manfred Zeller. 1999. "Placement and Outreach of Group-Based Credit Organizations: The Cases of ASA, BRAC, and PROSHIKA in Bangladesh." *World Development* 27, no. 12: 2123–2136.

Shefrin, Hersh M., and Richard M. Thaler. 1992. "Mental Accounting, Saving, and Self-Control." In *Choice over Time,* eds. G. Lowenstein and J. Elster. New York: Russel Sage.

Sobhan, Farooq, M. H. Kaleque, and Shamsur Rahman. 2002. "Factors Shaping Successful Public Private Partnerships in the ICT Sector in Bangladesh." Bangladesh Enterprise Institute.

Sobhan, Rehman. 2005. *A Macro Policy for Poverty Eradication through Structural Change*. Discussion Paper no. 2005/03, World Institute for Development Economics Research.

Steele, Fiona, Sajeda Amin, and Ruchira T. Naved. 2001. "Savings/Credit Group Formation and Change in Contraception." *Demography* 38, no. 2: 267–282.

Strauss, John, Germano Mwabu, and Kathleen Beegle. 2000. "Intra-household Allocations: A Review of Theories and Empirical Evidence." *Journal of African Economics* 9: 83–143.

Surowiecki, James. 2004. *The Wisdom of Crowds: Why the Many Are Smarter than the Few and How Collective Wisdom Shapes Business, Economies, Societies, and Nations*. New York: Doubleday.

Tagore, Rabindranath. 1998. "Sambaya Niti." In *Collected Works of Tagore*, Vol. 14, p. 313; translated from Bengali and quoted by eds. Binayak Sen and Atiur Rahman in *South Asia Poverty Monitor: The Bangladesh Chapter*, June.

Tietjen, Karen. 2003. *The Bangladesh Primary Education Stipend Project: A Descriptive Analysis*. Partnership for Sustainable Strategies on Girls' Education.

Todd, Helen. 1996. *Women at the Center: Grameen Bank Borrowers after One Decade*. Boulder, CO: Westview Press.

Uddin, Jamal. 2004. "Bangladesh Bank Advises Grameen Bank to Reduce Interest Rates and Distribute Dividends." *Daily Itefaq* (in Bangla), July 7.

Van Tassel, Eric. 2004. "Household Bargaining and Microfinance." *Journal of Development Economics* 74: 449–468.

The Village Phone. GrameenPhone Online. 2004. Available at http://www.grameenphone.com/modules.php?name=Content&pa=showpage&pid=3:11:1 (accessed September 29, 2005).

Wahid, Abu. 1993. *The Grameen Bank: Poverty Relief in Bangladesh*. Boulder, CO: Westview Press.

Woolcock, Michael. 1999. "Social Theory, Development Policy, and Poverty Alleviation: A Comparative-Historical Analysis of Group-Based Banking in Developing Economies." Unpublished Ph.D. dissertation, Department of Sociology, Brown University.

Wright, G. 1998. *Moving the Mountains: Savings as a Human Right in Bangladesh: The Case for Voluntary, Open Access Savings Facilities and Why Bangladesh's Largest MFIs are Slow to React.* MicroSave paper, UNDP.

Wright, Graham A. N., and Leonard Mutesasira. 2001. "The Relative Risks to Poor People's Savings." *Journal of Small Enterprise Development* 12, no. 3.

Wydick, B. 1999. "The Effect of Microenterprise Lending on Child Schooling in Guatemala." *Economic Development and Cultural Change* 47, no. 4: 853–869.

Yunus, Muhammad. 1998. "Alleviating Poverty through Technology." *Science* 282, no. 5388: 409–410.

———. 1999. *Banker to the Poor: Micro-lending and the Battle against World Poverty.* New York: Public Affairs.

———. 2002. *Grameen Bank II: Designed to Open New Possibilities.* Dhaka: Grameen Bank.

———. 2003a. "Expanding Microcredit Outreach to Reach the Millennium Development Goal: Some Issues for Attention." Paper presented at the International Seminar on Attacking Poverty with Microcredit organized by PKSF in Dhaka, January 8–9.

———. 2003b. Interview with the author, January 9.

———. 2004. *Grameen Bank at a Glance.* Dhaka: Grameen Bank.

Zaman, Hassan, et al. 2005. *The Economics and Governance of Non Governmental Organizations (NGOs) in Bangladesh.* Poverty Reduction and Economic Management Sector Unit, South Asia Region, World Bank.

Index

About the Authors

Asif Dowla is a professor of economics at St. Mary's College of Maryland. He did his undergraduate work in economics at the University of Chittagong, Bangladesh. He received an MA in economics from the University of Western Ontario, Canada, and a PhD in economics from Southern Methodist University in Dallas, Texas. Prior to joining St. Mary's College, he taught at Illinois State and Marquette universities. He has published articles on various subjects related to economics. Recently, he has published several articles on aspects of microfinance, such as leasing, savings mobilization, and social capital. In 1997 he received a fellowship to spend a year on sabbatical at Grameen Bank.

Dipal Chandra Barua is the Deputy Managing Director of Grameen Bank and the Managing Director of Grameen Shakti in Bangladesh. He has extensive experience in the fields of poverty alleviation, microcredit, rural development, and people's participation through his position as a core founder of Grameen Bank. He received undergraduate and graduate degrees in economics from the University of Chittagong. He has published articles and authored monographs on microfinance, cellular phone use, and renewable energy. He has served as consultant for the Venezuelan government, UNAIDS, the Building and Social Housing Foundation in London, and Grameen replication projects in China, Myanmar, South Africa, and Egypt. He serves on the Board of Directors of sixteen sister organizations of Grameen Bank, including Grameen Phone, the largest cell phone company in Southeast Asia, and Project Enterprise, a micro-lending program in New York.

Kumarian Press, located in Bloomfield, Connecticut, is a forward-looking, scholarly press that promotes active international engagement and an awareness of global connectedness.

◨ Also from Kumarian Press...

Microfinance:

Savings Services for the Poor: An Operational Guide
Edited by Madeline Hirschland

Pathways Out of Poverty: Innovations in Microfinance for the Poorest Families
Edited by Sam Daley-Harris

Housing Microfinance: A Guide to Practice
Edited by Franck Daphnis and Bruce Ferguson

Defying the Odds: Banking for the Poor
Eugene Versluysen

New and Forthcoming:

More Pathways Out of Poverty
Edited by Sam Daley-Harris and Anna Awimbo

**A World Turned Upside Down: Social Ecological Approaches
to Children in War Zones**
Edited by Neil Boothby, Mike Wessells, and Alison Strang

Humanitarian Alert: NGO Information and its Impact on US Foreign Policy
Abby Stoddard

NGOs in International Politics
Shamima Ahmed and David Potter

Development and the Private Sector: Consuming Interests
Edited by Deborah Eade and John Sayer

Visit Kumarian Press at www.kpbooks.com
or call toll-free 800.289.2664
for a complete catalog.